The
VIGIL
Series

Book Two

THE FRUITS OF SILENCE

A Journey into Praying the Scripture

by ALAN BOOKER

STUDENT'S NAME

Vigil Book Two: The Fruits of Silence and related materials:

Copyright ©2016 Alan Booker

All rights reserved. No portion of this book may be reproduced in any form, except for short excerpts for review, without written permission from the copyright holder. Published by Expedition Press.

All scripture quotations marked (NRSV) contained herein are from the New Revised Standard Version Bible, copyright ©1989 by the Division of Christian Education of the National Council of the Churches of Christ in the U.S.A., and are used by permission. All rights reserved.

All scripture quotations marked (NIV) are taken from the Holy Bible, New International Version®, NIV®. Copyright © 1973, 1978, 1984 by Biblica, Inc.™ Used by permission of Zondervan. All rights reserved worldwide. www.zondervan.com

All scripture quotations marked (KJV) are taken from the Holy Bible: Authorized King James Version.

ISBN: 978-0-9857591-0-0
Cover design by George Foster

For online resources to accompany this study, visit the Vigil web site at www.keepingvigil.org

To purchase copies of this book or related materials, visit Expedition Press at www.expeditionpress.com

Thou wilt keep him in perfect peace, whose mind is stayed on thee: because he trusteth in thee.

- Isaiah 26:3 (KJV)

My Lord, God, I have no idea where I am going.
I do not see the road ahead of me. I cannot know for certain where it will end.
The fact that I think I am following Your will, does not mean that I am actually doing so.
But I believe that the desire to please You, does, in fact, please You.
And I know that if I do this, You will lead me by the right road, though I may know nothing about it.
Therefore I will trust You always, though I may seem to be lost and in the shadow of death.
I will not fear, for you are ever with me; and You will never leave me to face my perils alone.

- A Prayer of Thomas Merton
From *Thoughts in Solitude*

Week 1 - Introduction

For God alone my soul waits in silence;
from him comes my salvation.

-Psalm 62:1 (NRSV)

AT THE AGE OF EIGHTEEN, standing in front of a tree whose branches had been stripped bare of leaves by the cold winds of winter, Nicolas Herman received a powerful vision of God's grace and provision. He had been born into a poor family in northeastern France in 1614, during a period of intense religious conflict between Catholics and Protestants that was creating war throughout Europe. Despite this, Nicolas did not see in the bare branches of the tree a reflection of the violence and death that surrounded him during his childhood. Instead, God allowed him to glimpse the inward life of the tree that would bring forth leaves and flowers in the spring. Nicolas realized this was a perfect picture of what God wanted to do inside of him. In that moment, he was overwhelmed by an understanding of the depth of God's love, an understanding that grew over time into an all-consuming desire to live every moment in God's presence.

At the age of 26, Nicolas joined a Carmelite monastery in Paris. Since he did not have the education or background to be a priest or cleric, he entered the monastery as a lay brother and dedicated himself to prayer and labor. He was given the new name of Brother Lawrence and began to work in the kitchen preparing food.

Through the years that followed, Brother Lawrence developed a simple yet profound way to live with his eyes fixed on God. He learned to keep a continual awareness of God's presence by making every action an act of service directed toward God. Each time he stirred a pot or washed a dish, Brother Lawrence saw it as an opportunity to serve the God who was right there with him the whole time. Once he grasped the reality of the constant companionship of the Holy Spirit, an ever-flowing conversation emerged in which Brother Lawrence spoke to God in prayer and then listened with inner silence as he worked.

Over time, this constant communion with God created in Brother Lawrence a deep wisdom that was recognized by those around him despite his lack of formal education. After his death, a collection of Brother Lawrence's letters, writings, and conversation were compiled, and became known as *The Practice of the Presence of God*. Still in print today, this book became a classic work of Christian literature because of its clear story of the love and peace to be found in God's presence.

As you begin this second book of *Vigil*, ask the Holy Spirit to grow in you the fruits that come from giving your full being to God, teaching you to be constantly aware of His presence and to hear His voice speaking in the silence. As you seek Him, the Spirit will lead you ever deeper along your own journey of finding the reality of the God that is always with you.

Extra Mile:

Arrange to spend the night outside one day this week. You will need a sleeping bag and ground pad if the weather is cold. Sleep out under the stars instead of in a tent if possible. Spend the last thirty minutes before you go to sleep in silence, watching as creation unfolds around you, talking to God and then listening as He speaks to you in the silence.

WELCOME TO BOOK TWO

Day 1

Since *Book Two* continues the practices started in the first book and builds on them, students who have not completed *Book One* will most likely find trying to start with the second book to be confusing and a bit overwhelming. Those new to *Vigil* should begin with *Book One: A Sacred Dwelling Place*, which covers the basics of *Lectio Divina* and establishes a daily time with God each morning.

For *Book Two*, each week contains several extra pages of reading material for Day One. As you plan your schedule for the week, include a time in the morning of Day One to go outside for *Vigil*, just as you would for each of the other days in the week. You will use your time on the morning of Day One to read the opening pages of the week. This will allow you to arrive at the weekly group meeting with the reading already accomplished, so you will be ready for the discussion.

WELCOME TO THE SECOND BOOK OF *VIGIL*. In this book, we begin looking at ways to carry your experience of God's presence out with you from your morning time of *Vigil* and into your everyday life. The flow of the second book will be much the same as the first, with your group meeting one day each week and your personal time the other six days of the week, preferably in the morning. The main change in this book will be the addition of a 5-8 minute time of prayer and reflection just before bed each evening, and an invitation to pause for a few seconds before each meal to bring God's presence back to mind. We will also be learning practices such as Breath Prayer and Welcoming Prayer to help you integrate your awareness of the spiritual into your moment-by-moment experience of the world.

For this week, you will simply be reading a couple of pages from this book each day. Go ahead and start going outside each morning to get back into the routine. After completing the reading for the day, take a few moments to pray and then move into *Contemplatio* for the remainder of your time. You will add your time of prayer before bed on Day Three of this week. Week Two will start back the daily practice of *Lectio Divina*.

If at all possible, take the time to read back through the first week of Book One, especially if it has been some time since you completed the first book. Now that you have practiced *Lectio Divina* for a while, you will find the material speaks to you at a different level and you may find things you missed the first time through.

Daily Time Commitment

Take a minute or two to plan out what time each day you are going to commit to doing *Lectio Divina*. As before, try to set aside a 30 minute period to give yourself enough time to not feel rushed. Day One will be the day your group meets each week. If your group meets on Wednesdays, then write this in as Day One, Thursday as Day Two, and so forth. Then record the time each day you plan to spend doing the morning part of *Vigil*. Don't worry about writing down a time for prayer each night, since you will simply do this in the last few minutes before you go to bed.

	Day of Week:	Time:
Day One	_____	_____
Day Two	_____	_____
Day Three	_____	_____
Day Four	_____	_____
Day Five	_____	_____
Day Six	_____	_____
Day Seven	_____	_____

The Extra Mile

Just as in Book One, you will find an Extra Mile option at the beginning of each week. You may find that some of the Extra Miles ask a little more of you, or push the edges of your comfort zones a bit further. Think seriously about doing the Extra Miles each week, even if they seem a little challenging. The world is full of people whose faith is all about reading and talking, but seldom about doing. Use the Extra Mile as a starting place to challenge yourself to concrete and specific actions in pursuit of living out what the Holy Spirit is showing you each week.

Finding Freedom During Lectio Divina

As you learned the daily practice of *Lectio Divina* in the first book, you may have found yourself falling into the pattern of working through each day in a set sequence, starting with *Lectio* and going straight through to *Contemplatio* without variation. If you look back at the diagram from the first week of *Book One*, you may remember that this represents only one possible way of doing *Lectio Divina*. The smaller arrows in the diagram are there to remind you that you are free to move back and forth between the different elements of *Lectio Divina* spontaneously.

Something you read in *Lectio* might bring an immediate response to mind, so that you speak back to God in *Oratio* before continuing to read the passage. A thought from *Meditatio* might bring God's presence so strongly to mind that you pause in *Contemplatio* for a few seconds before moving back to *Meditatio*, or feel yourself drawn back to part of the scripture passage in *Lectio*. As you continue in your practice of *Lectio Divina*, allow yourself the freedom to meet with the Holy Spirit in a sacred conversation that unfolds spontaneously moment by moment.

The outline for the daily practice of Lectio Divina from the end of the first book is included on page 223 as a reminder.

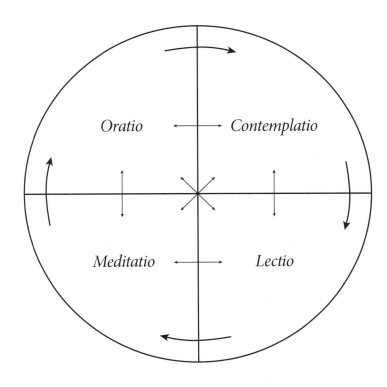

It is by no haphazard chance that in every age men have risen early to pray. The first thing that marks decline in spiritual life is our relationship to the early morning.

- Oswald Chambers

The Quotes Throughout this Book

You will notice a number of quotes scattered throughout the margin notes in this book. These quotes come from followers of the Christian path over the centuries and reflect their thoughts and experiences on their journeys. Following Christ changes the nature of your life fundamentally, transforming your view of the world from a perspective centered on self to one motivated by God's love flowing through you. Notice how each of these writers seems to come from a place of love and peace, regardless of the circumstances of their lives or the century in which they lived.

A RHYTHM OF SACRED PAUSES

THOSE WHO HAVE SOUGHT TO FOLLOW GOD throughout the centuries have found it impossible to isolate the spiritual from everyday life. Unless you weave your awareness of the sacred into the flow of life each day, you will almost certainly end up with a religion you leave at the church door when you exit. One of the more powerful ways to weave a mindfulness of God's presence into your day is to observe what has been referred to as *a rhythm of sacred pauses:* the practice of pausing at intervals throughout the day to bring your mind and spirit back into focus on God. Over time, this rhythm becomes like breathing. You pause to breathe in the presence of God and then return to your day, breathing out the love and peace of God through your actions.

The Seven Hours of the Divine Office

The early monastic orders realized a need to observe this rhythm of pausing throughout the day for spiritual reflection and used *Psalm 119:164* as a guide. In response to the statement of the Psalmist that "seven times a day do I praise you," they developed a system of pausing for prayer, reflection, and liturgy seven times a day. Since this practice was observed by priests and monks as part of the responsibilities of their office, it became known as the Hours of the Divine Office. Each of these seven times was given a name and specific practices were assigned to each.

Name	Traditional Time
Vigils (also called Matins)	During the night
Lauds (Morning Prayers)	At dawn, before breakfast (about 6:00 a.m.)
Terce (Mid-morning Prayers)	The third hour of the day (about 9:00 a.m.)
Sext (Mid-day Prayers)	The sixth hour of the day (about 12:00 p.m.)
None (Mid-afternoon Prayers)	The ninth hour of the day (about 3:00 p.m.)
Vespers (Evening Prayers)	At dusk, the lighting of the lamps (about 6:00 p.m.)
Compline (Night Prayers)	Immediately before bed

In ancient times, monks would often get up in the middle of the night to observe *Vigils*, but the more recent practice is to rise around 4:00 a.m. and not return to sleep afterward. *Vigils, Lauds,* and *Vespers* are often called the Major Hours since they can be longer than an hour each. The other four are the Minor Hours and are shorter in length, varying from fifteen minutes to half an hour.

Following such a schedule is quite rigorous, requiring complete commitment to the life of a monk or priest. The Catholic Church, which today runs the majority of Christian monasteries, acknowledges that only a few are called to such a life. Many Protestant denominations reject the idea that monastic life is appropriate for today, although a number of denominations still base their daily church schedules around these seven times of prayer and liturgy. Obviously, four to five hours of formal prayer and liturgy each day is not practical, and most likely not beneficial, for most people.

A number of Christians today are looking for a way to take these sacred pauses and integrate them into the flow of daily life while maintaining a healthy balance and not allowing the practice to become dry and mechanical. Spending time with God should be constantly fresh and new, always flowing from a desire for God's presence instead of a sense of duty or guilt.

Day 2

For more thoughts on using the pattern of the Hours of the Divine Office to help you keep focused on God's presence, see *Seven Sacred Pauses* by Macrina Wiederkehr.

Some parts of Eastern Christianity observe an eighth time of prayer between *Lauds* and *Terce* call *Prime,* but this is almost unknown in the Western Church.

Among those who continue to maintain the monastic tradition are several of the various congregations that comprise the Anglican Communion, including the Episcopal Church. The Anglican traditions were also instrumental in developing a practice of liturgy and personal prayer centered around the observance of the Hours of the Divine Office, which they began publishing in the mid-sixteenth century in a work that become known as *The Book of Common Prayer.*

A Rhythm of Sacred Pauses for Today

What should the rhythm of sacred pauses look like for the person today who is seeking after God but living with the hectic schedule that goes with modern life? As you found in the first book of *Vigil*, a time alone each day reading the scripture and praying is a foundational practice on the path of following Christ. Twenty to thirty minutes, preferably in the morning, gives you the time to slow down and really listen. You should make this a daily practice throughout your life. After you have completed this book, you may choose to continue using *Lectio Divina* during your daily study of scripture, or you may grow into other methods over time.

The Father spoke one word from all eternity and he spoke it in silence, and it is in silence that we hear it.

- St. John of the Cross

In this book, we will be using the idea of the seven sacred pauses to create a rhythm of returning our focus to God that is designed to fit into the flow of a normal day. You will continue to begin each day with your main time of *Lectio Divina*, just as in the previous book. Then, throughout the day, you will return for a few moments to inner silence by turning your face toward God, looking to Him as the source out of which your actions flow.

Starting the Day with Vigils & Closing with Compline

If at all possible, schedule your 20-30 minute time of *Lectio Divina* first thing as you get up in the morning. You may have already gotten into this habit in the previous book, or you may have found it hard to get up in the morning and decided to try another time. Consider pairing up with a friend to make sure you get up on time if this is a problem. Starting the morning with *Lectio Divina* is a strong way of setting the tone for your day. If your schedule doesn't permit you to spend this much time in the morning, at least take five minutes as you begin the day to pause for a moment of prayer and thankfulness.

The *Vigil* program is indeed named after the first Hour of the Divine Office, even though we do not get up quite as early as the ancient monks.

The second most important time of day to return your thoughts to God is in the evening just before you go to bed. The reading for tomorrow will outline for you how to spend five to ten minutes just before you go to sleep reflecting on your day and moving back toward inner quietness. In this way, you will start each day with *Vigils* and end with *Compline*.

Pausing A Few Moments Before Each Meal

A simple way to turn your mind back toward God throughout the day is to pause for a moment before each meal to pray. You may already have the habit of saying grace before each meal, or this may be something you never made a practice of doing consistently on your own. As you start into this book, make a commitment to pause for a minute before each meal to give thanks and then quiet your mind for about thirty seconds and simply sit with God in a brief time of *Contemplatio*. In this way, you will be observing your own version of *Lauds*, *Sext*, and *Vespers*.

Mid-day prayers, immediately before lunch, is a great time to observe one of the sacred pauses with your friends or family. Whether you are at school, work, or at home, it can be a blessing to pray with fellow Believers and then sit together in silence for a few moments before sharing a meal together.

Pausing Mid-morning & Mid-afternoon

If you follow the plan outlined above, you will observe five sacred pauses throughout each day. You may decide that this is all you are called to do right now, or you may want to go ahead and find a time to pause for *Terse* and *None*. You might chose a moment between classes or during a break at work to spend one or two minutes briefly praying and then sitting in the silence just long enough to move yourself back into awareness of God's presence. If these two additional times seem a bit much to you right now, put them aside and come back to them when you feel called.

COMPLINE

Day 3

Rᴇᴛᴜʀɴɪɴɢ ᴛᴏ Gᴏᴅ's ᴘʀᴇsᴇɴᴄᴇ ɪɴ ᴛʜᴇ ʟᴀsᴛ ᴍᴏᴍᴇɴᴛs before going to bed each night is an ideal way of preparing your mind and spirit to move peacefully into sleep. A brief time of reflecting on your day and talking to God allows you to unload the thoughts of the day and return to a place of interior stillness.

You should plan on observing *Compline* (pronounced *comp-lin*) during the last five to ten minutes before you climb into bed each night. Make sure to complete your evening routine before you begin, so you can simply finish *Compline* and go directly to sleep while maintaining the inner quiet that closes *Compline* each night. Start your practice of *Compline* this evening as you go to bed. You will find a small guide for *Compline* to follow each night in the margin at the lower right corner of each day's material.

Preparing a Space

If you did not set up a sacred space indoors during Book One, take a few moments to do it today. Pick a place that you can spend the last few minutes of your day alone and undisturbed. A bedroom, study, or even a closet can work well. It might be someplace you can sit at a desk or on the floor, or even kneel in front of an improvised altar. Make sure you have a Bible in your sacred space, since you will be using it to look up brief passages each evening.

Feel free to decorate your space in whatever way helps you express your intention to meet there with God each evening as you close the day. Some people find that lighting a candle during *Compline* helps set the time apart and adds a special element to this time of day.

Observing Compline

Before you begin *Compline*, make sure to complete all your other tasks and be ready for sleep. Finish any work that needs finishing, put your room in order, and get yourself ready for bed. If possible, darken the room except for a small light you will use to read during the first part of *Compline*. If you want to use a candle, light it just as you are starting each night. If the candle gives enough light, you might want to use it as the only source of illumination.

If possible, begin *Compline* each evening by stepping outside onto a porch or balcony for a few moments to reconnect with what God is doing in creation. Since you will be outside for only a minute or so, there is no need to get dressed for this, even if it is cold. Reach out with your senses and take in the patterns at work in the world around you. After a minute or two, go back inside to your sacred space.

The four stages of *Compline* that we will use are simpler and shorter versions of the stages of *Lectio Divina* you do each morning. You will start with a brief passage of scripture, either looking back at the passage from the morning or reading a new passage. Next is a form of *Meditatio* called Reflection on the Day, followed by a short time of prayer. Finally, you will return to the interior silence of *Contemplatio*. Each of these stages is outlined in more detail in the following sections. Spend one or two minutes on each stage. As you finish, turn off your light or blow out your candle and go to bed.

If it is dangerously cold outside (below 0 degrees F), you might simply look out a window instead of stepping outside. If it is raining, you might reach out your hand to feel the rain, but stay under the eaves in order to keep dry otherwise. Regardless of weather, make sure to be modestly dressed if you might be seen.

Scripture Reading & Reflection on the Day

The *Compline* sidebar at the end of each day will either give you a scripture reference to look up and read in your Bible, or ask you to read back over the scripture from that morning. Read slowly and carefully, almost as you would for *Lectio*, trying to allow the passage to soak into your spirit more than provoke a stampede of new thoughts running through your mind. Sit with the passage for a few moments, but allow yourself to enjoy its warmth more than analyze it intellectually. *Vigil* in the morning is the time to let your mind grapple actively with the scripture; *Compline* is the time to let the words help your mind move toward stillness.

As you finish reading, allow your mind to look back over the day. Examine your words, thoughts and actions to see if they were pleasing to God. Take note of anything you need forgiven so you can talk to God about it as you pray. Think about what was good about the day and what you want to do differently tomorrow. If you offended someone during the day and did not get the chance to make it right, make a specific plan for handling it tomorrow and then let go of it for the night.

Praying during Compline

As you move into prayer each evening during *Compline*, start by asking God's forgiveness for any place your thoughts or actions during the day were contrary to His will. Talk to God about your day, asking His help both for yourself and for those around you. Finish by taking time to be thankful for the blessings of the day and ask God to give you peace as you rest.

Closing Your Day with Silence

The last phase of *Compline* is to return to *Contemplatio* for the final minute or two. Close your eyes and turn your attention and intention fully toward God. In this place of listening, allow the Holy Spirit to heal the hurts of the day.

As you begin to practice *Compline*, you will notice it has a much different feel than *Vigil*. Whereas *Vigil* is a time of looking forward to the day, gathering your energy for the tasks ahead, *Compline* is a time of releasing, looking back over the day as it draws to a close. Allow yourself to unclench as you move through the last moments of *Compline*, relaxing into God's embrace and resting in silence.

Getting Started

Remember to begin observing Compline tonight as you get ready for bed. You can refer to the outline of *Compline* on page 224 to help you remember the steps as you get started. The sidebar to the right gives you the passage of scripture to read. Unless you are re-reading the scripture from the morning, you will need to look up the passage in your Bible since the passages for *Compline* are not printed in this book. The Reflection and Prayer sections give you some suggestions for these areas. Use them if they are helpful, but don't let them limit you. This time is between you and God, so go wherever the Spirit leads.

Don't worry if you are tired or not feeling fully awake when you come to do Compline. Just relax and let the words of the scripture passage soak in without trying to analyze too much. Let your time of night prayers be intimate with God, as if He were sitting with you beside your bed as you finish unwinding and getting ready for sleep, sharing about your day and simply enjoying each other's presence.

Compline

Reading: *Psalm 119:145-152*

Reflection: Look back over your day and see how many times you paused to remember God's presence.

Prayer: Ask God to help you learn to sense His presence throughout the day.

AWARENESS OF GOD'S PRESENCE

FOR MOST PEOPLE, A MOMENT-BY-MOMENT AWARENESS OF GOD'S PRESENCE seems almost impossible, something that is the sole province of monks and priests. But, as you will find, following a few simple practices can change your experience of the world deeply, resulting in a permanent shift toward an awareness of the Holy Spirit's presence within you. With this shift comes a sense of joy and peace that remains with you even when your world goes crazy or you find yourself in the middle of an emotional thunderstorm. Situations and the emotions they create are transient, but God's Spirit will be with you always.

Practicing the Presence of God

As Brother Lawrence discovered, the key to realizing God's presence is to make your life a constant conversation with Him. This discipline takes time to develop, but soon roots itself in your conscience so that your sense of God's presence is as constant as your sense of sight or sound. The first step in developing this sense is the observing of the sacred pauses, bringing your mind back to spiritual awareness throughout the day. The rhythm of seven sacred pauses each day forms the backbone of this practice. In the times between these pauses, three other practices are helpful in deepening your awareness: Prayers in Passing, Acts of Service, and Breath Prayers.

Prayers in Passing

You may have grown up with the idea that prayer must be a formal time during which you stop everything, close your eyes, bow your head, and speak to God with long and flowery words. While it is true that you should always address God reverently and should have times devoted strictly to prayer every day, stopping to close your eyes is not the only way to talk to God.

As you travel through your world today, try talking to God freely whenever the thought arises. You might silently say "*Thank You*" in a moment of realization of how God has helped you, or "*Please give me wisdom to handle this well*" when you run into a difficult situation. There is no need to stop and close your eyes, and those around you will never know you took a moment to talk to God. The more you practice these Prayers in Passing, the more it will become natural to include God in the conversation of even the smallest matters of life.

Acts of Service

Sometimes you may be called upon to do things you don't particularly enjoy, and find yourself tempted to have a bad attitude as you perform them. Next time this happens, use Brother Lawrence's example of making even the most menial tasks into an act of service directed toward God. Stop briefly to ask God to be with you as you begin and then listen to God with inner silence as you work. When you are tempted to do a poor job or slack off, remember that everything you do reflects God to those around you. Performing every task set before you, whether big or small, in a sacred way honors God and reveals His nature to everyone watching.

Day 4

If you have not started pausing for a few moments before each meal, try starting today. Give thanks for the meal, pray about anything that is on your mind, and finish with a few seconds of silence.

You may find it helpful to create a trigger for yourself to help establish the habit of pausing to talk to God during the flow of your day. Pick something that you do throughout the day, such as check your watch, look at your cell phone, or open a door, and use it as a reminder to do a Prayer in Passing. Once you have made it a natural part of your day, you will find you don't need to depend on an external trigger any more, and will find yourself spontaneously praying as you travel through your day.

Breath Prayers

A breath prayer is simply a short prayer you can say during a single breath, which is designed to be repeated throughout the day to return your mind to a specific thought or request you wish to direct toward God. Breath prayers are usually no more than a dozen syllables long and are often repeated silently as a form of inner prayer. Many of the breath prayers used through the centuries are either taken directly from scripture or inspired by scripture. For example, you might use the phrase "*His love endures forever*" from *Psalm 136* as a breath prayer if you wanted to meditate on God's love. Having selected this prayer, you would then repeat it through the day as a way of bringing your mind back to the reality of God's love.

Although the origin of breath prayer is not completely certain, it was most likely formalized during the fifth century in the desert monasteries of Egypt. The Eastern Orthodox Church adopted the practice and eventually developed a specific breath prayer know as the Jesus Prayer from *Luke 18:13*. The Jesus Prayer has a number of forms, with the most common being:

> *Lord Jesus Christ, Son of God, have mercy on me, a sinner.*

The Jesus Prayer would be repeated continually at intervals through the day to cultivate an inward yielding to the Holy Spirit. The Western church never adopted a standardized form of breath prayer, instead encouraging each person to use scripture as a guide in formulating prayers that met their personal needs. In this way, each person would move from one breath prayer to another as the circumstances of their spiritual journey evolved.

In creating your own breath prayers, you might use words or phrases from your scripture reading, sometimes shortening them so they easily fit into a single breath. The last two verses of *Psalm 139* might be turned into the breath prayer:

> *Lord, search me, know me, lead me.*

Some breath prayers contain explicit requests directed toward God, while others are simple statements of a promise found in scripture. Many people use the single word *Abba* from *Romans 8:15* as a breath prayer to remind them of God's acceptance of us as His children.

As you practice breath prayer, link your prayer to your physical breath, repeating the prayer once with each breath. Each time you return to the prayer through the day, repeat it several times, once with each breath, while directing your inner attention toward God.

Avoiding Mindless Repetition During Breath Prayer

Breath prayer is meant to help you return to an active remembrance of God, not to be just mindless repetition. Some religions use the repetition of words or phrases as a form of mantra designed to drive out conscious thought, but in *Matthew 6:7* Jesus warns against using the repetition of empty words as prayer. When you pray with words, your words should have the full attention of your mind and be a true reflection of your heart's desire expressed toward God.

Continue with a breath prayer only as long as it has true meaning for you. When you find that a breath prayer has become mere repetition, stop and think about why. It may be that something inside of you is resisting the prayer and needs to be yielded to the Holy Spirit, or that it is time to move on to another breath prayer.

Some example Breath Prayers:
Peace, be still.
Have mercy on me.
Not my will, but Yours.
I belong to You, O Lord.
Abide in me.
Lord, purify my thoughts.

You will probably find that the most natural way to link a breath prayer to your physical breathing is to say the prayer silently as you exhale. Remain inwardly silent as you inhale, as if listening, and then repeat the prayer the next time you exhale.

Compline

Reading: *Psalm 139*

Reflection: As you learn to remain aware of God in each moment, remember how much He thinks of you.

Prayer: Thank God for His constant presence with you, even as you sleep.

JOY & GRIEF

Day 5

We will use the concepts of *thoughts*, *emotions*, and *spiritual state* a number of times throughout this book, so understanding exactly how they are being used is important.

Thoughts refers to the words and images that move through your conscious mind.

Emotions are the transient feelings you experience as the result of both your conscious and subconscious mind responding to events, both external and internal.

Spiritual State refers to the underlying condition of your soul, which is determined more by the health of your spiritual relationships than by the changing winds of external events. Whereas the mind might experience the transient emotions of happiness or sadness, the soul experiences the more lasting states of joy or grief. Your soul might also grow toward a place of peace (versus inner turmoil), or loving-kindness toward others (versus self-centeredness or pridefulness), as your relationships with God, yourself, and those around you mature.

ONE OF THE INEVITABLE SIDE EFFECTS OF BECOMING more constantly aware of God's presence is that you will also become increasingly aware of your own internal spiritual state and more sensitive to the spiritual condition of others. As you deepen your spiritual sense through your daily practice of *Vigil*, you will come to realize that sin, both your own and that of others, creates grief and separation from God. The further you go down the path of the Spirit, the more sensitive you will become to the presence of grief inside of yourself, and to the presence of the sin that creates it.

This awareness is a critical part of your spiritual growth, because the Holy Spirit uses it to bring about deep change in your spirit. As you feel the presence of sin and grief more clearly, you will learn to release them to the Spirit so He can change the thoughts and desires that caused them. In return, the Holy Spirit will create in you a new heart with desires and motives that reflect God's purpose for you, and with this renewal of mind and purpose will come a sense of internal joy. If you practiced *Lectio Divina* consistently through the first book, most likely you have already subconsciously begun this process of releasing your sin and the grief it brings, giving them to the Spirit and allowing Him to give you internal peace in their place.

Thoughts & Emotions

If you have ever had someone repeatedly interrupt as you were trying to finish a task or watch a movie, you probably realize how quickly anger and irritation can raise their heads. Emotions often arise abruptly in response to circumstances, and then change just as quickly as they came. Your emotions are created as the events of the moment interact with your thoughts and inner spiritual state to form your perceptions of the world. Emotions can be powerful, but they are only transient reflections of the deeper nature of your inner self. Whether you react to an irritating situation with anger or calmness, for example, is a powerful indicator of what lies beneath the surface of your character.

As you become more aware of your own internal spiritual condition, you will learn to more clearly distinguish between the emotions you experience and the underlying spiritual state from which they arise. The Bible explains that the person who is following Christ has two natures that are in conflict with each other: the old nature that is separated from God by sin, and the new nature that is being transformed through God's grace into the image of Christ. The old nature creates grief, while the new nature given by the Spirit heals the grief of sin and replaces it with joy.

Emotions such as happiness and sadness are the surface images of your deeper self reflected on the ever-changing mirror of events. For the soul who has never known God, the happiness of the moment can feel hollow, because beneath it lies deep grief. For the one who knows God, even the sadness of a great loss is made easier to carry by an underlying joy that cannot be taken away.

The Sources of Grief & Bitterness

At its root, all grief is the result of sin. God created humans in His own spiritual image, to love and give just as He does. When mankind departed from this original purpose at the beginning of time, grief was born into the world. God designed you to love Him as He loved you, to love others just as you love yourself, and to have a caretaker's heart for His creation. Sin corrupts these priorities, teaching you to place yourself and your own desires at the center instead. Placing yourself first, however, denies the reasons for which God created you; it warps the very essence of your being so that your relationships can never bring you the joy God intended.

Since sin can best be defined as thoughts or actions that are contrary to God's nature, the most immediate result of your sin is that it separates you from fellowship with God. The spiritual nature you inherited from your ancestors is at odds with God's original design for mankind, and thus results in thoughts and actions that are destructive spiritually, mentally, and physically. These destructive thoughts and actions tear apart your relationships with everything God designed you to love. Grief is felt as the anguish of separation from those things God created you to have fellowship with, but that sin has cut you off from.

Your old, sinful nature bends your thoughts back toward yourself and corrupts your priorities, so the love God intended to flow freely out from you is directed inward toward the self instead, where it becomes toxic. These patterns of toxic thought are not all self-generated; many are learned from watching other people. Some of the most powerful are learned from parents and grandparents. Patterns of sin can be handed down from generation to generation unless they are dealt with through repentance and release to the Holy Spirit. If held inside, grief will create bitterness over time. Bitterness is the deep-rooted grief that grows from the regret of loss and the resentment of the ego to not having its desires fulfilled.

Your grief is the collection of unhealed wounds caused by sin, like broken bones that never healed properly, leaving you in constant pain and unable to even stand upright. The work of the Spirit is like that of a surgeon who must re-break crooked bones so they can be set properly and grow back straight. The healing process can be slow and difficult, but is necessary for you to be returned to full strength and health.

The Effects of Grief

The presence of grief creates a number of symptoms, the most obvious of which are the strong negative emotions that are triggered by the desires of your old nature. Whenever the wounds of grief or bitterness are touched, you may find yourself overrun by emotions such as anger, jealously, or hate. When you find yourself not feeling the need to be thankful or the desire to get out and fully engage in life, you are almost certainly experiencing grief.

The pain of grief can often sink your mind into a fog of inner turmoil and confused thoughts. Trying to push down the grief and ignore it doesn't make it go away, it just allows it to build up over time until it boils over into more hurtful emotions. If you follow the path of the Spirit, the pain and confusion of grief will bring you to a place where you realize all you have left to do is stop and listen into the silence to hear God's voice speaking to you words of healing and peace.

Releasing Grief & Accepting Joy

If you continue to deepen your spiritual awareness but don't release grief as it comes up, it will eventually come to overwhelm you. The Holy Spirit calls you to yield to Him, and works in response to your willingness to let go of your old nature and the grief it brings. God teaches you to have the mind of Christ by giving you the strength of will to release your own desires and to pursue what He wants for you.

Releasing your patterns of sinful thought and the associated grief is only the first half of the process. If you don't allow the Spirit to replace your old patterns with something new, you will find yourself slipping back into the old habits of thought and action that simply create more grief. Receiving the new mind being created in you by the Spirit is the other half of the process that allows you to accept the joy and peace God intends for you.

For some reason, some of the strongest patterns of sinful thought that are passed from one generation to the next involve prejudice or hatred. Wounds that have existed between nations or ethnic groups for generations, created by wars or conflicts hundreds of years ago, are still passed on in many communities today. These wounds have never been healed, and will continue to create conflict and hatred until they are dealt with and the grief they have caused is acknowledged.

You may occasionally meet someone who seems to have no visible grief or regret over sin, but who goes through life living for self and seeming to have all the good things the world has to offer. As you become more aware in your spirit, you will begin to sense the underlying desperation and spiritual need in people who live this way. They may not even be consciously aware of the grief themselves, all they know is that they are afraid to be still long enough to realize what they carry inside.

Compline

Reading: *1 Peter 1:3-12*

Reflection: God uses both joy and grief to grow you closer to Him. How have you felt joy or grief today? How have your emotions been related to the attitude of your spirit?

Prayer: Ask that God would use your grief throughout the next few weeks of this study to show you where you are holding on to things you need to release to Him.

THE WELCOMING PRAYER

As with the other practices in *Vigil*, Welcoming Prayer is best done outside, away from distractions, where you can more easily sense God's presence and hear His voice.

Day 6

Some examples of negative emotions are:
Anger
Frustration
Resentment
Hatred
Fear
Anxiety
Jealousy
Envy
Pridefulness
Selfishness
Shame

When experiencing habitual negative emotions, you may have become so accustomed to their presence in certain situations that you will first notice them by the effects they have on your body. Negative emotions almost always create either a tightness somewhere in your body, a change in your tone of voice, a change in your breathing pattern, or a combination of these.

The welcoming process can also be helpful in dealing with physical pain you experience in your body. Pain is a message from your body that something is wrong and needs your attention, whether it be a physical problem or an emotional issue that is creating stress. When you experience pain or discomfort in your body that doesn't have an immediately obvious source, stop and welcome it, trying to determine what it is telling you.

As the practice of *Lectio Divina* has found its way beyond the monastery walls, with it has come the need for an effective way to deal with the strong negative emotions that arise when the grief of sin bangs up against the modern world. Over the past few decades, the spiritual disciplines used throughout the centuries to help those in the monastic orders deal with negative emotions have been developed into a simple technique known as Welcoming Prayer that can be easily used by anyone.

The Welcoming Prayer in its current form was inspired by the reflections of a seventeenth century Jesuit priest named Jean-Pierre de Caussade in his book *Abandonment to Divine Providence*. The power of dealing with negative emotions in this way is that is does not try to suppress them or deny their existence. Instead, it encourages you to accept these feelings as messages from your inner self that tell you about what is happening deep within you. Emotions that are suppressed or ignored simply build up inside and create more grief. By listening carefully to the messages brought by your negative emotions, you allow them to pass through you harmlessly, releasing them to the Spirit instead of holding them inside and dwelling on them.

Noticing Your Negative Emotions

The first step in Welcoming Prayer is to notice the presence of a negative emotion and to allow yourself to simply experience it. Don't try to analyze it yet, or try to push it back down inside. Simply sit with the emotion and allow yourself to feel it. Notice also any way the emotion expresses itself in your body. Many negative emotions create a tightness or blocking somewhere in the body. See if you can localize how your body is responding, such as by clenching the jaw, tightening the fists, or changing your breath pattern.

If you can, name the emotion. You may find that you have a conflicting jumble of emotions that are hard to isolate and name. If so, either name the strongest of these emotions or simply let go of the idea of needing to put a name on what you are feeling. Once you have either named the emotion or not, just let yourself be present with what you are feeling and fully experience it.

Welcoming Your Feelings

The second step in the process might feel counter-intuitive at first: you welcome the negative emotion. If you realized that you are experiencing anger, you simply say *"Welcome, anger."* By welcoming the emotion, you begin the process of listening to what it has to tell you about the inner turmoil that is driving it. Welcome your negative feelings not as you would welcome a friend, but as you would welcome a messenger bringing you important information. You need to observe closely and pay attention in order to understand what it is telling you about what is happening inside of you.

At this stage, it is critical that you remember you are only welcoming the emotion, not any negative circumstances that created the emotion, and not any sinful thought that the emotion might try to provoke. For example, if someone in authority dislikes you for some reason and gives recognition you deserve to someone else, you might suddenly find yourself filled with anger and resentment. In this situation, you would not welcome the unfair circumstances, you would only welcome the feelings they create. You might also realize that your emotions are trying to create negative thoughts against those who wronged you. Don't confuse your emotions with the thoughts they produce. Your emotions consist of the raw feeling, while thoughts express themselves as words and images. You are welcoming the emotion, not the associated thoughts.

Be careful to separate negative thoughts from negative emotions and deal with the thoughts properly. During Welcoming Prayer, you should recognize negative thoughts just as you have practiced recognizing any thought during *Contemplatio*, and release them in the same way. Instead of using your sacred word to help release a negative thought, try repeating the welcome, such as "*Welcome anger, welcome resentment,*" to help bring you back to experiencing the raw feeling. As with any sinful thought, fighting with the negative thoughts and images brought about by strong emotion only gives them more energy. Gently release them and move past them so you can listen to the message coming from the emotion itself.

You may have to keep moving between the observing and welcoming processes for a while until the intensity of the emotion subsides and you are able to create some space between yourself and the feeling. Once you have allowed the emotion to pass through you in this way, you will be ready for the next phase of Welcoming Prayer.

Identifying Underlying Desires

The third step is to identify and name, if possible, any underlying desires that are causing your negative emotions. Sometimes emotions arise from an old wound being touched, other times from an ego desire being threatened. If the emotion comes from a wound inflicted by someone else, there may be no underlying ego desire you can identify since the wound came from somebody else's sin. Even if you can sense the emotion is coming from your own ego, you may still not be at a place where you can understand and name it. If you can identify and name an underlying motive or desire, do so. If not, don't worry about it; just go on to the next step.

Giving Your Feelings & Desires to God

The final step in Welcoming Prayer is to give your negative feelings and any associated desires or motives to the Holy Spirit in prayer, asking Him to take them from you and heal your spirit. You may find it helpful to involve your body in the releasing process, opening your hands upward toward God as an indication of your willingness to let go. At the same time, relax any tension in your body you noticed that is associated with the emotions, letting it flow out of you each time you exhale.

As you give your feelings and desires to God, also release control of the situation to Him as well. Accept whatever outcome God has for the circumstances. This doesn't mean that you fatalistically resign yourself to the situation never changing; it means you trust that God will use the situation for good in ways you could never understand in advance. Accepting God's plan doesn't mean you should stop praying or working toward resolution of the circumstances.

When You Don't Have Time for Welcoming Prayer

Sometimes you may find yourself in a situation where you can't stop right away and spend the time to go through Welcoming Prayer. Often, at school or work, you may not be able to walk outside and go through the whole process immediately. In these cases, use Breath Prayer to calm yourself down until you have time to return to Welcoming Prayer later.

Welcoming Prayer is a powerful tool, but it is not a substitute for the help of another person when needed. If at any point you find yourself becoming overwhelmed by negative thoughts or emotions, you should go talk to a minister, mentor, or counselor immediately.

Experiencing the emotion is part of the healing process. During the welcoming stage, you should:
1. Welcome the negative emotion and listen to its message.
2. Accept the situation.
3. Release any negative images or thoughts and return your focus to the raw emotion.

The three main desires that create negative emotions are:
1. The desire of the old, sinful nature to protect itself
2. The desire to have power or maintain control
3. The desire to gain the approval or affection of others

Some people feel a strong desire to express certain negative emotions with violence. If this happens to you, try releasing this urge the same way you release negative thoughts, while at the same time releasing the physical tension that goes along with the urge. Try releasing as you exhale, visualizing the violent thought flowing out through your feet and into the ground beneath you.

The process of Welcoming Prayer is outlined on page 224 so you can easily refer back to it as you go through this book.

Compline

Reading: *2 Corinthians 4:16-18*

Reflection: What caused you to lose your sense of peace today? How did you react?

Prayer: Ask God to help you give your negative desires and emotions to Him for healing.

A SPIRITUAL JOURNEY

Day 7

IF YOU HAVE EVER BEEN SITTING IN A RESTAURANT watching the people around you talking and eating, and suddenly realized they all seemed to be off in their own little worlds, trapped in the noise of their own thoughts, you may have experienced in that moment a sense of somehow being aware of a layer of reality everyone else was ignoring. Although you may still find yourself falling back into your old, narrower patterns of awareness, the practice of *Vigil* has most likely helped these glimpses of a larger perspective come with increasing frequency.

Looking through the eyes of the Spirit, you may at times feel disconnected from what others find important, but it is exactly this separateness that opens you to what is deep and real. Your mind is seeking a purpose beyond itself, and you find that you are traveling paths that lead to an altogether different destination. It is in these moments you begin to realize you are on a radically different journey from most of those around you.

A Life Fully Lived

Time spent with the Spirit changes your perspective and teaches you to move past distractions to pursue what really brings you fulfillment. Each day leads you ever deeper into an awareness of yourself and your relationships—deeper into a spiritual awareness of your connections to God, your family, your community, and the earth God made you to care for.

Our culture seems to broadcast the subconscious message that you must be constantly involved in lots of activities if you want to be successful. It is easy to fall into the trap of thinking that living fully means you must always be on the go or doing something. But allowing yourself to get overcommitted and overscheduled can simply get you too busy to really live.

Try to get in the habit of taking time at least once each month to think through your commitments and figure out what is really important. If you don't have time to spend each morning with God without feeling rushed, or time to sit and have meaningful conversations with those you love, or time to wander quietly through the wilderness for a day, then you have too much on your schedule. You are trapped on a treadmill of events and obligations that keeps you from slowing down enough to tend to the relationships that make life meaningful.

The Gift of Each Moment

One of the best ways to find time for what is important is to simply turn off the television and the video games, and to stop aimlessly surfing around the Internet. It is all too easy to get addicted to staring at all those screens, focusing on a distorted, filtered version of the world instead of spending time experiencing it directly.

If you haven't already, try turning off all those distracting gadgets for a while. Stop spending so much time staring at your cell phone, take the headphones off, and listen instead to the still, small voice of the Spirit speaking to you out of the quiet. If you are spending a lot of time on social media sites, log off and go spend real time with your family and friends instead.

If you really want to create space to hear the Spirit more clearly, consider giving up the television and video games for the next few weeks as you go through the second book of *Vigil*. Once you break the habit of using all the electronic devices to fill up spare moments, you will be surprised how little you miss them and how much time they were wasting.

Each moment of this life comes only once. Approach each day such that you can be at peace whatever God's plan is for you, whether He gives you many more years to live, or brings you face to face with your own death an hour from now. Each moment is a gift; spend it wisely.

Margin notes:

Although it is good to think ahead and plan for the future, always remember that life is what is happening right now. Don't get so stuck thinking about what you are going to do at some point in the future that you let it keep you from seeing what God has called you to do today.

Relationships that exist only via social media are just a hollow parody of the real thing. Social media can help you keep in touch with old friends who no longer live nearby, or help you organize getting together with friends, but it is no substitute for spending time directly with people without technology being stuck in the middle.

If you have a television set or video game in your bedroom, consider getting rid of it. You will rest better and reclaim a bit of quiet, reflective space from the constant noise and distraction.

Simplicity

When a storm knocks out the power for a few days, something interesting happens. People who have passed by each other for years actually start to talk to each other, to help each other, and to even make meals together. They get to know neighbors they have never met before, and the kids who are normally always inside come back outside to play together. For this brief time, it seems people almost remember how to act like a community again. Then the power comes back on, and almost immediately everyone goes right back to their old patterns.

Over the years, the world has just kept on adding more complexity, more distractions, more speed, more noise, more new things you must acquire. In the moments when something interrupts this pattern and you are pulled back to just the basics, the profound gifts found in the simplest joys of life reappear.

It seems that the more complexity you accept into your life, and the more stuff designed to fill your every whim you buy, the more empty and isolated you become. Jesus' answer to the distractions of the world was to own almost nothing, live simply, help others, and go to the wilderness so He could hear the Father's voice.

God alone is capable of making Himself known as He really is. We search in reasoning and in sciences, as in a poor copy. What we neglect to see is God's painting Himself in the depth of our soul.

- Brother Lawrence

Weaving the Tapestry of Shalom

In those moments when events such as a storm or other crisis bring your focus back to the most fundamental and important elements of life, you are quickly reminded that God did not design you to make the journeys of life in isolation. It is no accident that times of crisis quickly rekindle a sense of community and remind you of what a gift it is to have other followers of Jesus walking alongside you. While God's Spirit speaks directly into your heart through the scripture and the times of quiet you spend together, He also at times chooses to speak through the words and actions of other Believers in your community.

In *Romans 8*, Paul reminds us that when we enter a covenant relationship with God, we experience a spiritual adoption whereby we become His children. In becoming God's spiritual heir, you also gain an entirely new spiritual family. God's covenant with His children binds them together as brothers and sisters, and creates among them a shared responsibility toward one another.

The love and support found in spending time together with your spiritual family is foundational in your own growth, and creates the spaces where God can use you to help others in turn. The community that the Spirit seeks to create among God's children can only express itself fully when we treat each other according to God's commandments, acting out of the Spirit's love moving through us. When you walk with your spiritual brothers and sisters, together seeking to follow God's truth, He begins to weave among you a fabric of community that brings *Shalom*— God's own peace—to the daily experiences of life.

The principles found in the Bible involving how we are to treat each other as Believers are so critical to creating peace among the Church that we will spend the second half of this book looking at them in detail. Starting with Week Seven, we will look at passages that outline God's design for how we must behave toward each other as members of the body of Christ.

A Journey of Transformation

The journey of seeking after God is intense, and completely transformational. It transforms your mind, your thoughts, your desires, your actions, and your innermost being. It redefines the way you treat others, and how you see yourself. But, most of all, with each step along the way, it restores your relationship with the God who created you. The transformation of this journey is the inner working of the Spirit, conforming you ever more fully into the image of Christ.

The conclusion of the reading for Day 7, along with *Compline*, is on the next page. →

INTEGRATING THE SACRED INTO THE FLOW OF LIFE

God designed you so your awareness of the sacred would be present every moment of your day, permeating and informing your experience of the world. He then placed you in a world He created to remind you of Him and continually bring your mind back to His presence. The modern world often cuts us off from these reminders, its distractions and noise pulling our minds towards the priorities of our culture and away from things of the spirit. The disciplines we are developing in this book will start to bring the awareness of the spiritual back into the everyday. The points below will help you think about how to integrate these tools into the flow of life.

Day 7

- Start your day with *Vigil* each morning to set the focus for the rest of the day. As you finish *Contemplatio* and return your mind to looking forward to the tasks ahead of you during the few moments of Benediction, try to carry the awareness of the sacred out from your morning time with you into the world.
- Continue with getting ready for the day, cleaning up and preparing for work, school, or whatever lies ahead. As you come to breakfast, pause for a few moments to be thankful for the meal before you eat. As you finish your prayer of blessing, let your spirit move into the silence for several seconds, feeling God's presence and listening for His voice.
- In the same way, pause before lunch and dinner for a prayer of blessing followed by a few moments of returning to the silence. If you are eating with other Believers, you may wish to share the prayer aloud followed by a few seconds of quiet so that each person can turn inwardly back toward an awareness of the presence of God.
- If you feel moved to do so, find a time to work in a mid-morning and mid-afternoon prayer during which you again pause for a minute or two to return your focus fully to the sacred among the flow of life. Feel free to be creative during these moments, following whatever path the Spirit opens up for you. You may be called to pray, sing softly to yourself, bring the words of scripture back to mind, or just move back into interior stillness with your inward gaze fixed on God.
- Use Breath Prayers throughout the day to help you keep your awareness of God's presence or to call on His promises or provision.
- Whenever a situation arises where you want to talk directly to God for a moment, speak inwardly to God in a Prayer in Passing. You might express your thankfulness, ask for wisdom, or just pause to share a thought with your Creator.
- When you are faced with a task you find difficult or unpleasant, turn it into an Act of Service, keeping your focus on God's presence as you work. Make the task a sacrament by performing it as if it were being done for God Himself.
- If you run into a situation that creates negative emotions, use the Welcoming Prayer to deal with the feelings and release them to God's care. If the situation won't allow you to pause for Welcoming Prayer immediately, try using a breath prayer to calm yourself in the moment and then return to deal with the emotions with Welcoming Prayer as soon as you have the opportunity.
- Close the day with *Compline*, reflecting on what you learned during the day and how your walk with God was. Finish the day by returning to silence as your prepare for sleep.
- At any time during your day, if you come to a place where you feel difficulty in connecting with God's presence, try to go back outside and find a quiet space where the natural world can remind you of the Creator's hand at work around you. Put aside the noise and pace of the modern world for a while so you can ground yourself back into the reality of God's voice speaking to you in the silence.

Compline

Reading: *Psalm 119:153-176*

Reflection: How aware were you today of God's presence as you went about your daily tasks?

Prayer: Ask the Holy Spirit to help you develop an abiding sense of the spiritual reality of God's presence that deepens your awareness amid the noise and distractions of the world.

Week 2 - Pilgrimage

Then spake Jesus again unto them, saying,
I am the light of the world: he that followeth me shall not walk in darkness,
but shall have the light of life.

-John 8:12 (KJV)

JESUS' LIFE AND MINISTRY WAS A PILGRIMAGE. The gospels are the story of the God who walked among us, traveling from city to city on a sacred journey of teaching and healing that would eventually lead Him to a cross. Jesus did not build a temple to Himself and command everyone to come to Him; He went to where the people were, both physically and spiritually. As He walked among the people, the simple and everyday became sacred. He showed them that serving each other, sharing meals together, helping the sick, and even going fishing could be more profoundly spiritual than anything to be found in the synagogues. Jesus showed us the real journey is to be found in the everyday events of life, not sitting in a church building.

A *pilgrimage* is a journey to a sacred place. The ancient Hebrews would often travel to the Temple in Jerusalem on pilgrimage to join the annual festivals and offer sacrifices. During the Middle Ages, many Believers undertook difficult journeys to holy sites in a search for an encounter with God. Even today, Christians still travel to the Holy Land to see the places where Jesus lived and taught. These physical journeys often hold great meaning, but are really only a reflection of the deeper, spiritual journey of the life spent following Christ.

As a follower of Christ, you are called to make your life a pilgrimage: a spiritual journey through this world in search of the land that lies beyond. On this journey, you do not have to wait until the end to find what you are seeking. The God who called you to the journey, and whose country you seek, walks with you every step along the way, revealing Himself to you as you go.

Your journey will not look exactly like anyone else's. You may be called to another part of the world, or you may be called to walk across the room to talk to someone who is lonely. Your pilgrimage may lead you just down the street to help somebody you don't even know, or even find you seemingly lost for a while, unsure of whether you are on the right path. In the sacred pauses of life, when you are quiet enough to listen, God will reveal the path just ahead. God has laid out the road ahead of you, but you must get up and follow it. You won't find God by just sitting in a church service; you must make your search for Him a life-long pilgrimage.

The seasons are the focus for *Contemplatio* this week. The cycles of life and death driven by the seasons serve as a reminder of the constant unfolding of God's design. As we seek Him, we find that He was seeking us first, the unchanging God who reveals Himself in ever-changing patterns. We pass through this world only once, on pilgrimage toward our eternal home. Even as this life draws to a close, our journey with God is simply opening onto a new and higher path.

Extra Mile:

Plan and make a pilgrimage sometime in the next few weeks. You might visit the oldest church in your area, the site of an important event, or a place that has special significance in your spiritual journey. Make the journey sacred, praying as you go and pausing while there to reflect on God's hand at work in your life.

PILGRIMAGE

Day 1

The fact that entering into a covenant relationship with Jesus sets you onto an entirely new path does not mean that the path will be easy. You will almost certainly have times of significant struggle, of wandering off the path and feeling lost for a while, and of even doubting whether God is really there at all. God uses all of this to ultimately bring you to the place where you know Him in His fullness and learn to depend upon His love and provision, even when you can't clearly see the next steps lying ahead of you.

The word *liturgy* is sometimes used to refer specifically to a more formal style of public worship that has a prescribed format and a set pattern. In this section, *liturgy* is used to refer to all forms of Christian corporate worship, whether formal or informal. In the sense used here, *liturgy* also includes those times you spend alone in prayer, reading of scripture, or private fellowship with God.

Many people who have grown up in church have a hard time picturing the Christian life as a journey. Their experience is often one of going to church one or more times each week, usually to sit through a service or teaching time that seems mostly the same as the last week. Unless something spiritually real and deep is happening in their life outside of church, the practice of attending services, going to Bible studies, or even teaching them, can come to feel static and predictable.

This problem of getting stuck in the rut of *doing church* usually grows from not living with awareness of God's presence in the moment-by-moment flow of each day. You can't simply walk in the church door and turn on your awareness of the spiritual if you have been ignoring it the rest of the week. Your pilgrimage will require you to be on the spiritual journey every moment, not just for the few hours each week you are in a church building.

Faith Calls You to the Journey

The Bible uses the picture of the relationship between Jesus and the members of His church being like marriage. Just as a man and woman enter into a covenant by the exchange of marriage vows, we enter into a covenant with Christ when we call upon Him to receive us as His own. For some reason, though, many people fall into the trap of thinking of the experience of salvation as a single moment instead of a process that begins at that instant and continues throughout life. This is like claiming that everything important in a marriage happens during the wedding ceremony, and that nothing much important happens in the relationship afterward.

In a healthy marriage, the ceremony is simply a beginning point. The relationship deepens over time, as the couple spends time together and their love grows stronger over the years. Your relationship with Christ is the same: you give yourself to Him completely at the point of salvation, and the experience of that moment changes the path of your life entirely.

From that time forward, you will naturally seek to walk a path that leads ever closer to the mind of God. This kind of faith cannot help but change the way you think and act in every situation. As the Bible points out in the second chapter of *James*, the kind of faith that can save you is also the kind of faith that pushes you right out of your comfort zones and into radical acts of service for those around you.

The Cycle of Life & Liturgy

Going to a church building today is a very different experience from the early church practice of meeting together in homes. Increasingly, many churches are trying to make their buildings a center of community life, but for those who only show up for worship on Sunday morning, the ceremonies and rituals of the church can feel disconnected from the flow of daily life.

The first-century church had the advantage of being intimately integrated into the rhythm of the community, with groups of Believers often living close enough to share meals and gather several times throughout the week to pray and worship together. This closeness allowed the members of the community to move back and forth between the experiences of life and the times of prayer and reflection—both personal and corporate—that allow for these experiences to be understood and integrated. For many people today, the sense of isolation created by our rapid-transit, always-on-the-move world make it challenging to find this sense of community. Finding those who will walk beside you on this path, however, is critical. Take the time to seek out others who are on the same road; God gives them to you as companions for the journey.

The pattern God has created to strengthen and sustain you on your pilgrimage through this world is a two-fold cycle almost like breathing: you breathe in God's love and healing as you spend time with Him in liturgy, and you breathe out God's love and healing into the world as you walk through the experiences of everyday life.

Daily life is the part of the cycle that creates an awareness of God's Spirit at work in the world. The everyday moments are where God teaches you to see others as He sees them, and uses you as His hands and feet to carry His love into the world. When the weight of life begins to feel too heavy, liturgy provides time to allow you to reflect on events and respond to them. God ordained the liturgies and sacraments of the Church to help you integrate your experiences, to allow you to process and release your grief, and to provide you with the support of a community, so that you could receive spiritual healing when you are wounded by the battles of life.

Together, life and liturgy form a complete cycle. In the flow of each day, God gives you a series of challenges, making you constantly work to learn and grow. Liturgy provides the space to reflect on the journey and allows you to integrate this growth so you are ready for new challenges. Without this balance of life and liturgy, your journey will be much harder.

If you travel through the world constantly chasing spiritual experiences, opening yourself to an awareness of the spiritual aspects of the world, but neglect to take time to balance those experiences with times of quiet reflection and corporate worship, you will soon run into trouble. Without liturgy—both the shared liturgy of the community and the personal liturgy of daily times with the Spirit—spiritual experiences will open in you an awareness of your own grief without providing a way for you to process and release it.

On the other hand, if you spend time in liturgy without striving to follow God in daily life, you enter into liturgy with empty hands. Attempting the journey of a Christ-following pilgrimage without a habitual awareness of God at work around you will eventually lead you to a liturgy of empty prayer and empty worship. Empty liturgy in turn leads to becoming dogmatically attached to your intellectual ideas about God, since a lack of direct awareness of His presence means abstract ideas are all you have to hang onto.

You must follow God through the trenches of life in order for liturgy to be meaningful. As you seek God and taste the mystery of His presence, you realize you are ill-equipped to grasp God's nature with your mind alone, and soon learn to hold less tightly to the dogmas your mind creates in an attempt to define God and put Him in a box.

Although thinking about the cycle of life and liturgy can be helpful, the two are not, in reality, completely distinct. As you mature, the line between life and liturgy will begin to slowly blur, as you learn to carry the sacred space of liturgy with you throughout the ordinary experiences of your day.

Listening & Following

A common question for those starting on the journey of faith is how to know where God is leading. The simplest answer is that in order to follow, you must first listen. Learning to hear and distinguish God's voice develops from the type of listening found in the silence, and it is this type of listening that reveals the path ahead.

As you get to know the quality of God's presence, following becomes ever clearer. You hear Him speaking to you through the words of scripture, through the words of other Believers, and often through words spoken directly into your spirit as you sit with Him in stillness. As you look for the way He has ordained for you, the correct path will feel enlightened with His presence.

Carrying the name *Christian*, one who follows after and identifies with Christ, is a concept that has unfortunately been diluted over the years as the word has been picked up and used in a variety of other ways. Today it is often used to refer to anyone who attends a Christian church or who comes from a family who has a history of attending one. Throughout this book, the word *Believer* is used to refer specifically to a person who has entered into a covenant relationship with God through faith in Jesus Christ. In this sense, the term *Believer* excludes those who may attend a Christian church without having entered into a covenant relationship with God.

Although the word *liturgy* is used here to refer to time spent with God both privately and in the community of other Believers, the two are not interchangeable and each serve a unique purpose. God does not intend your spiritual journey to be a lonely one, and the support of other Believers is critical. On the other hand, times of corporate liturgy don't substitute for time spent alone with God each day, and can never create the personal intimacy with Christ that time alone with God creates.

Compline

Reading: *Acts 1:6-8*

Reflection: Are you on the journey that God called you to travel? Has your faith led you any place new and unexpected lately?

Prayer: Tell God what you think are the next steps in the journey He has laid out for you, then be still and listen for His guidance.

READING #1 - GENESIS 12:1-4

Throughout this book, the prayer that ends the preparation time will change to reflect each week's theme. Consider using part or all of this prayer as a breath prayer at least one day during the week.

Day 2

In this passage from Genesis, God calls Abraham to leave the country where he is living and follow God's lead into a new land. Through this journey, God set in motion the events that would eventually bring about Christ's birth. In this way, God fulfilled His promise to bless all the people of the Earth through Abraham's obedience to His call.

Are you willing to follow God where He leads you, whether around the world or in the ministry of everyday life? What has God called you to do that you haven't yet answered? What fears keep you from beginning the journey?

Preparation:

- Calm your mind and take a few deep breaths
- Start with a Prayer of Thanksgiving
- Continue with the prayer, "*Lord Jesus Christ, I choose to follow you. Guide my feet, guard my thoughts, and heal my spirit.*"

Lectio:

The LORD had said to Abram, "Leave your country, your people and your father's household and go to the land I will show you.
I will make you into a great nation and I will bless you; I will make your name great, and you will be a blessing. I will bless those who bless you, and whoever curses you I will curse; and all peoples on earth will be blessed through you."
So Abram left, as the LORD had told him; and Lot went with him. Abram was seventy-five years old when he set out from Haran.

- Genesis 12:1-4 (NIV)

Meditatio:

Oratio:

Ask God to show you the next steps He has for prepared for you in the pilgrimage of your spiritual journey. If you cannot see the next steps clearly yet, ask God to prepare you so that you will be ready for the path He will open ahead of you.

As you start back into your daily practice of Lectio Divina this morning, it would be a great time to set up a trigger to remind yourself to pause throughout the day for moments of prayer. Pick something simple, such a checking your phone or walking through a doorway, that can serve as a reminder to return to a Breath Prayer or take a moment to talk to God in a Prayer in Passing.

Contemplatio:

The progression of the seasons brings with it the changing cycles of life. Spring begins with an explosion of new life which grows and strengthens during the heat of Summer. Fall is a time of maturing, setting seed, and preparing for the cold weather to come. The shorter days of Winter are a time of dormancy and death, with the underlying promise of the rebirth of Spring just around the corner.

As you begin _Contemplatio_ today, look at the signs of the current season visible in the environment around you. The plants, animals, and the soil beneath you reflect where you are in the cycle of the year. Even the quality of light tells a story about the season. Think for a few moments about what the world around you is saying about life's journey from birth through to death. Remember that God has given you this one life to make your pilgrimage across the face of the Earth. As you move into wide-angle vision, quiet your thoughts and feel the rhythm of the seasons moving around you. Even in the depths of winter, the first hints of Spring are visible.

Benediction:

- Return slowly and peacefully from _Contemplatio_
- Take time to be thankful again
- Acknowledge that you have completed your time for today and ask God to go with you as you leave this time.

**Compline**

Reading: _1 Peter 2:9-11_

Reflection: How did you live out God's call on your life today? In what ways is God preparing you for the path ahead?

Prayer: Ask God to create in you a moment-by-moment awareness of His presence and of your spiritual journey through this world.

READING #2 - MATTHEW 9:9

Preparation:

- Calm your mind and take a few deep breaths
- Start with a Prayer of Thanksgiving
- Continue with the prayer, "*Lord Jesus Christ, I choose to follow you. Guide my feet, guard my thoughts, and heal my spirit.*"

Lectio:

Day 3

> As Jesus was walking along, he saw a man called Matthew sitting at the tax booth; and he said to him, "Follow me." And he got up and followed him.
>
> *- Matthew 9:9 (NRSV)*

Meditatio:

Imagine yourself in Matthew's place, as Jesus called him to leave his current life and follow a new path into the unknown. How would you have answered?

Oratio:

Talk to God about the path He is calling you to follow. Ask Him to show you the next steps on your journey and guide your feet as you go. Tell God about any fears that are holding you back and then give those fears to God.

There is meaning in every journey that is unknown to the traveler.

- Dietrich Bonhoeffer

Contemplatio:

Each season has its own distinctive sounds. The sound of the birds, the insects, and the wind in the trees all vary with the seasons. Differences in temperature and humidity affect the way sound carries through the air. The hot and humid air of summer seems to stifle sound, while noises seem to travel forever in the cold, dry air of winter. The winds rustling in the newly green trees of Spring or rattling the just-fallen leaves of Autumn also bring their own unique sounds.

Close your eyes and reach out your hearing as far as possible in every direction. Notice the way the sound carries through the air and think about how this relates to the season. Listen to the birds and notice how the season affects their behavior. Think about how the seasonal presence or absence of insects changes the sonic landscape. Let these sounds bring you into an awareness of God's unfolding work in the changing seasons around you. Then release the inward noise of your own thoughts and sit with God in the space of your interior silence.

Benediction:

- Return slowly and peacefully from *Contemplatio*
- Take time to be thankful again
- Acknowledge that you have completed your time for today and ask God to go with you as you leave this time.

Compline

Reading: *Matthew 10:37-39*

Reflection: How did you take up the cross and follow Jesus today? Are you willing to let go of your life so you can find it?

Prayer: Confess to God any things you are unwilling to let go of in order to follow Him.

READING #3 - MATTHEW 10:7-14

Preparation:

- Calm your mind and take a few deep breaths
- Start with a Prayer of Thanksgiving
- Continue with the prayer, "*Lord Jesus Christ, I choose to follow you. Guide my feet, guard my thoughts, and heal my spirit.*"

Lectio:

Day 4

These are the instructions that Jesus gave His disciples as He sent them out to travel from city to city and minister in His name.

As you go, preach this message: 'The kingdom of heaven is near.'
Heal the sick, raise the dead, cleanse those who have leprosy, drive out demons.
Freely you have received, freely give.
Do not take along any gold or silver or copper in your belts; take no bag for the journey, or extra tunic, or sandals or a staff; for the worker is worth his keep.
Whatever town or village you enter, search for some worthy person there and stay at his house until you leave. As you enter the home, give it your greeting. If the home is deserving, let your peace rest on it; if it is not, let your peace return to you.
If anyone will not welcome you or listen to your words, shake the dust off your feet when you leave that home or town.

- *Matthew 10:7-14 (NIV)*

Meditatio:

Visualize yourself standing with the other disciples listening to Jesus give you these instructions. How would you have felt as you set out? What would Jesus' instructions look like today if He stood before you and gave you a mission to fulfill in His name?

Oratio:

> Ask God to give you a clear understanding of the authority He has given you: authority to carry out His purpose and act in His name while here in this world.

> *You have chosen the roughest road, but it leads straight to the hilltops.*
>
> - John Bunyan

Contemplatio:

The seasonal changes in the air don't just affect the way sound carries; they also affect the way the air brings information to your skin. The cold, crisp air of Winter feels sharp against the skin, bringing a heightened awareness to your sense of touch. At times, the warm and humid air of Summer can feel like a blanket, smothering all but the closest of sensations. The more moderate periods of Spring and Fall invite the skin to open up and enjoy the warmth of the sun mixed with the coolness of the breezes.

Close your eyes and pay attention to how the air feels on your skin. Is it the cold, wet wind of a rainy Fall or Winter morning, or the warmer air of Spring or Summer? Think about what the direction of the wind tells you about the season. Where do the prevailing winds come from during this time of year? Notice your own body's reaction to the sensation of the air on your skin. Relax and accept the touch of the air without judgment. Bring your mind to stillness and turn your focus toward God as you let the sensations of the air play over your skin.

Benediction:

- Return slowly and peacefully from *Contemplatio*
- Take time to be thankful again
- Acknowledge that you have completed your time for today and ask God to go with you as you leave this time.

> *Compline*
>
> **Reading:** *Luke 24:13-35*
>
> **Reflection:** Jesus reveals Himself as you walk with Him and listen. Has Jesus walked with you today and you didn't recognize Him at the time?
>
> **Prayer:** Be thankful for all the ways God leads you and directs your path.

READING #4 - HEBREWS 11:8-10, 13-16

Preparation:

- Calm your mind and take a few deep breaths
- Start with a Prayer of Thanksgiving
- Continue with the prayer, "*Lord Jesus Christ, I choose to follow you. Guide my feet, guard my thoughts, and heal my spirit.*"

Lectio:

Day 5

Hebrews 11 begins by listing Abel, Enoch, and Noah as examples of those who had faith in God. Verse 8 continues by talking about the faith of Abraham. The statement in verse 13 that *all these died in faith* is a reference back to all these examples of great faith. In saying that they all died before they received the promise they were awaiting, the writer of *Hebrews* means that none of them lived to see the coming of Jesus in fulfillment of the promise of a Messiah.

By faith Abraham obeyed when he was called to set out for a place that he was to receive as an inheritance; and he set out, not knowing where he was going.
By faith he stayed for a time in the land he had been promised, as in a foreign land, living in tents, as did Isaac and Jacob, who were heirs with him of the same promise. For he looked forward to the city that has foundations,
whose architect and builder is God....
All of these died in faith without having received the promises, but from a distance they saw and greeted them. They confessed that they were strangers and foreigners on the earth, for people who speak in this way make it clear that they are seeking a homeland. If they had been thinking of the land that they had left behind,
they would have had opportunity to return.
But as it is, they desire a better country, that is, a heavenly one. Therefore God is not ashamed to be called their God; indeed, he has prepared a city for them.

- Hebrews 11:8-10, 13-16 (NRSV)

Meditatio:

Do your actions show that you live only for this world? Or that you desire the world to come, while still living every moment fully while here on Earth?

Oratio:

_____

Thank God for the fullness of life here on this Earth, and the even greater promise of an everlasting adventure with Him in the life beyond.

The process of sitting in silence each morning with God will inevitably begin to open you up to understanding the grief and negative emotions you carry with you as the result of sin. As you work your way through this second book of *Vigil*, it is very possible that you may come to a point when negative thoughts and feelings come into the open and ask to be dealt with. You may even be tempted to stop doing your time with God each morning because it seems easier than going through the difficult process of looking through clear eyes at your own inner self. Don't let yourself become discouraged if you hit this place, because it means that you are close to letting go of old thoughts and emotions so that the Holy Spirit can heal them. Keep moving forward, always asking God to help you along the way. Be sure to find someone who is spiritually mature who you feel comfortable talking with so they can support you as well.

Contemplatio:

Just as the seasons each uniquely affect the other senses, they also bring their own distinctive character to the smells carried on the wind and even the taste of the air. Close your eyes and smell the air, trying to see how many individual scents you can discern. Taste the air as well, and see if this combination of smelling and tasting brings out new information.

The smells and tastes on the air will, of course, be affected the most by the weather and man-made chemicals in the environment. But if you look further, you will begin to notice underlying scents and tastes in the air that belong to the season. The flush of new green in the Spring smells quite different from the decaying of leaves in late Fall.

As you move into the silence today, notice anything in your being that you are holding back from God or are afraid to open fully to Him. Don't judge yourself if you find it hard to let go of everything all at once. Just let go a little more each day, relaxing into God's presence.

Benediction:

- Return slowly and peacefully from *Contemplatio*
- Take time to be thankful again
- Acknowledge that you have completed your time for today and ask God to go with you as you leave this time.

Compline

Reading: *Psalm 121*

Reflection: *Psalms 120-134* are songs that were sung by the pilgrims on their way to the Temple in Jerusalem. *Psalm 120* was sung at the beginning of the journey, with each of the following Psalms representing another step in the journey until *Psalm 134* was sung when entering the Temple.

READING #5 - HEBREWS 12:1-2

Preparation:

- Calm your mind and take a few deep breaths
- Start with a Prayer of Thanksgiving
- Continue with the prayer, "*Lord Jesus Christ, I choose to follow you. Guide my feet, guard my thoughts, and heal my spirit.*"

Lectio:

Day 6

The passage you read yesterday was from *Hebrews 11*, a chapter that is sometimes called the Hall of Faith because it lists many of the great examples cf faith from the Old Testament. The phrase *great cloud of witnesses* used here in the first verse of *Hebrews 12* refers back to these examples of faith in the previous chapter.

> Therefore, since we are surrounded by such a great cloud of witnesses,
> let us throw off everything that hinders and the sin that so easily entangles,
> and let us run with perseverance the race marked out for us.
> Let us fix our eyes on Jesus, the author and perfecter of our faith,
> who for the joy set before him endured the cross, scorning its shame,
> and sat down at the right hand of the throne of God.
>
> *- Hebrews 12:1-2 (NIV)*

Meditatio:

Picture your life as a race that you must run with perseverance to reach the ultimate goal: a life beyond this one spent with the One who created you and saved you from the destructive power of sin.

Oratio:

> Confess to God the ways in which you are tempted to give up the race and just sit on the sidelines. Tell God what you find hard or intimidating. Give those fears to God and ask Him to give you the perseverance to run the race well.

> *We need to find God, and he cannot be found in noise and restlessness. God is the friend of silence. See how nature - trees, flowers, grass- grows in silence; see the stars, the moon and the sun, how they move in silence. We need silence to be able to touch souls.*
>
> - Mother Teresa

Contemplatio:

Start out today by laying on the ground and looking up at the sky. Use all your senses to take in what is happening around you, noticing how everything in the environment reflects the current season. Using wide-angle vision, look at the color of the sky and of the plants and trees. Listen to the movement of the air and the sound of the birds. Feel the earth beneath you and notice whether it feels awake or asleep. Taste and smell the air, noting any messages being carried to you by the wind.

Once you have all your physical senses engaged, reach out with your spiritual sense and feel the hand of God at work in the rhythm of everything around you. Let go of your own thoughts and simply watch God at work around you. Open yourself in a wordless invitation for the Spirit of God to work inside of you as well, healing your mind and spirit.

Benediction:

- Return slowly and peacefully from *Contemplatio*
- Take time to be thankful again
- Acknowledge that you have completed your time for today and ask God to go with you as you leave this time.

> ### Compline
>
> **Reading:** *Psalm 134*
>
> **Reflection:** Have your thoughts and actions today been a blessing to God?
>
> **Prayer:** Lift your hands up toward God and pray a prayer of blessing and thanksgiving.

REFLECTION

In picking a passage from the week to revisit on Day 7, feel free to use passages you read during *Compline* in addition to those from the main reading each day.

Day 7

Revisit Your Favorite Passage

Reflections on the Week

Compline

Reading: *Psalm 1*

Reflection: How has your understanding of your spiritual journey changed this week? What has God revealed to you about the path He has called you to follow?

Prayer: Be thankful for a God who walks with you and beside you.

Week 3 - The Sacrament of the Ordinary

For I received from the Lord what I also handed on to you,
that the Lord Jesus on the night when he was betrayed took a loaf of bread, and when he had given thanks,
he broke it and said, "This is my body that is for you. Do this in remembrance of me."
In the same way he took the cup also, after supper, saying, "This cup is the new covenant in my blood.
Do this, as often as you drink it, in remembrance of me."

-1 Corinthians 11:23-25 (NRSV)

Jesus instituted the sacrament of Communion as He shared the Passover meal with His disciples the night before He died. In the simple act of sharing a meal, Jesus created a powerful symbol of His sacrifice on the cross, a way for us to remember the price that He paid to save us. Each time we gather to share Communion, it returns our minds to the reality of Christ's gift of grace and forgiveness.

The word *sacrament* comes from the Latin word *sacrare*, which means to consecrate or make holy. The pace of modern life often pulls our thoughts away from the sacred and into the noise of the world around us. Although we most often think of sacraments as the formal rites or rituals of the church, any act that serves as a sign or symbol that returns our minds to the ongoing presence of God's work in our lives can be used as a sacrament if done in a sacred way.

Brother Lawrence, as he sought to live constantly aware of God's presence, learned the power of turning even the most ordinary of activities into a sacrament. By performing his tasks carefully, deliberately, and with humility, Brother Lawrence aimed to make all his actions into acts of service that radiated God's love. He did not view these Sacraments of the Ordinary as a duty or heavy burden, but as an opportunity to work alongside God and allow Him to lift the mental and spiritual load of life. As he followed this practice over time, Brother Lawrence found an ever-growing sense of joy and freedom.

Walking with God in this way slowly changes your priorities in life, bringing your thoughts and desires back into line with what God intended. The road is sometimes steep early in the journey, as you struggle against your old thoughts and desires. If you try climbing these mountains alone, you will soon become discouraged. As your rely on God to replace your old thought patterns with ones that reflect His thoughts and desires, you will find that following the commands found in scripture becomes increasingly more natural. This is the process through which the Spirit transforms you into the image of Christ.

For *Contemplatio* this week, you will be shifting your focus inward to your own breath. Since your mind is affected by your body, the way you breathe can influence how easy it is to calm your mind and quiet your thoughts. In addition to using your breath as a focus, you will practice moving your breathing back to a more natural, relaxing pattern. Returning to a natural way of breathing will help you keep your mind more focused throughout the day, and will allow you to move more easily into interior stillness during *Contemplatio*.

Extra Mile:

As an Act of Service, make a meal for your family or friends sometime this week. Put thought behind what you prepare and try to make it special. If possible, invite someone who needs a blessing right now, or who has been a blessing to you. Serve the meal yourself and lead in a prayer of thanks before you eat.

THE SACRAMENT OF THE ORDINARY

Ineluctable means *not able to be avoided or changed.* A *modality* is a way of thinking, acting, or perceiving. Thus, an *ineluctable modality* is a way of thinking or perceiving that you cannot easily escape or change.

Day 1

Your sacred pauses each day are not the only time you should think about protecting yourself from the noise and distractions of the world. If you want to develop a constant awareness of God's presence, you should work toward a state of inner quiet that you carry throughout the day. When you become caught up in your own thoughts and feelings, the noise begins to drown out your physical senses, which will tend to keep your spiritual sense shut down as well. When you find yourself lost in your own thoughts, slow down and return to a state of awareness. In time, you will learn to walk in the silence, allowing thoughts to arise when they are needed.

IN THE NOVEL *Ulysses*, JAMES JOYCE USES the cryptic phrase *ineluctable modality of the visible* to capture the idea that we as humans are almost completely stuck in the mode of creating our sense of reality from the information that comes in through our senses: primarily our eyes, but including the ears and other senses as well. The idea that only the world of the physical senses is immediate and accessible has become widespread in our culture, where we are told we can only trust what scientists can measure and quantify. Anything spiritual, if it is acknowledged at all, is often represented as being mystical and inaccessible, only to be found in far-away places or religious ceremonies.

As you have found in spending time quietly listening in silence each day, however, God has made your physical senses a doorway that helps open up your spiritual senses, revealing God's presence with you each moment. By exercising your spiritual senses, you allow God to teach you to escape the trap of seeing the world only with your physical eyes. Over time, this develops a new and deeper sense of reality in which this world is simply a reflection and echo of the unseen realm of spirit where God walks with you through the everyday moments of life.

Finding the God Who was Always There

For some reason, it's often tempting to imagine God's presence as limited to certain places: a church building, a lonely place in the wilderness, or a site of great beauty and majesty. Over the weeks you have been going outside each morning, you have probably grown to also think of the spot where you do *Vigil* each day as a place where God can be found. Other locations, however, can be more difficult. Although you may know intellectually that God is present in all places and all circumstances, you have likely noticed how challenging it is to remain mindful of God in places that seem more ordinary. In the noise and motion of a school, office building, or shopping center, God may seem far away and hard to hear.

Even harder can be remaining fully rooted in your spiritual awareness when you are faced with places that appear indifferent or hostile to God's presence. As your journey progresses, you will come to realize that God is every bit as present in a bar, strip club, or crime-ridden neighborhood as He is in the most beautiful cathedral or on the most remote mountaintop. If you pay attention to God only in the "special" places, you will miss much of what He is doing around you each day.

Learning Who God Really Is

If you wanted to get to know a person better, you would most likely arrange to spend some time together. You wouldn't invite a person over to visit and then ask them to sit in the corner while you read their biography. Why would you try to learn about a person second-hand when they are right there where you can get to know them personally? Developing a relationship with God is very much the same: first-hand time with God is the only way to know Him.

Sitting in school, you may come to think the way to learn about something is to study, but the reality of God is not found in theology textbooks. In fact, taking all the books too seriously can simply create confusion, as you focus more on other people's limited conception of God than on the very real presence of God Himself walking beside you right now. Reading about other people's experiences along the path can indeed be helpful, but it is never a replacement for direct time talking with God yourself. Study can result in you knowing a lot of facts about God, but only a relationship that is personal can lead you to know who He really is.

In this regard, time spent with the Bible is quite different than time spent with any other book. The Holy Spirit speaks to you directly through the words of scripture if you are listening for His voice as you read. It is certainly possible to approach the Bible with the intellect only, remaining closed to the Spirit's voice, so that all that results is an intellectual exercise in figuring out what the Bible says about a specific topic. This kind of reading of scripture is always shallow, often resulting in people arguing over minor points of theology instead of focusing on what is most important in God's view. Jesus leveled some of His most harsh criticism against the Pharisees, who had used the scriptures to create an elaborate system of rules to govern the most trivial aspects of life while ignoring God's primary commandments to love and care for each other.

It is through the constant cycle of life and liturgy that you come to know God personally and to realize what matters to Him most. You must run life's race fully aware and engaged every moment, but also remember to slow down and observe the rhythm of sacred pauses through prayer, study, and worship. The path of a life spent seeking God may have moments when you are called to great and heroic action, to climb to new spiritual heights or to fight major battles. But it is in the quiet moments of the average day, in the little things, that the Holy Spirit molds your soul into what God designed it to be.

Giving & Receiving

You encounter one of the most profound opportunities to turn the ordinary into the sacred each time you deal with another person. Since God has chosen His children to act as His hands and feet in this world, you are acting as an instrument of God Himself each time you talk to or help someone. When another person gives you comfort or help, God receives this kindness as if it were an act of service directed at Him. For this reason, you should always practice giving to and receiving from others in a sacred way.

As you give to others, do so graciously and generously, just as God has given to you. As you receive from others, receive graciously and with gratitude. By receiving graciously, you allow others to experience the blessing of giving.

A Life without Separation

As you live, make sure you don't allow walls to arise between the sacred and the secular, between your time focused on God's presence and your time out in the world. If you have communion with Christ, then you carry sacred space with you even as you travel through the most ordinary of places.

In the same way, any place where Believers meet together, work together, or live together, is also a sacred space. You should find no separation or disconnect between what happens in the church building and what happens in the rest of your life. When the church building becomes the sole focus of your spiritual life, it has become more of a problem than a blessing. What happens among the community of Believers outside of the church building is what frames those times of meeting together as a body and gives them meaning.

As Paul writes in *2 Corinthians 4:18*, when you look through the eyes given to you by the Spirit, you begin to see the eternal truths that remain unseen to earthly sight. The ability to see with spiritual eyes allows you to walk a path not visible to human eyes. This ability to see the unseen creates in you an awareness of God's presence and work in the everyday places of life that can turn even the most ordinary of moments into a sacrament.

The discovery of God lies in the daily and the ordinary, not in the spectacular and the heroic.
If we cannot find God in the routines of home and shop, then we will not find Him at all.

- Richard Foster

Week 3

Recognizing the sacred in the everyday does nothing to diminish the power, beauty, and mystery of the formal sacraments of the Church. Sacraments such as Communion and Baptism are an integral part of the liturgy that complements and completes the experiences of life in the cycle of life and liturgy discussed last week.

Compline

Reading: *Psalm 119:1-8*

Reflection: How consistently have you kept your mind fixed on God's precepts and presence today? At what points during the day is this easier or harder?

Prayer: Offer a prayer of thankfulness for the grace and wisdom God freely gives you in even the small moments of life.

Bible Reading #1 - Colossians 3:23-24

Preparation:

- Calm your mind and take a few deep breaths
- Start with a Prayer of Thanksgiving
- Continue with the prayer, "*Lord Jesus Christ, make my every act a sacrament in remembrance of you. Lead me as I seek to walk in your path.*"

Day 2

Lectio:

Whatever you do, work at it with all your heart, as working for the Lord, not for men,
since you know that you will receive an inheritance from the Lord as a reward.
It is the Lord Christ you are serving.

- Colossians 3:23-24 (NIV)

Meditatio:

What will you have to do this week that you will be tempted to have a bad attitude about? How could you turn this into something sacred by treating it as an act of service directed toward Christ?

Oratio:

Ask God to change your perspective on everyday activities this week, allowing you to turn them into sacraments that point others toward Christ.

Week 3

Contemplatio:

As you start *Contemplatio* today, close your eyes and pay attention to your breath. Notice which part of your upper body expands and contracts as you breathe. Most people have developed the habit of breathing into the upper part of the chest, expanding the chest and lifting the shoulders slightly during inhalation. This method of breathing makes it harder to fully fill your lungs with air, and also tends to keep your mind from settling fully into stillness.

Pick the spot about two inches below your navel, and imagine that your breath is travelling all the way down to this point as you inhale, shifting the expanding and contracting from your chest down to your stomach. This breathing pattern permits the diaphragm to fully open the lungs and allow in more air, which in turn allows the body and the mind to relax. Continue to breathe in this way as your thoughts move toward stillness, and then release your thoughts and allow your spirit to breathe in the presence of the Holy Spirit.

As you focus on your breath, try to breathe through your nose with your mouth closed if possible. If you find this difficult, try breathing in through your nose and out through your mouth. Relaxed breathing is more important than breathing through the nose, so do whatever you need so that your breathing is free and unrestricted.

Compline

Reading: *Psalm 119:9-16*

Reflection: God is not pleased by right actions for the wrong reasons. Were your motives as well as your actions pleasing to God today?

Prayer: Talk to God about the thoughts and motives that drove your actions today.

Benediction:

- Return slowly and peacefully from *Contemplatio*
- Take time to be thankful again
- Acknowledge that you have completed your time for today and ask God to go with you as you leave this time.

39

BIBLE READING #2 - MATTHEW 25:34-40

Preparation:

- Calm your mind and take a few deep breaths
- Start with a Prayer of Thanksgiving
- Continue with the prayer, "*Lord Jesus Christ, make my every act a sacrament in remembrance of you. Lead me as I seek to walk in your path.*"

Lectio:

Day 3

Then the king will say to those at his right hand,
'Come, you that are blessed by my Father,
inherit the kingdom prepared for you from the foundation of the world;
for I was hungry and you gave me food,
I was thirsty and you gave me something to drink,
I was a stranger and you welcomed me, I was naked and you gave me clothing,
I was sick and you took care of me, I was in prison and you visited me.'
Then the righteous will answer him, 'Lord, when was it that we saw you hungry and
gave you food, or thirsty and gave you something to drink? And when was it that we
saw you a stranger and welcomed you, or naked and gave you clothing?
And when was it that we saw you sick or in prison and visited you?'
And the king will answer them, 'Truly I tell you, just as you did it to one of the least of
these who are members of my family, you did it to me.'

- Matthew 25:34-40 (NRSV)

Meditatio:

God views the simple act of caring for those around you as a sacrament. How are you caring for the people who live in your neighborhood who need someone to care for them?

Oratio:

_____
_____
_____
_____
_____
_____
_____
_____
_____
_____
_____
_____
_____
_____
_____
_____
_____
_____
_____
_____
_____

Tell God about anything you are holding onto, such as possessions, self image, or fear, that keeps you from acting freely in your expression of love for Him or for others. Ask Him to help you release these fears and desires to Him so He can set you free.

Contemplatio:

Return to the pattern of breathing into your stomach today, keeping your chest and shoulders relaxed. Once your breath is relaxed and easy, close your eyes and notice the depth and speed of your breathing. Try to slow down your breathing so that each inhale takes about five seconds and each exhale also takes about five seconds. Slowing down in this way should also give you time to make your breath a little deeper, bringing more air into the lower part of your lungs.

The Bible calls the Holy Spirit the _Pneuma_, or Breath, of God. As you move your physical breath deeper and slower, invite the Breath of God's Spirit to move through your being more deeply, quieting your thoughts and giving you peace. Turn the attention and intention of your spirit toward the healing flow of God's breath around you and inside of you.

As you become more aware of your breath this week, try to integrate this awareness into your practice of breath prayer. Take a couple of moments a few times a day for two or three deep breaths, repeating a breath prayer silently on each exhalation, as if releasing yourself into God's presence.

Compline

Reading: _Psalm 119:25-32_

Reflection: What opportunities did you have today to express generosity? How did you respond?

Prayer: Ask God to help you hold lightly onto your possessions and give freely to those around you.

Benediction:

- Return slowly and peacefully from _Contemplatio_
- Take time to be thankful again
- Acknowledge that you have completed your time for today and ask God to go with you as you leave this time.

BIBLE READING #3 - ACTS 4:32-35

Preparation:

- Calm your mind and take a few deep breaths
- Start with a Prayer of Thanksgiving
- Continue with the prayer, *"Lord Jesus Christ, make my every act a sacrament in remembrance of you. Lead me as I seek to walk in your path."*

Lectio:

Day 4

The scripture for today describes the followers of Christ immediately after His resurrection and ascension into Heaven.

Now the whole group of those who believed were of one heart and soul,
and no one claimed private ownership of any possessions,
but everything they owned was held in common.
With great power the apostles gave their testimony to the resurrection of the
Lord Jesus, and great grace was upon them all.
There was not a needy person among them, for as many as owned lands or houses
sold them and brought the proceeds of what was sold.
They laid it at the apostles' feet, and it was distributed to each as any had need.

- Acts 4:32-35 (NRSV)

Meditatio:

What would happen in your church if everyone looked after each other so well that not a single person was lacking for anything? Why doesn't this happen? Are all the members of your church of one heart and soul? If not, what does this do to the power of the church's testimony?

Oratio:

> Ask God to help you find those around you with whom you can be of one heart and soul in following Christ. Thank Him for those friends whose faith supports your own desire to follow Him.

Contemplatio:

Spend a few moments re-establishing your breathing pattern from yesterday, taking about five seconds for each inhale and exhale as you breathe down into the space below your navel. Once you are breathing in this way comfortably, close your eyes and notice any tension you are holding in your body. On your next breath, let go of this tension as you exhale, allowing it to flow out of your body along with the air. Repeat this releasing of tension from the body each time you exhale, letting your whole body relax.

Remember that habitual tension in the muscles can be used to hold back recurring emotions you repressed and didn't allow yourself to fully experience. Using your breath to let go of habitual tension during *Contemplatio* can be a way of inviting these hurts and scars to emerge slowly and gently, so they can be given to the Holy Spirit for healing. Don't be surprised if old hurts come up during the silence; just hand them gently to God and allow Him to carry them for you.

> The method of breathing we are learning this week is not some esoteric religious practice, it is actually the proper biomechanical way your body is designed to work. The stress of modern life often leads to improper breathing habits. Breathing the way God designed helps return your mind and body to the state God intended.

Compline

Reading: *Psalm 119:33-40*

Reflection: Which of your friends are walking alongside you on your spiritual journey? Which of your friends tend to pull you from the path?

Prayer: Be thankful for the friends you have been given, and for those who encourage you along the way.

Benediction:

- Return slowly and peacefully from *Contemplatio*
- Take time to be thankful again
- Acknowledge that you have completed your time for today and ask God to go with you as you leave this time.

BIBLE READING #4 - 1 PETER 4:7-11

Preparation:

- Calm your mind and take a few deep breaths
- Start with a Prayer of Thanksgiving
- Continue with the prayer, "*Lord Jesus Christ, make my every act a sacrament in remembrance of you. Lead me as I seek to walk in your path.*"

Day 5

Lectio:

The end of all things is near.
Therefore be clear minded and self-controlled so that you can pray.
Above all, love each other deeply, because love covers over a multitude of sins.
Offer hospitality to one another without grumbling.
Each one should use whatever gift he has received to serve others,
faithfully administering God's grace in its various forms.
If anyone speaks, he should do it as one speaking the very words of God.
If anyone serves, he should do it with the strength God provides,
so that in all things God may be praised through Jesus Christ.
To him be the glory and the power for ever and ever. Amen.

- 1 Peter 4:7-11 (NIV)

Meditatio:

What does it mean to offer hospitality to other Believers? Jesus said that serving others, especially those in need, was the same as serving Him. Keeping this in mind helps turn every act of service and word of blessing into a sacrament.

Oratio:

Pray that you will see the needs of others around you today and be led to respond out of love.

If you haven't been pausing before meals for a few moments each day, try to start getting the practice integrated into your daily routine today.

Contemplatio:

Move back into your pattern of slow, deep breathing as you begin *Contemplatio* today. Close your eyes and turn your attention to the sensation of the air entering you nose and moving through your body on each breath. Notice the sensation of the air as it flows over the inside of your nose each time you inhale and exhale. Try to relax your breath and make the flow of air as smooth and unrestricted as possible.

You may notice that letting go of thoughts is easier as you exhale, almost like letting go of tension in your muscles. As you establish the habit of releasing tightness from your body each time you exhale, you will find it natural to let thoughts go at the same time. Over the course of ten to twenty breaths, let go of tightness in the body, along with any thoughts that arise. Then turn your inner attention to God's presence, releasing any stray thoughts as you exhale and resting fully in His arms.

Benediction:

- Return slowly and peacefully from *Contemplatio*
- Take time to be thankful again
- Acknowledge that you have completed your time for today and ask God to go with you as you leave this time.

Compline

Reading: *Psalm 119:41-48*

Reflection: Bring back to mind God's promise to give you strength to serve and words of blessing to speak.

Prayer: Be thankful for the small blessings of the day.

BIBLE READING #5 - COLOSSIANS 2:6-7

Preparation:

- Calm your mind and take a few deep breaths
- Start with a Prayer of Thanksgiving
- Continue with the prayer, *"Lord Jesus Christ, make my every act a sacrament in remembrance of you. Lead me as I seek to walk in your path."*

Lectio:

Day 6

So then, just as you received Christ Jesus as Lord, continue to live in him,
rooted and built up in him, strengthened in the faith as you were taught,
and overflowing with thankfulness.

- Colossians 2:6-7 (NIV)

Meditatio:

How can you actually follow the command to *live in Christ*? What does this look like in practice? What is something specific you could do today to grow toward a life rooted in Christ?

Oratio:

> Make part of your prayer today a visualization of the roots of your being growing down into the fertile soil of God's love and grace, drawing up nourishment and healing for your soul from the living waters below. Express this image to God as the desire of your heart.

> *In continuing the practice of conversing with God throughout each day, and quickly seeking His forgiveness when I fell or strayed, His presence has become as easy and natural to me now as it once was difficult to attain.*
>
> - Brother Lawrence

Contemplatio:

Spend your time today practicing the breathing pattern we have developed this week, breathing down into the space below your navel. Slow down your breathing a little more if you are comfortable doing so. Release the tension from your body, along with any stray thoughts, on each exhale.

Contemplatio should be a time of rest and peace, so be gentle with yourself if thoughts still arise more often than you would like. Simply let go of the thoughts without judging them and return to the silence. You may be tempted to grade yourself on how well you are doing with *Contemplatio*, but you should let go of this thought as well. Your intent to listen to God is much more important than any thoughts that might come into your mind. The thoughts will slowly diminish over time. Enjoy the moments of quiet union with God that come, and don't worry about the rest.

Benediction:

- Return slowly and peacefully from *Contemplatio*
- Take time to be thankful again
- Acknowledge that you have completed your time for today and ask God to go with you as you leave this time.

> ### *Compline*
>
> **Reading:** *Psalm 119:57-64*
>
> **Reflection:** How many times today did your thoughts return to God's presence? Did you spend the day looking selfishly inward, or lovingly outward?
>
> **Prayer:** Ask God to make your life an expression of His love flowing outward from you toward all those around you.

REFLECTION

Revisit Your Favorite Passage

Day 7

Reflections on the Week

Compline

Reading: *Psalm 119:65-80*

Reflection: Think back to the times over the week that God has seemed particularly near.

Prayer: Tell God about what you learned this week. Tell Him about the things that worried you and the things that brought you joy.

Week 4 - Mind, Body, & Spirit

Do you not know that you are God's temple and that God's Spirit dwells in you?
If anyone destroys God's temple, God will destroy that person.
For God's temple is holy, and you are that temple.

-1 Corinthians 3:16-17 (NRSV)

SINCE THE FORMATION OF THE EARLY CHURCH, much of Christian teaching has seemed to keep an uneasy truce with the fact that God created humans with a physical body. In fact, many churches almost never mention the human body unless it is in the form of a warning against sins such as lust, sexual immorality, or gluttony. The impression is often that the physical body is more of a curse than a blessing; the body being filled with desires that lead the spirit astray.

This negative view of the body does not actually come from scripture, but has grown out of the teachings of early Christian writers who were educated in Greek thought and who brought their Greek prejudices about the physical body with them when they converted to Christianity. Greek philosophers had developed a world view that considered all things physical to be corrupt reflections of perfect ideals that existed only in the nonphysical realm, and it didn't take long for people who came from a Greek background to start applying this thought to the teachings of scripture. They concluded that the body, being part of the physical world, was hopelessly imperfect and that only the spirit of a person had the ability to be made acceptable to a perfect God.

Where the original languages of the Bible clearly paint a picture of mankind being a unified whole creation, with the mind, body, and spirit together forming the whole self, they developed the idea that it was only our spirit that God cared about, and that the spirit would go to be with God when it finally escaped the physical body at death.

In the Bible's view, your body is a gift given to you by God to be used fully and joyously. As you read through the scriptures this week, think about how you have made use of the body God has given you. Have you developed your body to its full potential, or have you neglected it?

Since we are thinking about the body this week, we will use it as the focus for *Contemplatio*. In the haste of daily life, you may find yourself only paying attention to your body when something is wrong or when you don't feel well. Slow down this week and allow yourself to notice all the subtle messages your body sends you. Simply listening to your body lets you know when it is time to get up and move and when you need to rest, when it is time to eat or when you have eaten a bit too much. Noticing what is happening in your body can also help you understand why your mind seems distracted, you are having trouble concentrating, or you feel run down. Carry your awareness of how your mind, body, and spirit affect and support each other with you throughout the week, remembering that God created these three aspects of your being to work together powerfully so you can grab each day and live it fully.

Extra Mile:

Take care of your body this week by eating healthy meals and skipping all the junk food. Don't eat processed sugars or starches, and try to stick to real, whole foods. Drink only water and try to do something physically active each day. Spend some time thinking about how you should be taking care of the body God gave you.

MIND, BODY, & SPIRIT

Science is a powerful tool that allows us to understand more of God's creation, and does not have to be the enemy of faith when used properly. But, as the product of human minds, its viewpoint is limited and unable to fully comprehend the mysteries of the spirit.

Day 1

One of the most influential sources of the Greek idea of the physical world being an imperfect reflection of eternal ideals that exist only in the nonphysical realm is the *Theory of Forms* developed by Plato. This theory holds that forms such as *human* or *chair* exist first as perfect ideals outside of time and space, and that all real examples of these ideals in the physical world are merely corrupted reflections of these unchanging ideal forms. For example, no circle that can exist in the physical universe is absolutely perfect, and it is therefore a corrupt version of the perfect, ideal circle.

The Greek word *sarx* (σάρξ) used in these verses in *Romans* can actually be used in a variety of ways. It can be translated as *flesh, carnal, worldly, sinful nature,* or even *ancestry* according to context. Although it is sometimes used to refer specifically to the soft tissue of the physical body, it is just as often used to refer more generally to human nature or the spiritual attributes shared by all mankind.

ONE OF THE MAJOR ANALYTICAL TOOLS OF WESTERN SCIENCE is the process of breaking down complex phenomena into their component parts so they can be studied separately. When you look at how science approaches the problem of studying the human body, you find that the body has been divided down into an array of specialities: cardiologists work with the circulatory system, neurologists with the nervous system, psychologists with behavior and cognition, and so forth.

If you stop for a moment to simply feel your own body, however, you will realize that your body is much more than a collection of parts that can all be understood separately. Your body is instead an amazingly integrated system in which the parts all interact in subtle and intricate patterns to form a whole. When you expand your awareness to include your mind and spirit at work along with your body, you find that the wholeness of your being is actually a creation of profound complexity, a singleness of form that cannot be divided.

The human mind developed the tools of science in an effort to grapple with this complexity, but science still can't adequately explain how your mind and body work together, much less how your spirit fits into the picture. Modern science, much of which has grown out of ancient Greek thought, is slowly realizing it must reassess its deconstructionist approach to human nature.

The Greek View of the Body & the Spirit

The Greek view of the spiritual and physical aspects of humans has its roots around the fifth century B.C. with the teachings of Plato, whose theories postulated a kind of physical/spiritual dualism. As Plato's ideas were developed over the following centuries, the spiritual realm came to be seen as the "real" world and the physical world as just an imperfect projection of this ideal realm. Because of this, many schools of Greek and Roman philosophy began to view the physical body as a temporary dwelling place in which an eternal spirit was trapped during the period of life on Earth. Death was seen as the spirit finally escaping the body and transcending to the spiritual realm.

The practical conclusion of this world view was to consider the physical body as beyond redemption. For the Greeks, the best you could hope for was to leave the body behind. As those influenced by this line of thought began to accept Christianity during the first century, they brought with them a very different view of the relationship between the spirit and the body than is found in the Bible.

This idea eventually went so far that a belief called *docetism* emerged, which claimed that Jesus could not have been born with a physical body because it was impossible for the perfect spirit of Jesus to reside in an earthly body. This idea was firmly rejected by the early church, but much of this bias against the physical body made its way into Western thought and has been responsible for much of the misinterpretation of what scripture teaches about the body.

The Biblical Picture of the Whole Self

The most common misapplication of Greek thought about the body is probably found in the interpretation of the word often translated as *flesh* throughout the New Testament. The most well-known example is found in *Romans 7-8*, where Paul contrasts those who walk "according to the flesh" with those who walk "according to the spirit." The temptation for those coming from the Greek viewpoint is to say that the word *flesh* represents the physical body and that the word *spirit* represents the soul, but this interpretation doesn't match up with the way the Bible

50

actually uses these concepts. When you look at the context, it becomes clear that Paul is using the word *flesh* to mean the old, sinful nature, not to refer to the physical body. In just the same way that the Bible uses the word *heart* to refer to your inner self, not to the organ that pumps your blood, it also uses the word *flesh* to refer to your sinful human nature, not your physical being.

When you look back carefully at the original language of scripture, it shows that the Bible doesn't see the mind, body, and spirit as divisible. Instead, your mind, body, and spirit are intimately tied together to form your whole self. It is for this reason that God has promised to save all of you, not just your spirit. Whenever scripture talks about the resurrection, it includes the resurrection of your physical body, not just of your soul. The Biblical picture of your whole self reaffirms the oneness that God created when He knit you together in your mother's womb.

Mind, Body, & Spirit

Since your mind, spirit and body are all intimately connected, whatever happens to one deeply affects the other two. You have probably noticed that when you are physically sick or have allowed yourself to get out of shape, your mind can't think as clearly and you often have trouble concentrating on matters of the spirit. Similarly, when your spirit is overwhelmed with grief that you have not yet released, your mind will seem constantly distracted and your body will feel sapped of strength. This connection is also part of the reason that it is difficult to maintain your spiritual awareness when you don't pay attention to your physical senses.

In order to follow God's path for your life, you must take care of your whole self. You simply can't be as strong in your spirit as God intended unless you keep your mind and body in top condition as well. God has given you the power to act as His hands and feet here on Earth. He has given strength to your body to do good work, strength to your mind to perceive the truth, and strength to your spirit to carry His blessings into the world.

Keeping the Body Strong

Living in a culture that keeps you sitting inside all the time and that makes it easy to eat nothing but cheap junk food, you may find it difficult to figure out how to stay active and care for your body while balancing the rest of your schedule. If you haven't already, the first step is to reclaim the time wasted sitting in front of the television, video games, or computer. In addition to keeping you sedentary, they fill your mind with unhealthy body images. Instead of fighting with these images, stop letting them get into your head in the first place. Learn to turn off all the electronics when you aren't doing something important with them, and get back to actually engaging in life directly instead of through a screen.

God has given you your body to use for His purpose, so you should develop your body to its full potential. This starts with taking the time to eat real food instead of settling for eating processed junk. Second, you need to stay active. There is a big difference between working out just for vanity and working out to build functional strength and stay healthy. This doesn't only mean going to the gym or playing sports. Remember to get outdoors where God designed you to be and take time to explore.

Each person's body comes with its own unique strengths and unique challenges. Be thankful for the body God has given you, imperfections and all. Your body is a gift that allows you to express God's love in tangible ways as you journey through this world, so take time to develop and care for it in a way that gives you strength to live each day to the fullest.

The thought patterns of modern culture still reflect the body/spirit dualism of early Greek thought. Many people still subconsciously think with this framework, and thus are tempted to think about the spiritual parts of their life as somehow separate from the rest of life. As the Spirit carries you farther into an integrated understanding of self, you will find that these artificial divisions fade and that you experience life with a singleness of purpose.

As you have found in practicing *Contemplatio*, the posture of the body can greatly affect the mind and the spirit. Something as simple as opening your hands upward to God can help you let go with your mind and spirit.

Don't neglect any of the gifts, talents, or abilities the Holy Spirit has given you, whether of your mind, your body, or your spirit. You need every form of strength God has given you to follow the path He has prepared for you.

Compline

Reading: *1 Corinthians 15:40-58*

Reflection: Your physical body is an integral part of your whole self. Do you treat it as God's creation that will be transformed into an immortal body at the resurrection?

Prayer: Give thanks for being alive today and for the ability to call out to God in prayer.

READING #1 - ROMANS 12:1-2

Preparation:

- Calm your mind and take a few deep breaths
- Start with a Prayer of Thanksgiving
- Continue with the prayer, "*Lord Jesus Christ, I give my whole self to you. Guard my mind, strengthen my body, and purify my spirit.*"

Lectio:

Day 2

Therefore, I urge you, brothers, in view of God's mercy,
to offer your bodies as living sacrifices,
holy and pleasing to God—this is your spiritual act of worship.
Do not conform any longer to the pattern of this world,
but be transformed by the renewing of your mind.
Then you will be able to test and approve what God's will is
—his good, pleasing and perfect will.

- Romans 12:1-2 (NIV)

Meditatio:

Imagine what it would feel like to treat your body in a sacred way: staying in good shape, eating well, keeping yourself pure sexually, and using the strength God has given you in service to others. How would it affect your mind and spirit if you decided to use your body in that way all the time?

Oratio:

Carry the image of using your body in a sacred way into *Oratio* and offer this image to God as a picture of your desire to make yourself into a living sacrifice. Ask God to show you how He wants you to use your body in service to Him.

*Christ has no body on Earth
but yours,
no hands but yours,
no feet but yours.
Yours are the eyes through which
Christ's compassion for the world
is to look out;
yours are the feet with which
He is to go about doing good;
and yours are the hands with
which He is to bless us now.*

- St. Teresa of Avila

Contemplatio:

Sit in such a way that you can close your eyes and focus on the sensation of inhabiting your own body. Check in with your breath and make sure you are breathing the way you practiced last week. Release any tension from your body as you exhale a few times. As your body settles, spend a few minutes enjoying being in your own body. Notice how the sense organs of your body bring a constant stream of information about the world into your mind. If any part of you is uncomfortable or experiencing pain for some reason, just accept the sensation without judgement.

Once you are fully aware of your physical body, shift your focus to include your spiritual sense of God's presence both around you and inside of you. Sense God's Spirit and your spirit touching in the unnamed place deep inside of you. Release your thoughts and enjoy the silent communion of your mind, body, and spirit with the Spirit of God inside you.

Benediction:

- Return slowly and peacefully from *Contemplatio*
- Take time to be thankful again
- Acknowledge that you have completed your time for today and ask God to go with you as you leave this time.

Compline

Reading: *Psalm 63:1-8*

Reflection: Was the way you used and treated your body today an act of worship?

Prayer: Confess any way in which you treated your body today that fell short of making yourself a living sacrifice. Thank God for the gift of a body and the strength to live today.

READING #2 - 1 CORINTHIANS 6:19-20

Preparation:

- Calm your mind and take a few deep breaths
- Start with a Prayer of Thanksgiving
- Continue with the prayer, *"Lord Jesus Christ, I give my whole self to you. Guard my mind, strengthen my body, and purify my spirit."*

Lectio:

Day 3

The paragraphs leading up to this passage talk specifically about staying away from acts of sexual impurity. Paul reminds us that we carry the Holy Spirit with us at all times, and that we should therefore be careful what we do with our bodies.

Do you not know that your body is a temple of the Holy Spirit,
who is in you, whom you have received from God?
You are not your own; you were bought at a price.
Therefore honor God with your body.

- 1 Corinthians 6:19-20 (NIV)

Meditatio:

The mind and the spirit are greatly affected by what happens to the body. In addition to sexual impurity, what else should you avoid doing with your body? How should you treat your body so that it honors God?

Oratio:

Be thankful for the body you have been given. Talk to God about how He wants you to use your body to honor Him.

Contemplatio:

In addition to the five senses most often talked about, the body has a number of other senses that work together to produce information about how your body is oriented in space (such as which way is up) and how your body is arranged in relationship to itself (whether your arm is folded in next to your body or stretched out away from you, for example). This *proprioceptive sense*, as it is called, also gives you your sense of motion or stillness.

Close your eyes and notice how your mind provides a picture of how your body is situated in space even though you can't see it. You know which way is up, can sense how your body is arranged, and know whether any part of you is moving. Slow down your thoughts and allow your awareness of your body to deepen. Allow the presence of your body to ground you into the reality of the moment, and then draw in your senses to focus on God's presence inside of you. Relax into God's presence with both your body and your spirit.

Proprioception is produced by the brain combining information from a number of sources. The inner ear provides information about balance, motion, and the direction of gravity. Special nerve receptors in the muscles and joints tell the brain about the orientation of the joints and how extended the muscles are. Changes in the stretching of the skin and blood flow to different parts of the body are also taken into account as the brain builds a picture of how the body is moving through the world.

Compline

Reading: *1 Thessalonians 5:23*

Reflection: Did you carry the thought of being a temple of the Holy Spirit with you through your day? What did you do with the sacred space of God's temple today?

Prayer: Make *1 Thessalonians 5:23* into a prayer for yourself.

Benediction:

- Return slowly and peacefully from *Contemplatio*
- Take time to be thankful again
- Acknowledge that you have completed your time for today and ask God to go with you as you leave this time.

READING #3 - ROMANS 8:9-11

Preparation:

- Calm your mind and take a few deep breaths
- Start with a Prayer of Thanksgiving
- Continue with the prayer, "*Lord Jesus Christ, I give my whole self to you. Guard my mind, strengthen my body, and purify my spirit.*"

Day 4

Lectio:

You, however, are controlled not by the sinful nature but by the Spirit,
if the Spirit of God lives in you.
And if anyone does not have the Spirit of Christ, he does not belong to Christ.
But if Christ is in you, your body is dead because of sin,
yet your spirit is alive because of righteousness.
And if the Spirit of him who raised Jesus from the dead is living in you,
he who raised Christ from the dead will also give life to your mortal bodies
through his Spirit, who lives in you.

- *Romans 8:9-11 (NIV)*

Meditatio:

How does having the Holy Spirit living in you change your relationship with your own body? Are you happy or unhappy with the body God gave you? What should you be doing to form your body into an instrument fit to serve God and be a temple for His Spirit?

Oratio:

Ask God to make you content with the body you have been given, and to help you care for it in a way that honors His presence in you. Tell God about any desires of the flesh (i.e. the old sinful nature) that try to control your thoughts, asking Him to replace these desires with thoughts motivated by perfect love.

Brother Lawrence's practice of turning everyday tasks into Acts of Service is an excellent way to bring your mind, body, and spirit together in an act of worship that involves your whole being. Look for opportunities today to turn an otherwise ordinary task into an Act of Service.

Contemplatio:

God designed the human body to be one of the most beautiful, adaptable, and powerful machines in creation. Take a few moments to look closely at the design of your body. Notice how your feet, ankles, knees, and hips are all designed to work together to allow you to walk, run, and even dance. Notice as well how a strong, flexible spine allows you to twist and stretch, enabling you to move in an almost endless number of ways as you work and play.

Move your attention to your hands. Throughout scripture, the hands serve as a symbol of our ability to work in this world on God's behalf. God designed our hands to put forth great power when needed, but still be able to handle the most delicate of work. As you look at your hands, begin to slow down your thoughts and allow them to bring your awareness to the Holy Spirit living inside you, who wants to direct your hands to bring about sacred works. Surrender your hands and your whole self to God in silence.

Benediction:

- Return slowly and peacefully from *Contemplatio*
- Take time to be thankful again
- Acknowledge that you have completed your time for today and ask God to go with you as you leave this time.

Compline

Reading: *Romans 8:18-27*

Reflection: Did you hold back any part of yourself from God today? Were you able to give your whole mind, body, and spirit to God completely, or did something make you hold part of yourself back?

Prayer: Ask the Holy Spirit to help you pray in the way you most need to pray tonight.

READING #4 - 1 CORINTHIANS 10:31

Preparation:

- Calm your mind and take a few deep breaths
- Start with a Prayer of Thanksgiving
- Continue with the prayer, "*Lord Jesus Christ, I give my whole self to you. Guard my mind, strengthen my body, and purify my spirit.*"

Day 5

Lectio:

So, whether you eat or drink, or whatever you do,
do everything for the glory of God.

- *1 Corinthians 10:31 (NRSV)*

Meditatio:

Does what you eat and drink bring glory to God? Do you use your mind and body in selfish ways or as an expression of love toward others? Do you take good care of yourself so you will be able to care for others as well?

Oratio:

> Pray that God will give you the wisdom and the will to develop and discipline your mind, body, and spirit so they are powerful tools that can serve those around you.

> *The morality of clean blood ought to be one of the first lessons taught us by our pastors and teachers. The physical is the substratum of the spiritual; and this fact ought to give to the food we eat, and the air we breathe, a transcendent significance.*
>
> - William Tyndale

Contemplatio:

In addition to the systems that make up your proprioceptive senses, your body has a variety of sense organs that form the *interoceptive senses*, which give you information about what is happening inside your body. Nerve receptors inside your body tell you all about your internal state, such as when your intestinal tract is upset, about the movement of your internal organs, and even when your bladder is full.

Sit comfortably and close your eyes so you can focus on the sensations inside your body. As you begin to slow down your interior dialog, your sense of what is happening inside your body will deepen. Take a few breaths to help you relax your body and let go of tension. Notice all the information that comes to you from inside when you pause to listen. Join this awareness with the awareness coming to you from your ears and skin to complete the picture of what is going on both inside and outside of you. Let go, becoming aware of what God is doing in and around you.

Benediction:

- Return slowly and peacefully from *Contemplatio*
- Take time to be thankful again
- Acknowledge that you have completed your time for today and ask God to go with you as you leave this time.

> **Compline**
>
> **Reading:** *1 Corinthians 9:24-27*
>
> **Reflection:** What is the Holy Spirit calling you to do differently with your body, whether in what you eat, in how you exercise and take care of yourself, or in sexual purity?
>
> **Prayer:** Tell God about anything you need to change about the way you care for your body.

READING #5 - EPHESIANS 2:19-22

Preparation:

- Calm your mind and take a few deep breaths
- Start with a Prayer of Thanksgiving
- Continue with the prayer, "*Lord Jesus Christ, I give my whole self to you. Guard my mind, strengthen my body, and purify my spirit.*"

Lectio:

Day 6

The image Paul uses here is of each of us bringing our minds, bodies, and spirits to God so He can build us all together into a community of people who love Him, support each other, and act as a beacon to those searching for God. Together we form a living temple, resting on the foundation of Christ, in which God dwells in this world.

So then you are no longer strangers and aliens,
but you are citizens with the saints and also members of the household of God,
built upon the foundation of the apostles and prophets,
with Christ Jesus himself as the cornerstone.
In him the whole structure is joined together and grows into a holy temple in the Lord;
in whom you also are built together spiritually into a dwelling place for God.

- Ephesians 2:19-22 (NRSV)

Meditatio:

This passage says nothing about organized churches or denominations. Everyone who lives in Christ is a member of God's household. Do you ever let the fact that someone is from a different church or denomination keep you from embracing them as a brother or sister in Christ? Take a few moments to picture all followers of Christ, regardless of where they are from, as living stones in the temple built by the Holy Spirit, with God dwelling among you all and binding you together with His love—a love that is expressed in a unique way through each member.

Oratio:

Thank God for knitting your mind, body, and spirit together in a way that allows you to know and love Him. Surrender your whole being to the Holy Spirit and ask Him to join you deeply into the fellowship of those following Christ, growing you together into a temple fit to welcome the presence of God Himself.

Contemplatio:

Start _Contemplatio_ today by taking a minute to return your breath to the slow, deep pattern you practiced last week. Close your eyes and notice how changing your breathing pattern changes the way you feel inside your body, which in turn affects your thoughts and feelings. Relax your body each time your exhale, welcoming any negative emotions that come up as you let go of your tension and releasing them to God as they arise.

Move your mind toward stillness, letting go of your interior dialog and simply observing how your mind and spirit occupy your body. As you breathe, notice how God's Spirit seems to breathe inside of you as well. As you surrender your whole self to the Spirit, you will come to rest in a place where your body, mind, and spirit fuse into oneness, the edges blurring. God's presence inside you, pulling you back into harmony with His nature, will bring you back into harmony with all the parts of yourself.

Benediction:

- Return slowly and peacefully from _Contemplatio_
- Take time to be thankful again
- Acknowledge that you have completed your time for today and ask God to go with you as you leave this time.

Compline

Reading: _Re-read today's passage_

Reflection: Do your closest friends follow Christ in such a way that you are all being built together by the Spirit into a dwelling place for God?

Prayer: Ask God to help you find companions along your spiritual journey with whom you can travel the deep paths of the Spirit.

REFLECTION

Day 7

Revisit Your Favorite Passage

Reflections on the Week

Compline

Reading: *Psalm 16*

Reflection: Changing habits is always easier with support from a friend. Who could you partner with to help you keep any commitments you made this week?

Prayer: Thank God for the blessings of the week.

WEEK 5 - PRAYER & FASTING

So I turned to the Lord God and pleaded with him in prayer and petition,
in fasting, and in sackcloth and ashes. I prayed to the LORD my God and confessed:
"O Lord, the great and awesome God,
who keeps his covenant of love with all who love him and obey his commands,
we have sinned and done wrong. We have been wicked and have rebelled;
we have turned away from your commands and laws."

-Daniel 9:3-5 (NIV)

THE PRACTICE OF FASTING has become somewhat rare in the modern church. As western cultures have increasingly compartmentalized the spiritual and physical into separate spheres over the centuries, the idea of involving the physical body deeply in the spiritual arena of prayer has become seen as a bit weird or extreme. For many people, prayer is a mental and spiritual exercise only, practiced in a vague inner space that floats comfortably disconnected from the real world around them.

The Bible paints a very different picture of prayer: of Jacob wrestling with God to obtain His blessing, of David dancing before God in joy, of Daniel sitting in ashes to express his sorrow over the people of Israel turning away from God. Throughout the Bible, we see no separation of the body from the act of prayer, no holding back of the physical expression of the inward spiritual struggles and triumphs. The biblical picture of prayer is the bringing of your whole self to God, expressing your mental and spiritual journey of seeking God in the physical actions of life. Whether you are dancing to God with all your might, or crying out to Him in sorrow and repentance, bring your whole being fully and completely to each moment.

Biblical fasting most often involved refraining from eating for a period of time in order to focus on God. By putting your spiritual needs ahead of your desire for food, fasting brings your body deeply into the process of prayer. Disciplining your body through fasting moves your focus off your own temporary desires and opens your mind and spirit to be more sensitive to the presence and leading of the Holy Spirit.

Just as with the other spiritual disciplines, fasting should not be allowed to become something you do merely out of a sense of obligation or simply because it has become a habit. Fasting should always be a conscious act of seeking after God, whether in repentance, in response to a loss, or out of a desire to hear Him more clearly. Allow fasting to become a natural part of your prayer life, expressing itself when you feel moved to engage the Holy Spirit more deeply, crying out to God and then listening closely with your whole being.

During *Contemplatio* this week, you will focus on the edges and boundaries in the ecosystems around you. God made the edges in the world some of the most diverse and productive parts of nature. As you think about the richness that occurs at the boundaries of the natural world, remember also the fertile soil God has created at the edges where your mind, body, and spirit meet. Ask the Holy Spirit to open up the ground of your being to new growth and deeper life.

Extra Mile:

Spend one day fasting this week, eating nothing and drinking only water. If, for medical reasons, you need to eat to maintain blood sugar levels, eat only small, plain meals. Make sure to drink enough to stay well hydrated. Spend your normal meal times in prayer and contemplation.

PRAYER & FASTING

Day 1

In James 5:16, the Bible gives us a remarkable promise: that God will listen to the prayers of the righteous, making them powerful and using them to accomplish great things. When those in your community are sick or need spiritual healing and forgiveness, you are to pray for them so they can be healed. What makes this promise puzzling at first is that God, who knows what they need far better than you ever could, chooses to act in response to your requests, even though they often come from an incomplete understanding or may even be misguided. Why would God choose to act in this way, when He already has perfect knowledge of every need?

The answer seems to be that the Holy Spirit uses the simple act of asking for God's help to teach you to see through God's eyes and to understand what God wants to accomplish. As you ask God to help you, He teaches you to desire for yourself those things He desires for you. As you pray for others, you learn to see them as God sees them, and to want for them those things God knows will benefit them most. Prayer, like fasting, is an act of will, and your choice to pray or fast in pursuit of knowing God's purpose changes you profoundly.

Prayers of Blessing & Peace

Prayers of gratitude or praise to God often seem to come much more easily than prayers of intercession or supplication. We often feel in the beginning that we do not even know what to ask for, and can even become afraid we are asking for the wrong things. But you are promised in scripture that the Spirit will help you as you pray, using your willingness to seek God's purpose to reveal to you the mind of God Himself.

As you learn to know the mind of God, your prayers will come to have ever more power, as your own desires and concerns become closer to those of Christ. Prayers that are contrary to God's purposes lack power, but prayers that reflect God's perfect will accomplish much because they ask for those things that will truly bring blessings and peace, and that God wants to give in abundance.

What you ask for changes as you realize God is more concerned with returning His children to a right relationship with Him than He is in their temporary physical or emotional comfort. In His love, God sometimes allows His children to go through great pain and suffering in order that they may find eternal blessing. As you learn to see the journey through this life as preparation for what lies beyond, you will learn to look past the suffering of the moment to see God's long-term plan. Sometimes the most powerful prayer is that God will use painful circumstances to help someone grow, instead of simply praying for the circumstances to be changed.

Prayer Beyond Words

Learning to see with God's eyes results in more than prayers that can be expressed in words. In *Romans 8:26-28*, God also promises that the Holy Spirit will help you pray even when what you need to ask cannot be captured with spoken language. As you go deeper into the inward silence of sitting quietly with God, the Spirit will teach you to pray beyond words. In the sacred space of inner attention to Him, the Holy Spirit touches your soul directly and enables you to communicate with God in a way that bypasses the clumsiness of trying to express your innermost thoughts and desires verbally.

God calls you to bring your whole self into this prayer beyond words, and you may find that at times this will include the act of fasting. Disciplining the body through fasting can help you open your spiritual senses more fully so that you can pray from the place beyond language.

Some of the ways to bring your body more fully into prayer include:

Fasting
Dancing
Singing
Speaking aloud
Crying or weeping
Opening your hands
Raising your arms
Kneeling
Laying prostrate

Reasons for Fasting

Throughout the Old and New Testaments, three main reasons for fasting appear over and over. First, fasting is often a response to a loss or a great disaster. In *Judges 20*, the people of Israel fast to mourn the civil war that has arisen between them and the tribe of Benjamin. In *2 Samuel 12*, David fasts after his son becomes sick. You may also find that in times of great sorrow, you feel called to fast as a means to express a whole-body cry to God for help.

Second, fasting is often an expression of deep grief and repentance for sin. In the passage from *Daniel 9* that opens this week, Daniel pleads with God to forgive the nation of Israel for their disobedience that has resulted in God allowing them to be taken into captivity in Babylon. Sin builds a wall between you and God, hiding His face from you. As you realize the damage caused by your sin, both to yourself and to others, you may find your natural response is to accompany your prayers asking God's forgiveness with fasting to express your repentance with your body as well as your mind and spirit.

Third, fasting is used to discipline the mind, body, and spirit in order to hear God more clearly, to express your desire to know Him more deeply, or to ask for wisdom or clarity when faced with a major decision.

As you think about when and how to fast, be sensitive to why you feel called to fasting in each specific instance. Fast only when it is an organic response to circumstances, not just because you feel it is the "spiritual" thing to do. At first, fasting may seem strange or even a little intimidating, but over time, fasting will become a natural part of your walk with the Spirit.

The Practice of Fasting

If you have never fasted before, start with shorter periods of time and pay attention to what your body is telling you during the fast. Biblical fasting usually involves not eating for a period of time, while drinking plenty of fluids to ensure you stay hydrated. For shorter fasts, you should drink only water instead of any flavored or sugary drinks.

You may want to start by simply skipping a meal or two, praying during the times you would normally be eating. Gradually work your way up to 24 hours without food (for example, after dinner one evening, do not eat again until dinner the next night). Most people can fast for a full day without major problems, but you should talk to your doctor before fasting if you have any medical condition that might cause problems with blood sugar levels.

For longer fasts, it is wise to find someone who has experience with fasting for multiple days. You should never undertake a fast of more than 48 hours without some guidance. While the human body can actually handle fasts lasting for several weeks, this requires special care. For most people, the worst hunger comes during the second or third day of the fast, after which the sensation of hunger usually subsides. During these longer fasts, you may feel weak or even light-headed at times, especially if you exert yourself. Some people drink diluted fruit juices to help their body through the process. After a fast lasting two days or more, you must be careful when you resume eating. The stomach will not be able to handle foods that are hard to digest. You should break your fast with soft foods that are easy on the stomach. After longer fasts, you may need to start with diluted grape juice before you progress to very soft foods.

Although fasting most often involves refraining from food, it can also involve refraining from anything that has become a distraction. When choosing how to fast, ask what one thing is most standing in the way of your journey to follow Christ and consider fasting from that.

The truth of the matter is, we all come to prayer with a tangled mass of motives altruistic and selfish, merciful and hateful, loving and bitter. Frankly, this side of eternity we will never unravel the good from the bad, the pure from the impure. God is big enough to receive us with all our mixture.

- Richard Foster

When you feel called to fast, carefully consider how long you will keep the fast. In most cases, a shorter fast of a day or less will give you the time and space you need. Most people will never find the need to fast for more than 48 hours, and longer fasts carry some risk. The length of a fast should flow from the reason you are fasting, not from the idea that longer fasts are somehow more "spiritual."

Remember that fasting is a private spiritual practice. While you shouldn't hide the fact that you are fasting from someone who needs to know, or create awkward situations by trying to hide the fact that you are fasting from those around you, fasting should be done in a way that does not draw attention to itself. If someone needs to know you are fasting, tell them simply and quietly, and then move on.

Compline

Reading: *1 Timothy 2:1-6*

Reflection: Do you find within yourself the desire to pray for all people, even those who treat you poorly? In what ways do you hurt yourself if you hold back from praying for those whom you dislike?

Prayer: Ask for the wisdom and love to pray genuinely for all those around you, that they would find God's truth.

READING #1 - MATTHEW 6:16-18

Preparation:

- Calm your mind and take a few deep breaths
- Start with a Prayer of Thanksgiving
- Continue with the prayer, "*Lord Jesus Christ, let Your Spirit breathe in me. I yield the desires of my mind and body to You.*"

Lectio:

Day 2

"When you fast, do not look somber as the hypocrites do,
for they disfigure their faces to show men they are fasting.
I tell you the truth, they have received their reward in full.
But when you fast, put oil on your head and wash your face,
so that it will not be obvious to men that you are fasting,
but only to your Father, who is unseen;
and your Father, who sees what is done in secret, will reward you."

- Matthew 6:16-18 (NIV)

Meditatio:

Fasting is not to be done as a display of how pious you are, but as a true expression of calling out to God. Are you ever tempted to do things just so those around you will be impressed by how "spiritual" you are? When is it appropriate to publicly express what is happening in your spirit, and when should you keep it between you and God?

Oratio:

Talk to God about ways in which you are tempted to do the "right" things for selfish reasons. Ask God to change your thoughts and motives such that your actions flow out of love and not selfishness.

As you think about the act of prayer this week, try to expand your thinking to include all the ways God has given you to communicate with Him. Think beyond the typical "bow your head and close your eyes" praying to also include breath prayers, prayers in passing, the prayer of silence, and prayers that involve the body, such as fasting or even dancing before God. Remember also practices such as Welcoming Prayer that help you deal with strong emotions as they arise.

Contemplatio:

In the natural world, the boundaries between different types of environments are often the most diverse and productive areas. Edges—such as where the forest meets the meadow or the lawn meets the hedge row—provide a unique habitat where two diverse ecosystems interact. Species of plants and animals from both ecosystems, along with additional species unique to their intersection, all inhabit the space along edges.

Look at the edges in the environment around you: the lawn meeting a line of bushes or trees, the land meeting a lake or river, anywhere there is an abrupt change in the landscape. Notice what is happening along these boundaries, using wide-angle vision to take it all in. Look for God's weaving of the diverse tapestry of life into a dynamic whole that joins the landscape together seamlessly, even at these edges. As you move your mind toward silence, open your spirit to God's work around you in a wordless invitation for Him to knit you together into the fabric of His thoughts manifesting around you.

Benediction:

- Return slowly and peacefully from *Contemplatio*
- Take time to be thankful again
- Acknowledge that you have completed your time for today and ask God to go with you as you leave this time.

Compline

Reading: *Isaiah 58:3-12*

Reflection: Were your actions today motivated by selfishness or by love? Did you do anything simply to impress someone else today?

Prayer: Name any selfish desires that you found in yourself today and give them to God.

READING #2 - MARK 2:18-20

Preparation:

- Calm your mind and take a few deep breaths
- Start with a Prayer of Thanksgiving
- Continue with the prayer, "*Lord Jesus Christ, let Your Spirit breathe in me. I yield the desires of my mind and body to You.*"

Lectio:

Day 3

Now John's disciples and the Pharisees were fasting; and people came and said to him,
"Why do John's disciples and the disciples of the Pharisees fast,
but your disciples do not fast?"
Jesus said to them, "The wedding guests cannot fast while the bridegroom is with them, can they? As long as they have the bridegroom with them, they cannot fast.
The days will come when the bridegroom is taken away from them,
and then they will fast on that day."

- Mark 2:18-20 (NRSV)

The Bible uses the image of the church as the bride of Christ. Jesus says that during the time He was with His disciples on Earth, they would not fast, but after His death and resurrection they would fast until He returned.

Meditatio:

When you pray and fast, in what way are you remembering Christ's life and death? In what way are you also looking forward to the fulfillment of the promise of Christ's return?

Oratio:

> As you pray today, engage your whole self in remembrance of Christ's sacrifice for you and the promise of life with Him at the end of your journey through this world.

Contemplatio:

If your normal spot is not already situated along a boundary between two different environments, get up and move so that you are sitting at a place where two unlike environments meet. If you are in a neighborhood, it might be where a lawn meets a row of trees or bushes. Even the edge between a lawn and flower bed will work. Try to pick the most distinct boundary in the area around you. The more different the two environments, the stronger the interactions at the edge.

Sit right on the edge between the two areas, facing one and with your back toward the other. Close your eyes and notice the different feel on your skin front and back. Listen to the different quality of sound coming from each direction. After a minute or two, turn around to face the opposite direction and observe the difference this makes. Relax and allow yourself to occupy the edge between two spaces. Releasing your thoughts, expand your awareness toward the edge where your spirit meets God's Spirit in silence.

Benediction:

- Return slowly and peacefully from *Contemplatio*
- Take time to be thankful again
- Acknowledge that you have completed your time for today and ask God to go with you as you leave this time.

Compline

Reading: *Psalm 35:11-18*

Reflection: What was your reaction to those who treated you poorly today? Did you want to respond in the same way, or pray and fast on their behalf?

Prayer: Pray for those who were unkind to you today. Ask God to help you see their spiritual needs so you can pray for them more clearly.

READING #3 - MATTHEW 17:18-21

Preparation:

- Calm your mind and take a few deep breaths
- Start with a Prayer of Thanksgiving
- Continue with the prayer, "*Lord Jesus Christ, let Your Spirit breathe in me. I yield the desires of my mind and body to You.*"

Lectio:

Day 4

Some ancient texts omit the last sentence from this passage, so some modern translations do not include it. The King James Version and other older translation include verse 21, while a number of newer translations simply skip over verse 21 and continue with verse 22.

And Jesus rebuked the devil; and he departed out of him:
and the child was cured from that very hour.
Then came the disciples to Jesus apart, and said, Why could not we cast him out?
And Jesus said unto them, Because of your unbelief: for verily I say unto you,
If ye have faith as a grain of mustard seed, ye shall say unto this mountain,
Remove hence to yonder place; and it shall remove;
and nothing shall be impossible unto you.
Howbeit this kind goeth not out but by prayer and fasting.

- Matthew 17:18-21 (KJV)

Meditatio:

How does the practice of prayer and fasting affect your faith? Why do you think involving your body in prayer is so important?

Oratio:

> Ask God to remove any blocks you have to involving your body in the practice and discipline of spiritual growth. Ask Him to help you understand when to use fasting in your journey of knowing Him.

> *Prayer is not asking. Prayer is putting oneself in the hands of God, at His disposition, and listening to His voice in the depth of our hearts.*
>
> - Mother Teresa

Contemplatio:

Every environment across the landscape interacts with the wind in a unique way. Flat, open land allows the wind to move freely, picking up dust and debris when it is blowing fast enough. A dense forest can absorb a strong wind at its edge and reduce it to a gentle breeze within a few hundred feet. At the boundaries, the wind's interactions can become even more complex, moving in different directions at different altitudes, speeding up when going through narrow spaces, dropping what it is carrying when slowed by leaves and foliage.

As you begin *Contemplatio* today, return to the edge you visited yesterday. Look for evidence of how the wind is affected by the edge and how the wind affects conditions along the edge. If the wind is moving, notice its interaction with the edge where you are sitting. Slow down your thoughts and relax into the inner breath of the Holy Spirit moving inside you, cleansing the old, stale air from the innermost parts of your spirit and replacing it with something new and fresh.

Benediction:

- Return slowly and peacefully from *Contemplatio*
- Take time to be thankful again
- Acknowledge that you have completed your time for today and ask God to go with you as you leave this time.

> ### Compline
>
> **Reading:** *Acts 13:2-3*
>
> **Reflection:** When was the last time you were serious enough about a decision that you prayed and fasted to better discern the answer?
>
> **Prayer:** Commit to God that you will seek Him in all circumstances, even when you are called to fast to hear Him clearly.

Reading #4 - Luke 18:9-14

Preparation:

- Calm your mind and take a few deep breaths
- Start with a Prayer of Thanksgiving
- Continue with the prayer, "*Lord Jesus Christ, let Your Spirit breathe in me. I yield the desires of my mind and body to You.*"

Lectio:

Day 5

He also told this parable to some who trusted in themselves
that they were righteous and regarded others with contempt:
"Two men went up to the temple to pray, one a Pharisee and the other a tax collector.
The Pharisee, standing by himself, was praying thus,
'God, I thank you that I am not like other people: thieves, rogues, adulterers,
or even like this tax collector. I fast twice a week; I give a tenth of all my income.'
But the tax collector, standing far off, would not even look up to heaven,
but was beating his breast and saying, 'God, be merciful to me, a sinner!'
I tell you, this man went down to his home justified rather than the other; for all who
exalt themselves will be humbled, but all who humble themselves will be exalted."

- Luke 18:9-14 (NRSV)

Meditatio:

Jesus clearly says that the tradition of the Pharisees fasting twice a week is meaningless unless it is done out of a true desire to hear and see God. Is there anything you are doing out of routine or habit simply to look like you are following God? Why is it important that outward actions line up with inward motives?

Oratio:

Talk to God about any way in which you are feeling called to fast. Ask Him to help you be humble and motivated by a pure desire to follow Him.

Contemplatio:

Return again to the edge you visited yesterday and sit in wide-angle vision. Reach out with your senses of hearing and touch as well, bringing in as much information as you can about the energy and activity along the edge. Once you have relaxed into the space created by the edge, pause to notice the additional edge that exists at the boundary between you and the world around you.

Think for a moment about how the landscape around you is changed by your presence. Notice how the pattern of the wind is affected in the space right around you, how you affect the pattern of light and shadow, and how the birds and animals react to your presence. God created you to be a blessing to His creation. When you act humbly and care for the Earth, you return to a right relationship with the place God designed you to live. Let your mind, body, and spirit take on the attitude of the Creator, wanting to bless the whole of creation. As you take on the mind of Christ, feel the edges between yourself and God fade as He fully inhabits your being.

Benediction:

- Return slowly and peacefully from *Contemplatio*
- Take time to be thankful again
- Acknowledge that you have completed your time for today and ask God to go with you as you leave this time.

Compline

Reading: *Psalm 109:21-31*

Reflection: Was your attitude more like the Pharisee or the tax collector today?

Prayer: Make the prayer of the tax collector your own tonight. Go to bed praying *God, be merciful to me, a sinner.*

READING #5 - JOEL 2:12-15

Preparation:

- Calm your mind and take a few deep breaths
- Start with a Prayer of Thanksgiving
- Continue with the prayer, "*Lord Jesus Christ, let Your Spirit breathe in me. I yield the desires of my mind and body to You.*"

Day 6

Lectio:

Yet even now, says the LORD, return to me with all your heart,
with fasting, with weeping, and with mourning;
rend your hearts and not your clothing.
Return to the LORD, your God, for he is gracious and merciful,
slow to anger, and abounding in steadfast love, and relents from punishing.
Who knows whether he will not turn and relent, and leave a blessing behind him,
a grain offering and a drink offering for the LORD, your God?
Blow the trumpet in Zion; sanctify a fast; call a solemn assembly…

- Joel 2:12-15 (NRSV)

Meditatio:

Is there something in your life you habitually hold back from God or are afraid to let go of? What would happen if you were to turn it over to Him with fasting and weeping?

Oratio:

_____

Confess to God anything you are holding onto, afraid to give to Him. Ask for courage to trust Him to forgive you and take away your sense of shame and guilt.

Whenever the insistence is on the point that God answers prayer, we are off the track. The meaning of prayer is that we get hold of God, not of the answer.

- Oswald Chambers

Contemplatio:

Return to your normal spot today if you had moved to another place to be at an edge over the past three days. Close your eyes and spend a moment bringing your awareness back to your own body. Make sure you are breathing using a slow, deep pattern. Just as you did last week, notice what it feels like to occupy your own body and live with the rhythm of your own breathing.

Once you are comfortably relaxed into your body, take a moment to observe the edges between your own mind, body, and spirit. God created each part of you with a distinct essence, but joined these parts together to form one being. For those who follow Christ, these parts are knit together by the Holy Spirit to form a temple in which God Himself dwells. Move toward inward silence as you turn your gaze toward the innermost edge of your being where your spirit and the Holy Spirit meet. Sit at this edge in perfect stillness and receive healing.

Benediction:

- Return slowly and peacefully from *Contemplatio*
- Take time to be thankful again
- Acknowledge that you have completed your time for today and ask God to go with you as you leave this time.

Compline

Reading: *Jonah 3:1-10*

Reflection: What has been God's response when you have called to Him for forgiveness?

Prayer: Be thankful for God's mercy and grace in dealing with your sin. Ask Him to protect your mind and purify your spirit through the night and during the day tomorrow.

REFLECTION

Revisit Your Favorite Passage

Day 7

Reflections on the Week

Compline

Reading: *Psalm 103*

Reflection: What did God teach you this week about the role fasting should play in your spiritual journey?

Prayer: Pray whatever is on your heart tonight, bringing your body into the prayer in some way.

WEEK 6 - AN EXTRAORDINARY LIFE

So again Jesus said to them, "Very truly, I tell you, I am the gate for the sheep.
All who came before me are thieves and bandits; but the sheep did not listen to them.
I am the gate. Whoever enters by me will be saved, and will come in and go out and find pasture.
The thief comes only to steal and kill and destroy.
I came that they may have life, and have it abundantly."

-John 10:7-10 (NRSV)

OVER THE CENTURIES, people have tried to take Jesus' command to *pick up your cross and follow Me* and make it somehow less demanding. The emphasis has slowly been shifted onto all the things the Bible says we should avoid, and away from the many calls to action found in scripture. In an effort to make the challenge of following Christ's positive commands seem easier, many teachers have turned them into vague, sweeping generalities that are pleasantly safe: we should love God, love each other, and pray for God's will to be done. We can all shake our heads in agreement without too much thought, since it is kept so broad that we can safely avoid asking the harder, more specific questions about whether we are actually doing what Jesus expects of us. Are you showing your love toward God in your thoughts and actions today? Are you taking care of the person living at the end of the street who needs your help? When was the last time you sacrificed eating a meal so somebody who was truly hungry could eat?

Jesus said in *John 10:10* that He came to give you a life that is *abundant*. It is easy to simply read past this and let it fall into the same category of pleasant but somewhat vague thoughts you hear in church each week. But when you dig into what Jesus is really saying, you find something a bit startling. The Greek word translated as *abundantly* in the passage above is *perissos*, which literally means being in number or amount beyond what is required or even needed. Jesus says He intends for you to have a life that is well beyond the ordinary, completely overflowing, and surpassing everything you need. By using this word, Jesus implies a life of vitality and action, not one of passivity. Your call to follow Christ requires you to get up and move, to take action, to make the story of your journey through this life extraordinary.

The abundance of which Jesus speaks has little to do with physical possessions or comfort, which are only temporary. The life spent seeking God overflows with abundance precisely because it is full of challenges and sacrifices. The joy is sometimes deepest in the moments you are at the end of your own capabilities and yet still finding strength to move forward through the love that ties you to God and in your relationships with those close to you.

To help deepen your focus on the abundance that flows out of God's designs, we will think about the diversity found throughout creation during *Contemplatio* this week. The natural world is rich and endlessly varied, untamed and always beyond our control. To find God's design for your life, you must venture past the edges of the places built by man and into the wild places through which the journey to follow God passes.

Extra Mile:

Live fully this week. Laugh and weep with your whole being. Do something a little bit crazy just for fun. Dance to the Lord at least once. Spend an hour or more helping someone you don't know very well. Hug your family and friends all at least three times each over the week. Make a task you don't like into an Act of Service. Pray with all your strength. Enjoy living in God's presence.

LIVING AN EXTRAORDINARY LIFE

Day 1

GOD IS AN EXPERT IN ABUNDANCE. He creates overflowing abundance in a wide variety of forms and packages. The first step in embracing the fullness of life God has designed for you is to realize that it won't necessarily look like you expect, or look like what you see in somebody else's life.

You may pass through times of quiet growth which outwardly look rather ordinary, but that creates something new and deep in your spirit. You may be called on wild adventures, taking you around the world or into places you would normally be afraid to go. You may go through times of sorrow and grief, challenges the world would never think of as living in abundance, but that develop inside you a strength of faith that leads to the deepest abundance of all.

All these seasons of life become a part of your journey to become who God designed you to be. If you listen closely to the voice of the Spirit and follow where He leads, you will one day look back over your life and realize that God has made it into something extraordinary.

Breaking Free from Ruts

If you walk the same path through a trackless wilderness more than two or three times, you will start to see a visible rut forming. If you keep traveling the same path, this rut soon becomes a worn-in trail you can follow without having to consciously think about where you are going. In the same way, the thoughts and actions you follow each day can quickly form ruts you mindlessly follow simply because they have become habit. Although certain habits can be helpful, others can trap you into ruts that keep you from growing. Learning to listen to God's Spirit through inner silence, and constantly asking yourself whether your actions are in alignment with God's design for your life, are the first steps in identifying habits that are becoming ruts.

A simple way to move yourself into a mind-set that breaks up ruts in thinking is to spend more time outdoors paying attention to what God is doing. The environment inside most buildings is designed to be comfortable and static, allowing you to easily fall into thoughtless patterns of behavior. Outside everything is always changing, reminding you that you were designed to grow, not just stay still.

When you find yourself stuck in a rut, don't just try to break the pattern without bringing in something new to replace it. Trying to break an old habit without replacing it with something better will just leave a void that will quickly be filled, often by simply falling back into the old pattern. Pray that God will show you a new challenge to fill the space instead.

Finding a Mentor

Having a mentor can be valuable at any stage of life. The person you consider to be your mentor should be the same gender as you. The job of mentoring younger men falls to the older men, and mentoring of the younger women falls to the older women. Because they are so emotionally close to their children, a parent should not try to act as a mentor to their own child. The two relationships are very different, and the fact that a mentor can act as more of a neutral party often times is important. If you are in your mid-twenties or older, you should also consider being available as a mentor to someone younger than yourself. Mentoring someone younger will encourage you to keep growing yourself.

One of the most powerful ways to strengthen your walk with God is to find a person who can act as a mentor. Look for someone at least ten years older than you who is a mature follower of Christ, someone you know will encourage and challenge you. A good mentor will ask the types of questions that help you bust out of your ruts, and will keep you accountable to your commitment to follow Christ. Getting to know your mentor will give you an example of what it looks like to seek after God, and will give you someone to talk to when you need some wisdom.

Find someone you know and respect, and talk to them about being your mentor. If you both agree it feels right, you should both pray about it for a few days. If at the end of this time the Spirit tells you to go ahead, formally ask the person to mentor you. Mentoring relationships have become rare today, so you and your mentor will both probably have much to learn as your relationship deepens.

Being Fully Alive

If you let them, the routines and ruts of the day can leave you in a state of almost sleepwalking through your life. Looking back over the past weeks and months, you may sometimes feel it all blurs together almost like one long, unremarkable day. God did not design you to have a boring life, even when walking through ordinary circumstances. When you follow the path of the Spirit, doing what He shows you in each moment, you will have an unending stream of remarkable experiences, even when travelling through the most well-worn terrain.

Getting to know God through practices such as *Lectio Divina* will begin to fill you with the desire to live a life that is fully alive. As you have learned during *Contemplatio*, God is always unfolding something new, always calling you deeper into the mystery. Strive to carry this same awareness with you at all times, experiencing each moment fully. Don't miss the power of the small things; instead, try to see the depth of God's purpose at work in all parts of creation.

When you find a cold mountain stream and, setting aside your possessions, you jump in, submerging your whole body in the tumbling waters, you feel in that instant what it means to be fully alive. The cold almost takes your breath away, but in that moment every fiber of your mind, body, and spirit are present and connected. As you break back through the surface and instinctively gasp for air, you begin to realize that this is what you were made for: not sitting in a room hiding from life, but out living it in all its abundance. You were designed to be this fully alive all the time, even in places where others might only see the ordinary and everyday.

The decision to grow always involves a choice between risk and comfort. This means that to be a follower of Jesus you must renounce comfort as the ultimate value of your life.

- John Ortberg

Seeking Adventure

The life fully lived is full of adventures, some small and some epic. You can find small adventures around you each day, whether in watching a spider weave a web or in meeting someone new. Look for opportunities to try new things. Remember that God designed your mind to always be learning, not just in school or at work, but simply out of curiosity. Keep your eyes open for the big adventures that will be sent your way. Seek them out and embrace the growth that these new challenges bring.

Hang out with people who push you outside of your old comfort zones in a good way, people who encourage you to fully develop the gifts the Spirit has given you. Even when circumstances make it difficult, fight to keep your body healthy and in great shape. You will feel much more able to take on the challenges and adventures of life when you keep your body in prime condition.

Living with All Your Might

Living with all your might can seem scary, especially when you have been conditioned to believe you are never allowed to fail. If you don't have permission to fail, then you don't have permission to really live. You will only feel free to attempt what you know you can succeed at on the first try. If you live in God's presence, though, His love will bring you past these fears and help you take moments that others would classify as failure and see them as some of your points of most profound growth.

As you learn to live fully, you will come to experience both the joy and the pain of life more deeply, becoming more authentically yourself as God reveals the purposes for which He designed you. Letting God dig around the roots of your being uncovers the bad along with the good, but it also allow Him to heal you and move you through the grief to the joy beyond.

Compline

Reading: *1 Timothy 6:11-19*

Reflection: Were your actions today directed toward storing up treasures in heaven or here on Earth?

Prayer: If you desire to take hold of the life that really is life, open yourself up to the Holy Spirit and cry out to Him, making this the prayer of your whole being.

READING #1 - DEUTERONOMY 4:29

Preparation:

- Calm your mind and take a few deep breaths
- Start with a Prayer of Thanksgiving
- Continue with the prayer, "*Lord Jesus Christ, help me live fully in each moment, taking hold of each new day and living it with all my strength.*"

Lectio:

Day 2

In this passage, Moses gives God's promise to Israel that, even when they have wandered far from Him, He will always be found if they search for Him with all their strength.

From there you will seek the LORD your God,
and you will find him if you search after him with all your heart and soul.

- Deuteronomy 4:29 (NRSV)

Meditatio:

Is your life an adventure in search of God? Or do you just wander aimlessly much of the time? What would your life be like if you were searching for God with all your heart and soul?

Oratio:

Pray that God would give you the courage to live fully today, enjoying and caring for the world He has given you to live in, loving those around you, and seeking Him with all your heart and soul.

Contemplatio:

The modern concept of a lawn is very controlled and tidy. The lawn is dominated by neatly mowed grass with a few trimmed bushes or flowers along the edges. Modern humans always try to take the richness and diversity of God's creation and tame it into something we can control. The result is an impoverished landscape that is never really under our control anyway. When we allow nature to express the diversity that God designed into it, it creates fertility and abundance, often in ways that seem untidy or chaotic to our limited way of perceiving.

Look around at the diversity of life that surrounds you. If you are surrounded by lawn, look out toward the wilder areas around the edges. Where would you rather live: in the man-made landscape with its illusion of control, or in the wild areas alive with God's abundance? As you move into silence, reach out with your spiritual senses and feel the power of God working in the wild and untamed edges of life.

If you haven't fully internalized the practice of breathing more deeply into your body during *Contemplatio* yet, you may find it helpful to begin each day by taking a few moments to focus on your breathing, relaxing your chest and shoulders as you breathe lower, into the space below your navel. Once you have the pattern established, you should find that it helps greatly with settling the mind into the silence.

Compline

Reading: *Philippians 1:20-30*

Reflection: In what ways did the Holy Spirit use you today? What blessings did the day bring? What challenges?

Prayer: Be thankful for the blessings and the challenges of the day.

Benediction:

- Return slowly and peacefully from *Contemplatio*
- Take time to be thankful again
- Acknowledge that you have completed your time for today and ask God to go with you as you leave this time.

READING #2 - 2 SAMUEL 6:5

Day 3

Preparation:

- Calm your mind and take a few deep breaths
- Start with a Prayer of Thanksgiving
- Continue with the prayer, "*Lord Jesus Christ, help me live fully in each moment, taking hold of each new day and living it with all my strength.*"

Lectio:

Throughout the Psalms that he wrote, you can see that David expressed himself without holding back to God, whether in sorrow or in joy. Because of this, the Bible says that David was a man after God's own heart (*1 Samuel 13:14*). In this passage, David and the people of Israel dance as they bring the Ark of the Covenant back to the city of Jerusalem.

David and all the house of Israel were dancing before the LORD with all their might, with songs and lyres and harps and tambourines and castanets and cymbals.

- 2 Samuel 6:5 (NRSV)

Meditatio:

Have you ever danced or sung to God with all your might? If not, imagine yourself doing so. What holds you back from expressing yourself fully to God? Are you afraid of what others might think or scared of what might happen if you opened up fully? Where does this fear come from?

Oratio:

_____

Ask God to take away any fear that keeps you from pursuing Him, and to replace it with a profound trust in His love. Picture yourself standing before God with your heart fully open, and then offer this image to God as a symbol of your desire to trust Him completely.

How little people know who think that holiness is dull. When one meets the real thing it is irresistible.

- C. S. Lewis

Contemplatio:

Like many other parts of God's creation, the diverse range of natural sound can at first seem random and confusing. If you listen for a while, however, you will begin to detect the underlying patterns that weave these sounds into a dynamic tapestry through which all the life around you communicates. During the wild chorus of sound heard in the forest at sunset, for example, you will find that all the different birds, animals, and insects use their own distinct range of pitches so that each can be heard among the vast range of noises.

Close your eyes and listen past the man-made noises to the natural sounds around you. Even if you are in an urban environment, a diversity of sounds made by the wind in the trees, the birds, and the insects is always present. Quiet the noise of your own thoughts so you can listen to the wild and untamed sounds of God's creation calling you to remember the extraordinary life found beyond the edges of your own control.

Benediction:

- Return slowly and peacefully from *Contemplatio*
- Take time to be thankful again
- Acknowledge that you have completed your time for today and ask God to go with you as you leave this time.

Compline

Reading: *Ecclesiastes 3:1-8*

Reflection: Was today for you a time to laugh or a time to weep? A time to dance or a time to mourn? Or perhaps a mixture of both? What did God teach you in the events of today?

Prayer: As you pray, bring your body into the prayer in some way, maybe even by dancing in a way that expresses how you feel tonight.

READING #3 - MARK 12:28-34

Preparation:

- Calm your mind and take a few deep breaths
- Start with a Prayer of Thanksgiving
- Continue with the prayer, "*Lord Jesus Christ, help me live fully in each moment, taking hold of each new day and living it with all my strength.*"

Lectio:

Day 4

The passage for *Compline* this evening is *Deuteronomy 6:4-9*, the Old Testament passage from which Jesus takes what He says is the greatest commandment. The second, to love your neighbor as yourself, is contained in *Leviticus 19:18*.

One of the teachers of the law came and heard them debating.
Noticing that Jesus had given them a good answer, he asked him,
"Of all the commandments, which is the most important?"
"The most important one," answered Jesus, "is this: 'Hear, O Israel, the Lord our God,
the Lord is one. Love the Lord your God with all your heart and with all your soul and
with all your mind and with all your strength.'
The second is this: 'Love your neighbor as yourself.'
There is no commandment greater than these."
"Well said, teacher," the man replied. "You are right in saying that God is one and there
is no other but him. To love him with all your heart, with all your understanding and
with all your strength, and to love your neighbor as yourself is more important than all
burnt offerings and sacrifices."
When Jesus saw that he had answered wisely, he said to him, "You are not far from the
kingdom of God." And from then on no one dared ask him any more questions.

- Mark 12:28-34 (NIV)

Meditatio:

What would it look like to live each day following the commandment to love the Lord with all your heart, soul, mind, and strength? Imagine a life packed with happiness and sorrow, deep fellowship and profound loss, journeys to the tops of the mountains and through the deep shadows of the dark valleys. Are you ready to follow God all the way, trusting that He will give you joy to sustain you even when the road is difficult?

Oratio:

Give a prayer of thanks today that God has called you to love and follow Him. Ask Him to fill you with perfect love that will pour itself out back to Him, and overflow toward those around you.

Contemplatio:

The natural world exhibits a wide variety of patterns throughout its design: spirals and whorls, branching and nets, waves and flows. Look at all the natural objects around you and notice the wide range of patterns you see in the trees, plants, clouds, birds, and forms of the landscape. You will soon realize that almost nothing is perfectly straight or forms perfect rectangles. Creation is a beautiful collection of arcs and spirals, dynamic forms, and intricate branching patterns. In comparison, man-made objects such as cars and buildings seem flat and lifeless.

The diverse patterns of creation reveal something of the mind of their Creator. Each need is served by the simple yet elegant unfolding of basic forms working together to create a complex and perfectly functional whole. As you move into the silence today, use these patterns to help you focus on the presence of the Creator, the one God whose creative power unfolds in an endless variety of forms.

Benediction:

- Return slowly and peacefully from *Contemplatio*
- Take time to be thankful again
- Acknowledge that you have completed your time for today and ask God to go with you as you leave this time.

Compline

Reading: *Deuteronomy 6:4-9*

Reflection: How is God's commandment to love Him a reflection of His love toward you?

Prayer: Spend time tonight telling God why you love Him.

READING #4 - LUKE 6:22-23

Preparation:

- Calm your mind and take a few deep breaths
- Start with a Prayer of Thanksgiving
- Continue with the prayer, "*Lord Jesus Christ, help me live fully in each moment, taking hold of each new day and living it with all my strength.*"

Lectio:

Day 5

The teachings of Jesus found in *Luke 6:20-49* are also contained in the Sermon on the Mount recorded in *Matthew 5-7*. The parallel of this passage is found in *Matthew 5:11* at the end of the Beatitudes. Jesus refers to Himself here as the *Son of Man*.

Blessed are you when men hate you,
when they exclude you and insult you
and reject your name as evil,
because of the Son of Man.
Rejoice in that day and leap for joy, because great is your reward in heaven.
For that is how their fathers treated the prophets.

- Luke 6:22-23 (NIV)

Meditatio:

What is your normal reaction when people hate you, exclude you, insult you, or reject you? What kind of change in mind-set would it take for you to rejoice when you were rejected because your way of life didn't match up with the rest of the world's? Do people notice anything different about you because you follow Christ? If so, what kind of people does this attract into your life, and what kind of people does it cause to reject you?

Oratio:

Ask God to make your life such a clear reflection of His love that you will attract those who follow Him into your life. Ask for the wisdom to pray for those who reject you because they have rejected God and they see His reflection in you.

Contemplatio:

Nature is always in motion. Even in the quietest of landscapes, something is always moving, even if slowly. At other times, during a storm or high wind, the whole world can appear to be a riot of movement, with trees rocking and leaves blowing along the ground.

Move into wide-angle vision and watch the motion in the landscape around you. Notice how distinct each type of motion appears: the swaying of leaves in the breeze, the slow rolling of clouds through the sky, the quick darting of birds in and out of the bushes, the coming and going of people busy with life. Let these many types of motion remind you of the variety of ways God works in the world, sometimes quietly and slowly, other times quickly and with great power. Relax into God's presence and accept the rhythm of His will unfolding in your life. As your thoughts become still, direct your intention toward the Holy Spirit moving within you, allowing yourself to be carried in the stream of His divine will.

Benediction:

- Return slowly and peacefully from *Contemplatio*
- Take time to be thankful again
- Acknowledge that you have completed your time for today and ask God to go with you as you leave this time.

Compline

Reading: *Acts 6:1-15*

Reflection: Have you been rejected or ridiculed this week because you follow Christ? Has your relationship with God drawn you closer to anyone?

Prayer: Ask for the wisdom to see the spiritual need behind the rejection of those who exclude you because of your faith.

READING #5 - PHILIPPIANS 4:12-13

Preparation:

- Calm your mind and take a few deep breaths
- Start with a Prayer of Thanksgiving
- Continue with the prayer, "*Lord Jesus Christ, help me live fully in each moment, taking hold of each new day and living it with all my strength.*"

Lectio:

Day 6

I know what it is to have little, and I know what it is to have plenty.
In any and all circumstances I have learned the secret of being well-fed and of going hungry, of having plenty and of being in need.
I can do all things through him who strengthens me.

- Philippians 4:12-13 (NRSV)

Meditatio:

Being content during the good times is easy. How content are you when life gets tough? Why does God let you go through periods of hardship? What do periods of difficulty and sorrow develop in your character?

Oratio:

> Pray that God will give you the faith to trust Him as you go through the dark places along the road of life. Be thankful that He has promised to use these periods of difficulty to build His strength into your spirit as He conforms you into the image of Christ.

> *There are believers who by God's grace, have climbed the mountains of full assurance and near communion, their place is with the eagle in his eyrie, high aloft; they are like the strong mountaineer, who has trodden the virgin snow, who has breathed the fresh, free air of the Alpine regions, and therefore his sinews are braced, and his limbs are vigorous; these are they who do great exploits, being mighty men, men of renown.*
>
> - Charles Spurgeon

Contemplatio:

As you start today, close your eyes and imagine the vast number of possible paths your life could have taken thus far, and the many possible paths that diverge ahead of you. Although the events of life can sometimes seem random, God has worked everything that has happened to you, both good and bad, together to bring you to where you are today. Even though billions of people are alive on the Earth today, the path that God has laid out for you is unique. Just like a father's relationship with each of his children is different and brings out different parts of his personality, every child of God has a unique relationship with Him that brings forth the character of God in unique ways.

Turn your attention fully to God's presence with you at this very moment. Use your sacred word if you need to release your thoughts, and then simply hold your intention on dwelling with God in stillness for these few moments, a sacred pause in the journey of life.

Benediction:

- Return slowly and peacefully from *Contemplatio*
- Take time to be thankful again
- Acknowledge that you have completed your time for today and ask God to go with you as you leave this time.

Compline

Reading: *John 15:1-11*

Reflection: Did you depend upon your own strength today, or did you draw upon the strength that comes from abiding in God's presence?

Prayer: Be thankful for the calling God has made for you to live an extraordinary life. Ask Him to abide in you each step of the journey.

REFLECTION

Revisit Your Favorite Passage

Day 7

Reflections on the Week

Compline

Reading: *Psalm 66*

Reflection: Do you feel that nothing extraordinary happened in your life this week? Don't overlook the power of God at work in even the small things.

Prayer: Say a prayer of blessing to God, thanking Him for His steadfast love.

Week 7 - Integrity

"Again, you have heard that it was said to the people long ago,
'Do not break your oath, but keep the oaths you have made to the Lord.'
But I tell you, Do not swear at all: either by heaven, for it is God's throne; or by the earth, for it is his footstool;
or by Jerusalem, for it is the city of the Great King.
And do not swear by your head, for you cannot make even one hair white or black.
Simply let your 'Yes' be 'Yes,' and your 'No,' 'No'; anything beyond this comes from the evil one."

-Matthew 5:33-37 (NIV)

OVER THE CENTURIES LEADING UP TO JESUS' TIME, the Pharisees had developed an elaborate set of rules for interpreting and applying the Old Testament Law. They had rules for exactly how far you could walk on the Sabbath, exactly how you had to pay your tithe, and even rules for which type of oaths were more binding than others. Swearing by the altar was not considered binding, but swearing by the sacrifice on the altar was.

As Jesus laid out His teachings during the Sermon on the Mount, He systematically attacked all these rules the Pharisees had built up in order to give themselves the appearance of righteousness. When He came to the subject of the Pharisees' rules on oaths, He said they had totally missed the point. What God requires is complete integrity: speaking the truth and living up to your commitments, acting with honesty and fairness in all your dealings. Jesus leaves no room for hiding behind made-up rules and double-talk.

Most people think of the word *integrity* as simply meaning the quality of being honest, but the concept of integrity that is developed in the Bible is much stronger. *Integrity* literally means the quality of being complete and undivided, of being strong and sound structurally, of being reliable and without defect. When you say that a building has integrity, you mean that it is properly built and can handle the winds and the rains of the fiercest storms without leaking or falling down. The character of a person with integrity is the same: it will handle the storms of life without falling.

The root word from which we get *integrity* is also the source of the word *integrated*, meaning that all the parts of a whole fit together and work as one. As you follow Christ, you will find this kind of integrity manifesting itself in you. Your heart, mind, emotions, and body will slowly be transformed so they are no longer in conflict with each other, but work together as God intended.

As you practice integrity both inwardly and outwardly, you will find yourself becoming increasingly undivided in your thoughts and actions. The gap between what you claim to believe and how you live will gradually disappear.

If you pause to look at the natural world God built for us, you will find a design of incredible integrity. Each part works exactly as God intended, fitting together with the other elements of the Creation to create the constantly regenerating patterns of life. We will use these interconnections as the focus for *Contemplatio* this week, thinking about how the seamless working together of nature provides a picture of how God wants to create in you a harmony of mind, body, and spirit that results in a powerful life lived with integrity.

Extra Mile:

Practice integrity in your commitments this week by fulfilling them to the best of your ability. Be on time and give your best in all your responsibilities. If you fail in keeping a commitment, apologize to the person you let down and make it right. Practice integrity in your words by speaking only truth. If you have misled anyone in the past week, go to them and set it straight.

FINDING PEACE IN COMMUNITY

Day 1

The Old Order Amish feel that the trade-off of doing without modern technology in order to pursue a more spiritually grounded life and a healthier community is well worth it. What does it say that many people who claim to be a follower of Christ find that getting up on time each Sunday morning is asking too much? Would you be willing to forgo some of the things now thought of as standard parts of modern life if you realized this is what it would take to find true community?

WHEN YOU THINK BACK TO THE TIMES IN YOUR LIFE THAT WERE THE MOST MEMORABLE, the times when you felt most alive, the times that felt the most critical in shaping the person you have become, you will most likely find that these memories intimately involve other people. God created you not only to have a relationship with Him, but to live in deep relationship with others. God intended that the most powerful experiences in your life be relational, that His grace and blessings would most often flow out to you through your relationships with family and community.

God seldom calls a person to live the extraordinary life of faith alone. Instead, He designed the life of faith to unfold in the company of a community of Believers who support and encourage each other along the way. As modern culture becomes ever more fragmented and scattered, people are increasingly looking to find faith communities that provide relationships based on something less shallow and transient than the things the world puts forward as important. They are looking to fulfill the basic human need to be part of a community that creates lasting relationships based on things of eternal value.

A Community of Faith

For most people, any mention of the Amish immediately calls to mind the image of a horse and buggy rolling down a rural road in Pennsylvania, carrying plainly dressed passengers who reject the use of modern conveniences such as cars, telephones, or electricity. To our modern sensibilities, choosing to go without these things we consider necessities seems downright odd or unfathomable. For some reason, though, this picture of a simpler life can also call up thoughts of what it might be like to belong to the kind of tight-knit community that seems so hard to find today.

If you look past the surface of the Old Order Amish tradition, you will find their choices of what technologies they decide to use has less to do with a blanket rejection of anything new than with a practice of asking careful questions about what will keep their families and communities strong. The Old Order Amish believe that working together to produce the basic staples of life—growing food, sewing clothes, joining together to build their own homes—is critical in maintaining the connections that form the backbone of their culture. In traditional Amish communities, church meetings don't involve going to a building and sitting in a pew along with hundreds of other people who barely know each other. Instead, it is a time of gathering in their homes with the people they work with in the fields or workshops each day, with whom they prepare meals and share the everyday burdens of life.

You don't have to give up all your modern conveniences to see a key Biblical truth illustrated by the Amish way of life: the kind of community that God intended is not just a group of people who meet for a few hours every week in a church building; it is the kind of community formed when people live, work, and fellowship together intimately every day. This is the same pattern of community seen in the first century churches throughout the book of *Acts*. Believers living side by side in this way form the true community of the Church.

In fact, churches of a century ago often had many of these elements, being mostly smaller congregations comprised of people who lived and worked close together. Meeting at the church building served simply to supplement the spiritual communion experienced during the week by providing a time of meeting together for the purposes of worship, teaching, and focusing on God's presence and work in the community.

Over the past few decades, as population centers have shifted and become more suburban, the members of the average church have become increasingly spread out and more likely to see each other only when they drive to the church building. As a result, many churches are now finding it hard to provide the kind of close-knit relationships that God intended. With many churches becoming larger, they sometimes end up with a group of core members who are well connected with each other, but with a large group of isolated and unconnected members around the edges.

As churches have become increasingly defined by buildings and programs, it has also become easier for church congregations to grow more cliquish and self-oriented, creating an atmosphere of distrust and separation from those who might happen to attend other churches or belong to other denominations. We must always remember that distinctions of denomination are the product of the human mind, not of God's creation. The Bible sees all those who follow Christ as part of His *ekklēssia*, as a member of the body of God's people, called out and set apart from the world, who together form the community of the Church.

Your community of faith isn't just the group of people who show up at a church building together a couple of times each week. It bridges across divisions caused by denomination, church membership, ethnicity, or other man-made barriers. Your sense of community should reach out to include all those with whom you share the challenges and joys of daily life, all those who are seeking to travel the same spiritual path in search of God's truth.

The Biblical Precepts that Bring Shalom

As churches have grown and changed over the last century, and an increasing number of people have begun to attend for purely social reasons, many churches have come to tolerate behavior clearly condemned by the Bible. Increasingly, many Believers are being driven away from churches by the internal politics and the way they are treated by other members. Some people who profess to be Christians now even refuse to go to church because of the series of wounds they have sustained through their experiences at the various churches they have attended. There is no excuse for our churches to function in this way when the Bible gives us clear instructions for how we are to love and support each other.

Starting this week, we will look at a set of eight core precepts from scripture that tell us how to live together in peace as a community of faith. The Hebrew word *shalom*—meaning *peace*—paints a beautiful picture of what it looks like for God's peace to exist within a community. Although *shalom* does indeed mean the absence of internal discord, backbiting, or agitation, to the ancient Hebrews it meant much more than simply the absence of conflict. To them, *Shalom* also implied the presence of peace, wholeness, health, harmony, and safety. When we as Believers follow the Bible's precepts for how to treat each other, we build the foundations of *shalom* upon which our communities of faith are built.

As we work to restore *shalom* in our communities, we must find ways to restore the daily fellowship required for community to have space to grow. The types of relationships that create community are those that revolve around meeting primary needs, such as feeding each other, caring for the children, and helping each other through problems and crises. Simply hanging out together to have fun or socialize doesn't build these types of powerful relationships. Your community of faith must exist in the space of the everyday and practical in order to function.

The study of integrity this week starts us off with one of the most fundamental of the Precepts of *Shalom*. Until we deal with each other honestly, openly, and justly, we will never learn to apply the other precepts consistently in our communities.

Throughout this book, the word *church* (lower case) is used to indicate an organized congregation of people who regularly meet together, whether they identify themselves with a specific denomination or not. The word *Church* (upper case) is used to indicate the body of all those people who follow Jesus and who have entered into a covenant relationship with God. The phrase *community of faith* is used to indicate the group of all those Believers with whom you fellowship and share your spiritual journey, whether or not they are a member of your specific church or denomination.

Week 7

A *precept* is a rule or direction for personal conduct. The precepts outlined this week and in the following weeks are the commandments laid out in scripture that, when followed, will create *shalom* among those in your community of faith.

Since these precepts are reflections of God's love, they also help Believers live in peace with those who do not follow Christ, even if they do not follow these principles themselves.

A summary of all eight precepts can be found on pages 220-222. You may find this summary helpful as a reminder.

The conclusion of the reading, along with today's *Compline*, is on the next two pages. →

WALKING WITH INTEGRITY

Watch your own reactions to each of the eight precepts as we discuss them in turn over the next few weeks. Notice which of them you like and which ones tend to push your buttons. Pay special attention to those precepts that you are tempted to think of as difficult or impractical to integrate into your everyday life. Ask yourself why these particular things seem so hard for you. And remember that growing into fully following these principles is a journey that will see you fail many times along the way. Simply confess your failures to God and release them to the Spirit so you can continue to move forward in a good way.

Jesus reserved His harshest criticism for religious leaders who used God's law simply as a way to appear righteous, but who failed to search out the real meaning behind God's commands. Jesus repeatedly called them hypocrites and blind guides. You will read what Jesus had to say about the hypocrisy of the Pharisees in the passage from *Compline* tonight.

Scripture warns specifically against lying about other people, or *bearing false witness against your neighbor* as it is called in the Ten Commandments. A lie told for selfish reasons or to get out of trouble can end up destroying another person's reputation and create negative consequences for that person that can last for decades. Even when lies about a person are later disproved, the lie has already done its damage and created lingering doubts in the minds of others that can never be erased.

The Roots of Hypocrisy

One of the most common criticisms non-Christians level against churchgoers is that they are hypocritical: they claim to believe the Bible's teaching, but do not reflect it in the way they live.

The word *hypocrite* comes from the Greek word for an actor who puts on a mask in order to assume another identity while on stage. Today we use the word to refer to people who claim to believe something in order to impress others or to feel better about themselves, but whose actions show they don't really believe what they claim.

The problem is that the actions of a person who is truly trying to follow Christ but who has sinned because of weakness can sometimes be mistaken for hypocrisy. To discern the difference between someone who is hypocritical and someone who is really trying to follow Jesus, you must look at their response when they sin. Those who are following Christ will be convicted when they sin, and call out to God for help, while the hypocrite experiences no such conviction and keeps right on sinning.

The reason that even those who try the hardest to follow Jesus can sometimes appear hypocritical is that their old, sinful nature causes actions that conflict with the new spiritual nature being created in them by the Holy Spirit. You may know with your conscious mind what is right, but if the motives of your heart have not been made holy through the healing work of the Spirit, you will find yourself actually desiring something completely different from, or even opposed to, what you know to be God's will.

Although we like to think that we choose how to act out of logic and reason, more often than not our actions arise from the inward desires of the heart and then the mind simply rationalizes the heart's motives. Until God heals the motives and desires of your heart, you will always wrestle to make your actions conform to what you profess to believe.

Speaking Truth

The Bible has some amazingly strong words to say about lying. It warns that *lying lips are an abomination* to God (*Proverbs 12:22*) and that God *abhors those who are deceitful* and will *destroy those who speak lies* (*Psalms 5:6*). God hates dishonestly so much because it destroys trust between His children and renders them powerless. Once you get into the habit of lying, you soon find yourself speaking half-truths and outright falsehoods almost without thought. Those who lie to others soon learn to deceive themselves as well.

To the best of your ability, speak only truth. Avoid even the "small" lies designed to let you slide by in conversation or to smooth over social situations. An important part of spiritual maturity is to learn to speak the truth with love and sensitivity so that your words are a blessing.

Let Your "Yes" Mean "Yes"

In the Sermon on the Mount, Jesus addresses integrity by saying that your "Yes" should mean "Yes" and your "No" should mean "No" (*Matthew 5:37*). If you speak with integrity, people will soon learn that they can accept what your say as straight-forward and trustworthy without having to parse your words to figure out whether you mean what you seem to be saying. Letting your "Yes" mean "Yes" means people can trust what you say without feeling they need to extract promises or vows from you in order to be sure you will carry through on what you say. Instead, your words will carry integrity, being undivided, reliable, and reflecting God's love of truth.

You may at times be tempted to try working around the Bible's command to not lie by instead telling a carefully edited version of the truth—but painting a false picture by giving the facts selectively is still lying. Those around you should never have to wonder whether you are giving them the whole story, or whether there is a hidden agenda behind your words.

You don't actually have to make false statements in order to lie; a lie can just as easily be told by speaking only that which is factually true. A lie is any intentionally inaccurate representation of reality, whether the inaccuracy comes from making false statements or by using carefully selected true ones to construct a misleading picture. Lying by omission or by leaving out what is required to tell the whole truth is still deception. When you speak, let what you say reflect the truth to the best of your ability, without evasion, omission, or misdirection.

Keeping Commitments

As cell phones and instant messaging have become ubiquitous, changing plans at the last minute has become increasingly easy. When it is so simple to send a quick text saying your plans have changed, it becomes tempting to only let your commitments last until you change your mind or until something better comes along. But an important part of letting your "Yes" mean "Yes" is thinking your way through commitments before you make them and then honoring the commitments you have made.

Practicing integrity means following through when you tell someone you will be somewhere or will help them out. Your friends should be able to count on you when you commit to something. There are real consequences when you don't hold up your end of a commitment, because others are depending on you. Resist the temptation to back out on a commitment just because something better comes along. Once you make plans with someone, do your best to be there.

The pace of modern life makes it easy to become over-committing, so be thoughtful about not taking on more than you can reasonably handle. It is better to be faithful in a few commitments than to take on so much that you can't do any of it well. Try to make it a habit to be on time and to really be present when you arrive, not letting your mind be off somewhere else.

As a follower of Jesus, your actions and attitudes should be a reflection of His nature, especially in the tough situations. Do your best in every task you set your hand to do, and ask the Spirit to help you keep a positive attitude even when circumstances make it difficult. When you are faced with a commitment that you don't enjoy, simply try turning it into an Act of Service.

In all your dealings, never cheat or shortchange others, but instead give beyond what is required. God has given to you in abundance, so give to others in the same way.

Integrity in Mind, Body, & Spirit

Just as with all the other precepts we will study over the next few weeks, living with integrity is not something that you will become perfect at overnight. Selfishness and deception are such deep parts of the sinful nature that they will take repeated yielding to the Holy Spirit's healing to root them out. Growing into a person who refuses to compromise the truth and who is known as trustworthy with commitments is part of the larger spiritual journey.

When you allow God to create in you a new mind that reflects His truth, and to change your heart so that it purely expresses his love, integrity will come naturally. You will find your whole being—mind, body, and spirit—transformed by the desire to make every footstep on your path through this world a reflection of God's unfailing love and faithfulness.

Once you make a commitment, be faithful to honor that commitment unless something unexpected arises that prevents it. In the event you must change plans, contact the people or person you committed to and explain the situation. Ask them to reschedule with you if this is possible. Asking to reschedule helps communicate that you value your commitment and value them.

Different cultures perceive time in very different ways, so the importance of being on time varies in different places. In the U.S. and many western cultures, keeping someone waiting communicates a lack of regard or respect, while certain cultures in other parts of the world perceive time much more flexibly. Try to be trustworthy with your commitments in whichever way is best expressed in your particular circumstances.

Compline

Reading: *Matthew 23:1-36*

Reflection: Have you been hypocritical in some way this week? What do you say you believe, and what do your actions show you really believe?

Prayer: Ask God to change your thoughts and motives so that the source of any hypocrisy is removed from your spirit.

Reading #1 - James 2:14-23

Preparation:

- Calm your mind and take a few deep breaths
- Start with a Prayer of Thanksgiving
- Continue with the prayer, "*Lord Jesus Christ, make the words of my mouth, the meditations of my heart, and the work of my hands all wholly conformed to Your will, so that I may walk with integrity the path you have laid before me.*"

The opening prayer this week is inspired from Psalm 19:14.

Lectio:

Day 2

What good is it, my brothers and sisters, if you say you have faith
but do not have works? Can faith save you?
If a brother or sister is naked and lacks daily food, and one of you says to them,
"Go in peace; keep warm and eat your fill," and yet you do not supply their bodily
needs, what is the good of that? So faith by itself, if it has no works, is dead.
But someone will say, "You have faith and I have works."
Show me your faith apart from your works, and I by my works will show you my faith.
You believe that God is one; you do well. Even the demons believe—and shudder.
Do you want to be shown, you senseless person, that faith apart from works is barren?
Was not our ancestor Abraham justified by works when he offered
his son Isaac on the altar? You see that faith was active along with his works,
and faith was brought to completion by the works.
Thus the scripture was fulfilled that says, "Abraham believed God,
and it was reckoned to him as righteousness," and he was called the friend of God.

- James 2:14-23 (NRSV)

Meditatio:

True faith in God produces a change in the desires of your heart, which changes your motives and patterns of thought. Your words and actions flow out of your mind and spirit, so any true change in your character will automatically show up in how you talk and what you do. The ultimate result is true integrity, where your heart, mind, words, and actions are all in perfect harmony with each other in expressing God's love.

Oratio:

> Ask to be shown any place in your life that you are harboring the kind of false faith that does not result in godly actions. Ask the Holy Spirit to replace any false faith with the kind of true faith that changes your thoughts and desires to reflect those of Christ.

Contemplatio:

The more you look at the creation, the more you realize the deep interconnections between all its parts. The sun heats the land, which warms the air and causes it to rise. The warm air carries moisture from the trees and helps seed the clouds with dust, which in turn creates rain. The rains spread the waters across the face of the Earth so the plants can drink. The plants take in the water and the energy from the sun, creating new growth that shelters and feeds the birds and animals, who then scatter seeds and help bring fertility to the soil. God's design is a perfect example of integrity: all the parts work together as intended to create a rich tapestry of life.

Look around at the patterns of interconnection in the landscape surrounding you. Remember that the God who created everything you see also created all parts of you to work together—the desires of your heart, the thoughts that move through your mind, the words that you speak, and the work of your hands—to bring His will into being on the Earth. Move into the silence, allowing the Holy Spirit to work whatever change in you is needed to restore you to wholeness.

Benediction:

- Return slowly and peacefully from *Contemplatio*
- Take time to be thankful again
- Acknowledge that you have completed your time for today and ask God to go with you as you leave this time.

Compline

Reading: *Proverbs 4:23-27*

Reflection: Has your life this week displayed integrity in both faith and actions?

Prayer: Pray that your faith would be the kind that automatically produces in you words and actions pleasing to God.

READING #2 - DEUTERONOMY 25:13-15

Preparation:

- Calm your mind and take a few deep breaths
- Start with a Prayer of Thanksgiving
- Continue with the prayer, "*Lord Jesus Christ, make the words of my mouth, the meditations of my heart, and the work of my hands all wholly conformed to Your will, so that I may walk with integrity the path you have laid before me.*"

Lectio:

Day 3

In Old Testament times, weights and measures were often used in the market to insure trades where completed fairly. Dishonest merchants would often have a rigged set of weights and measures they could use to short-change a customer.

> You shall not have in your bag two kinds of weights, large and small.
> You shall not have in your house two kinds of measures, large and small.
> You shall have only a full and honest weight;
> you shall have only a full and honest measure,
> so that your days may be long in the land that the LORD your God is giving you.
>
> *- Deuteronomy 25:13-15 (NRSV)*

Meditatio:

A life of integrity is marked by never holding double standards, by never having two different sets of measures to use with different people or under different circumstances. God commands that you treat everyone fairly and honestly, whether they are a friend or an enemy.

Oratio:

If you have realized you are sometimes guilty of using two sets of weights and measures when dealing with people, then visualize yourself giving your false measures to God and allowing Him to replace them with the full and honest measures that flow from His grace.

Integrity is the glue that holds our way of life together. We must constantly strive to keep our integrity intact. When wealth is lost, nothing is lost; when health is lost, something is lost; when character is lost, all is lost.

- Billy Graham

Contemplatio:

Lie on the ground and feel the soil beneath you. We often take the thin layer of soil that covers the Earth for granted, but it is from the soil that almost all plant life grows. Without the plants and trees, we would not be able to live.

God designed the interconnections between the plants and the soil so that the soil feeds the plants, and the plants repair and replenish the soil. When the soil is too compacted, certain plants grow that repair the compaction. When the soil is too acid or alkaline, other plants grow that repair the imbalance. When the soil lacks key nutrients, yet other plants grow that use deep roots to pull up the nutrients from deep underground and make them available.

Close your eyes and remember for a moment how God designed cycles of growth and healing into all parts of His creation. As you move into silence, turn your inner attention toward the Holy Spirit, who works at the place where mind, body, and spirit meet to bring healing and growth.

Benediction:

- Return slowly and peacefully from *Contemplatio*
- Take time to be thankful again
- Acknowledge that you have completed your time for today and ask God to go with you as you leave this time.

Compline

Reading: *Luke 11:33-35*

Reflection: Visualize the picture Jesus paints of integrity: all parts of your being-mind, body, and spirit-filled with His light, with no darkness in any part.

Prayer: Ask the Holy Spirit to illuminate your whole being, freeing you from any selfishness or pridefulness that would keep you from giving yourself fully to His love.

READING #3 - ZECHARIAH 8:16-17

Preparation:

- Calm your mind and take a few deep breaths
- Start with a Prayer of Thanksgiving
- Continue with the prayer, *"Lord Jesus Christ, make the words of my mouth, the meditations of my heart, and the work of my hands all wholly conformed to Your will, so that I may walk with integrity the path you have laid before me."*

Lectio:

Day 4

> "These are the things you are to do:
> Speak the truth to each other,
> and render true and sound judgment in your courts;
> do not plot evil against your neighbor,
> and do not love to swear falsely.
> I hate all this," declares the Lord.

- Zechariah 8:16-17 (NIV)

Meditatio:

Do you try as best you can to always speak the truth, or do you occasionally find yourself lying for some reason? In what situations are you tempted to speak falsely or be unfair? What inner desire creates the temptation?

Oratio:

Release any habitual desires that tempt you to speak untruths or deal with people unfairly. Ask God to give you a clear mind and pure motives so you can act with integrity even when it is difficult.

Contemplatio:

Sit in wide-angle vision, looking at the landscape surrounding you again, noticing how the connections between the plants, animals, and soil work together to form the web of life. The bacteria and fungi in the soil interact with the roots of the plants, giving the plants the nutrients they need and receiving food in the form of starches and sugars in return. These starches and sugars are created by the plants using the energy from photosynthesis, and also form the foundation of the food chain that feeds all the animals on land. The animals, in turn, eat the plants and return the fertility to the soil through their manure.

As you sit in silence today, simply let the complexity and inter-connectedness of creation wash over you. Make sure to return your breathing to a slow, deep pattern to help you relax fully into God's presence. In the quietness, feel the hand of God at work in the dance of life all around you.

Benediction:

- Return slowly and peacefully from *Contemplatio*
- Take time to be thankful again
- Acknowledge that you have completed your time for today and ask God to go with you as you leave this time.

Compline

Reading: *Colossians 3:9-10*

Reflection: Have you done your best to speak only truth this week? Have you found yourself saying something untrue without really intending to? Why does this happen?

Prayer: Commit to set right any untruth you have spoken in the last week.

READING #4 - 1 SAMUEL 12:1-5

Preparation:

- Calm your mind and take a few deep breaths
- Start with a Prayer of Thanksgiving
- Continue with the prayer, "*Lord Jesus Christ, make the words of my mouth, the meditations of my heart, and the work of my hands all wholly conformed to Your will, so that I may walk with integrity the path you have laid before me.*"

Lectio:

Day 5

Samuel had been God's appointed judge over Israel for around 25 years when he was called by God to anoint Saul as king. In this passage, Samuel speaks to the people of Israel as he is handing over authority to Saul. He asks if anyone has any claim of not being treated fairly and honestly, promising to make right anything he has ever done wrong. Samuel had treated the people with such integrity that nobody was able to accuse him of a single act of dishonesty or favoritism.

Samuel said to all Israel,
"I have listened to everything you said to me and have set a king over you.
Now you have a king as your leader. As for me, I am old and gray, and my sons are here with you. I have been your leader from my youth until this day. Here I stand.
Testify against me in the presence of the LORD and his anointed.
Whose ox have I taken? Whose donkey have I taken? Whom have I cheated?
Whom have I oppressed? From whose hand have I accepted a bribe to make me shut my eyes? If I have done any of these, I will make it right."
"You have not cheated or oppressed us," they replied.
"You have not taken anything from anyone's hand."
Samuel said to them, "The LORD is witness against you,
and also his anointed is witness this day,
that you have not found anything in my hand."
"He is witness," they said.

- 1 Samuel 12:1-5 (NIV)

Meditatio:

What would the people that know you say if they gave an honest account of your honesty and integrity in daily life? In what areas would you deserve blame for how you have treated others? In what areas would those who know you rightly give you praise?

Oratio:

_____

Pray for wisdom to deal fairly and honestly with those around you, so that everyone will be forced to agree that you are blameless and beyond reproach.

Contemplatio:

The narrative of modern life often paints a picture of us as humans being somehow separate and apart from the rest of creation, as if God put the Earth here merely for us to exploit to feed our own selfish desires. The Bible says, however, that God created the Earth and everything in it and said that it was good, that it had value and worth simply because it came from His hand and was a reflection of His love. God then placed us on the Earth to act as an integral part of His creation, to care for the Earth and be a blessing to it.

Reach out with all your senses and feel how deeply you are connected to the Earth beneath you and the sky above you. Remember that, although God made mankind unique in all creation, being formed in His image, you are also designed to connect deeply with the Earth that God created to support you. Relax and breath, allowing your body to rest on the Earth that God has created to sustain it, and allowing your spirit to rest in the peace that comes from God's Spirit.

Benediction:

- Return slowly and peacefully from _Contemplatio_
- Take time to be thankful again
- Acknowledge that you have completed your time for today and ask God to go with you as you leave this time.

**Compline**

Reading: _Acts 20:17-38_

Reflection: What will those who know you say about you when it is time for you to leave them? Will they be able to say you lived a life filled with integrity?

Prayer: Try holding your hands with the palms turned upward as a sign of openness to the Holy Spirit as you pray tonight.

READING #5 - JOB 27:3-6

Preparation:

- Calm your mind and take a few deep breaths
- Start with a Prayer of Thanksgiving
- Continue with the prayer, *"Lord Jesus Christ, make the words of my mouth, the meditations of my heart, and the work of my hands all wholly conformed to Your will, so that I may walk with integrity the path you have laid before me."*

Lectio:

As long as my breath is in me
and the spirit of God is in my nostrils,
my lips will not speak falsehood,
and my tongue will not utter deceit.
Far be it from me to say that you are right;
until I die I will not put away my integrity from me.
I hold fast my righteousness, and will not let it go;
my heart does not reproach me for any of my days.

- Job 27:3-6 (NRSV)

Meditatio:

Day 6

God had pointed out Job to Satan as an example of a man who lived with integrity. Satan persuaded God to let him test Job by taking away all Job's possessions, killing his children, and striking his body with boils. Job's three friends repeatedly accused him of having sinned against God to deserve such a fate. His wife encouraged him to curse God for what had happened. This passage is part of Job's response. Read the first two chapters of *Job* to better understand the beginning of the story.

Are you ever tempted to blame God when circumstances get tough? How would you respond if God let you be tested in the same way that Job was tested? Would you let go of your integrity, or hold fast no matter what?

Oratio:

> Remember as you pray that your breath and life flow from God, and that He understands your circumstances far better than you. Pray that you will have the courage and strength to walk with integrity even when you don't understand what God is doing in your life.

> *Courage is not simply one of the virtues, but the form of every virtue at the testing point.*
>
> - C. S. Lewis

Contemplatio:

The interconnection between the spiritual and the physical is something of a mystery. Although the ancient Greeks and many of the cultures that followed them wanted to believe the two were completely separate, the Bible seems to paint the picture of a world in which the spiritual and the physical lie alongside each other, touching in some way beyond our comprehension. When mankind sinned against God, it resulted in corruption of both the spiritual and physical bodies. The spiritual act of Jesus' sacrifice on the cross was so powerful that it caused the Earth to shake and resulted in darkness in the middle of the day. Even God's promise of salvation extends beyond just a spiritual resurrection to include a new and perfect body.

As you move toward inner stillness today, close your eyes and extend your spiritual senses to rest on the place where your mind, body, and spirit meet. For the Believer, this is the point where the Holy Spirit dwells, knitting together your whole being into a form pleasing to God.

Benediction:

- Return slowly and peacefully from *Contemplatio*
- Take time to be thankful again
- Acknowledge that you have completed your time for today and ask God to go with you as you leave this time.

> **Compline**
>
> **Reading:** *Psalm 26*
>
> **Reflection:** Has anything tempted you to let go of your integrity this week? What desire provoked this temptation?
>
> **Prayer:** Release your desire to hold onto what you think belongs to you, and trust that God will provide what you really need, even when it doesn't seem like it at the moment.

REFLECTION

Revisit Your Favorite Passage

Day 7

Reflections on the Week

Compline

Reading: *Psalm 15*

Reflection: Have you ever experienced circumstances where holding onto your integrity seemed to get you nothing but pain or hurt? What was God building into you as you fought your way through the situation?

Prayer: Be thankful that God sometimes uses the hardest times to complete the deepest work in your life.

WEEK 8 - PEACE

You will keep in perfect peace
him whose mind is steadfast,
because he trusts in you.

-Isaiah 26:3 (NIV)

THE MODERN WORLD'S CONCEPT OF PEACE is another place where we have inherited a way of thinking that began with ancient Greek philosophy and which remains with us today. What began with Plato's view of a world divided between the "real" world of thoughts and ideas, and the "distorted" world of the physical realm, has resulted in a modern conception of peace as an abstract ideal, static and unchanging, mostly characterized by a lack of internal or external conflict or warfare.

Not surprisingly, God's picture of peace is much richer. God's peace is not static. Although God's nature never changes, the expression of His nature is always fresh and new, always changing and revealing itself in new ways. Living in peace by God's definition is a process of constant growth that takes you on a life-long journey through the dynamic unfolding of God's design for all His creation, even when the larger picture is hidden behind the chaos of the moment.

The first reflection of God's peace in the life of a Believer is the growing sense of inward peace that comes from the work of the Holy Spirit. This kind of peace is the ultimate expression of integrity: the state of the mind, body, and spirit being in perfect alignment with each other and with God's will. This state of inner alignment grows as you journey deeper into surrender, consciously and continuously yielding to the Holy Spirit, allowing Him to return your innermost being to a place of harmony with God's original intent.

The outward peace of the Church living together in community grows out of the inner peace the Holy Spirit nurtures in each of us individually. Even through times of trouble and great hardship, the people of God have peace within themselves and with each other because they all listen to this same inner voice. Because of the indwelling power of the Holy Spirit, we can have peace even when the world around us is consumed with conflict and war.

For those who think of peace merely as the absence of conflict, there will always be fear of the next conflict or hardship, because external events can rob them of their peace. For those whose peace rests in God, no circumstance can take away their peace. Even as you come to die, you can be at perfect peace because you know where your journey ends.

We will think about the cycles of life and death this week during *Contemplatio* to focus our minds on the peace God provides us as we walk life's journey, knowing our steps are ordained by the one who loves us most. Whether God gives you today to live with all your strength, or chooses today as your last, He will give you His peace always.

Extra Mile:

Spend 20-30 minutes sometime this week practicing *Contemplatio* in a noisy place such as a shopping center or crowded restaurant. When you are tempted to be irritated by the noise, simply relax and accept it. When you are finished, think about what it means to carry God's peace with you always as you travel through the noise and distraction of the world.

WORDS & ACTIONS THAT FLOW FROM PEACE

Day 1

Jesus' promise of peace is found in *John 14:27*. The story of Jesus washing the disciples' feet is recorded in *John 13:1-17*.

You have a responsibility to develop the discipline of guarding your conscious mind through the process of surrendering to the Holy Spirit, but this discipline by itself will not root out the unrighteous thoughts and motives which your sinful nature will constantly cause to be at work in your subconscious mind. Do not worry: the Spirit will purify your subconscious mind over time, as you spend daily time in fellowship with God and allow Him to replace your old, sinful nature with a new nature that flows from Him. Concentrate on taking your conscious thoughts captive to the will of Christ, knowing that He is even now purifying your whole being, including your subconscious motives and desires, and making you anew in His image.

As the time approached that He would go to the cross, Jesus began to prepare the disciples for a time when He would no longer be with them. Jesus told them that, although He would not be there to walk with them physically, the Holy Spirit would remain with them, reminding them of His words and revealing God's truth. He promised that the Spirit would give them *His* peace, the same peace that Jesus knew as He walked as one in fellowship with the Father, a kind of peace that the world could never offer or even understand.

The world's concept of peace often involves one group conquering or subjugating another, preventing conflict by coercion or threat of force. Jesus' idea of peace was precisely the opposite. Just before He promised that all those who follow Him would inherit His peace, He painted a perfect picture of what God's peace looks like: He took a towel and wash basin and, taking on the role of a servant, washed the feet of His disciples. God's peace flows from a place of strength—not just the strength to conquer, but the strength to love and serve each other.

When you offer water to someone who is thirsty, or words of comfort to one who is hurting, whenever your actions express God's love, you are creating the fabric of peace—of *shalom*—in your community. The tapestry of *shalom* is woven from the threads of words and deeds that flow naturally out of God's children each moment as they walk with Him. The *shalom* that God intended for His Church to create here on Earth arises from His people serving each other, caring for those who are in need, and enjoying the blessings of God's creation.

Part of the covenant you enter when you join the community of Believers is the responsibility to be part of this fabric of peace that creates the sacred space where God's presence can be seen even in the midst of a sinful and imperfect world. God has given clear precepts for how we are to treat each other and deal with each other to create the safe and healing space that surrounds any gathering of those who walk by the Spirit. As you read the scriptures this week and reflect on these precepts, ask the Holy Spirit to make you an instrument of His peace.

Speaking & Acting from a Place of Peace

Most people go through their day with a stream of unguarded thoughts, images, and emotions filling their head. If you let unguarded thoughts run unchecked through your mind, however, your actions will never reflect God's peace. You must develop the discipline of guarding your mind, striving to capture any improper thought before it manifests itself in your words or deeds. For many reasons, *Contemplatio* turns out to be a powerful tool in developing this discipline.

As you continue your daily practice of *Lectio Divina* over time, you will find that *Contemplatio* begins to develop in your spirit a deep capacity for silence and listening that changes the way your mind operates. The ability to be silent and listen begins to slowly extend beyond just the times of *Contemplatio*, as you learn to carry it with you into the ordinary spaces of life.

The full fruit of this practice comes as you learn to allow listening and maintaining awareness of God's presence to become your baseline state. As you make this transition, thoughts and words begin to arise only when needed, and then to recede when their work is done, returning you to the quiet sense of the Spirit's presence within you.

This baseline of peace creates a yardstick that measures your thoughts against the quality of God's presence. Heard against the background of the inner peace given by the Spirit, any movement of your mind contrary to God's indwelling purpose reverberates like the sound of a car crash shattering the stillness of a quiet morning. When your mind is drawn forward by the Spirit's leading, on the other hand, your thoughts and actions will seem to harmonize with the silence out of which they arise, and leave behind blessings as they return to rest.

A foundation of inner silence leaves no place for sinful thoughts to hide, so it becomes much easier to discern when your actions are no longer reflecting God's will. Taking negative thoughts captive and rejecting them before they erupt into sinful acts will allow you to live in such a way that others sense the richness and power of the peace that Jesus gives you through the Spirit. As you learn to stand in stillness before God and listen to His voice even amidst the chaos of everyday events, your words and actions will flow ever more fully from the place of peace within, where your spirit and God's Spirit dwell together in fellowship.

When You Don't Have Peace

On your journey through this world you are guaranteed to face situations, both internal and external, that pull you out of peace. Your own pride and selfishness often create desires that brew up strong negative emotions when they are not met. Situations where someone hurts you, your family, or your friends can also trigger strong emotions that tempt you to lash out in response. If you do not deal with these emotions immediately, as they occur, they will produce damaging thoughts and images that bounce around inside your mind and become almost impossible to control.

Learn to watch yourself and notice when you begin to get pulled out of your place of peace. Many times your body will alert you when something starts to go wrong. The moment you notice that your voice is becoming harsh, that you are suddenly developing tension somewhere in your body, or that your body has developed an odd sensation of things not being right, you should stop and figure out why.

Watch closely for any thoughts or emotions that tend to pull you away from God's peace. Try to catch emotions such as anger, pridefulness, or impatience early, before they become lodged in your mind. As soon as you realize a negative emotion is welling up inside of you, deal with it using Welcoming Prayer, giving it over to the Spirit before it is allowed to take root and affect your words and actions.

When you realize you don't have peace, the best strategy is to stop speaking and acting until you address the problem. You can't do anything helpful when you don't have peace; you will just throw your emotional junk into the situation and make things worse. If possible, excuse yourself and go be alone with God, seeking His help in understanding your own feelings and bringing your thoughts and emotions back in line with His will.

When the situation doesn't allow you to go through Welcoming Prayer immediately, try using a breath prayer to help you calm down until you have a chance to deal with it fully later. Consider going outside to your *Vigil* spot when you need to work out emotions. Simply sitting on the earth and returning your awareness to God's presence in Creation can help put things into perspective.

You are ready to resume speaking and acting once you have separated yourself from negative emotions to the point of being able to see the situation clearly, and can address it from a place of peace and love for all those involved. This does not mean that you cannot be angry about something that is clearly wrong, but that you shouldn't let your anger rule you.

Learn to not be overly sensitive, always looking for reasons to be offended by others. When someone throws something hurtful at you, try to see past the surface to perceive the spiritual need that created the hurtful words or actions. In many cases, when another person lashes out at you it has little to do with you and more to do with their own spiritual pain or sinful desires; you are just a convenient target for their negative emotions.

Lord, make me an instrument of Your peace. Where there is hatred, let me sow love; where there is injury, pardon; where there is doubt, faith; where there is despair, hope; where there is darkness, light; where there is sadness, joy.

O, Divine Master, grant that I may not so much seek to be consoled as to console; to be understood as to understand; to be loved as to love; For it is in giving that we receive; it is in pardoning that we are pardoned; it is in dying that we are born again to eternal life.

- A Prayer of St. Francis of Assisi

Ask the Spirit to give you wisdom to understand the spiritual need that is driving any attack you face. You will find it much easier to forgive those who attack you when you understand the spiritual wounds causing the pain and grief driving them, and ask the Spirit to allow you to see the situation through God's eyes.

No matter how hard it is to let go, don't hold onto bitterness or frustration over being wronged; it will end up hurting you more than the person you are holding the grudge against, and will create even more pain in the long run. Any bitterness you hold will slowly creep into everything you do, causing you to hurt those you love for reasons you don't even understand.

One of the hardest, but most important, places to practice the principle of peace is with your own family. The emotional closeness of familial relationships can trigger responses to members of your own family that are stronger than with most anyone else. When dealing with family, you must make the time and space to find peace when peace is hard.

Holding Responsibility for Your Words & Actions

When you sin, the impact on your community is like a stone dropped onto the still surface of a pond that sends out ripples of agitation in all directions. These ripples affect all those around you and often provoke further harmful words or actions in response, each of which sends out their own ripples of disturbance across the landscape. If allowed to continue, this sequence of provocations and responses can become a chain reaction that ultimately undermines the *shalom* of the entire community.

You must take responsibility for the results of your own words and actions. If you cause somebody else to be pulled out of peace, or do something wrong that affects another person, your responsibility is to go to that person and try to make it right. If at first they won't accept your attempts at reconciliation, try praying about the situation as you continue to attempt finding a way to resolve it. If all your attempts to make things right are rejected, and your prayers bring you peace that you have done all you can do, then you have fulfilled your responsibility and should give the situation over to the Holy Spirit instead of dwelling on it.

God has also given each of us a place of responsibility in caring for His creation. He gave us the Earth and everything in it to provide for our physical needs. God blessed the natural world with beauty and abundance that remind us of His great love for us. To the extent that you damage or degrade the Earth, you dishonor God's gift and steal from your own grandchildren by robbing the land of the fertility and abundance God intended to sustain them. In your decisions, you should always consider the long-term impact your actions will have on the land God has given your community to steward, and on the Earth as a whole.

In addition to your own actions, you are ultimately responsible for all those things done by others on your behalf as well. What does it say when you buy clothes from a designer you know abuses its workers, or support a company that destroys the Earth for profit? These are not comfortable questions for most people in today's consumer culture, but those who follow Christ must not shy away from dealing with what they pay others to do on their behalf.

This problem is so large that it seems almost impossible to address, since these practices are wide-spread in the modern world. You should make the best choices you can, but these issues ultimately must be addressed corporately by the Church since the scale of the problem is so large. If those who follow Jesus would stand together and only spend money with those businesses that acted in accordance with God's law, it would create a market for goods and services produced in a just manner.

When someone else sends waves of agitation in your direction, try to let them pass through you instead of responding with your own agitation. Ripples of agitation coming in your direction usually have little to do with you; often you are just a convenient target. Try to learn to stop the chain reaction instead of spreading it.

Believers must reject the idea that needless consumption is acceptable. For most people raised in a consumer culture, consumption is reflexive. They have consumed so much for so long without giving it any thought that they no longer realize exactly how much they have or how much they use up every day. Not only does this pattern destroy the gifts of nature that God created for us, it takes our focus off of God and places it on all the *stuff*. There is wisdom in learning that more happiness can be found in having less and making do without.

Tending the Altar Fire

In the sixth chapter of *Leviticus*, God gives Moses instructions for how the priests were to tend the altar fires and how they were to offer the sacrifices unto the Lord. Under the Old Testament law, the altar represented the people's way to God. When Jesus brought forth a new covenant through the shedding of His blood, the offering of burnt sacrifices on a physical altar was abolished and God's covenant was written anew on our hearts. Under the New Covenant, your place of communion and sacrifice is now within your own heart and, just as in the time of Moses, you must always be sure to keep the altar fire of your heart burning brightly.

Your first responsibilities are tending your relationship with God and taking care of your own self in mind, body, and spirit. As hard as it can seem at times, you must place the needs of others, even your own family, behind tending your own relationship with God and doing what is necessary to keep yourself strong.

When the Bible says that you are to prefer others over yourself, it means you should place a lower priority on your own *wants* and *desires* than those of others, not that you should neglect those things you *need* in order to tend your own fire. If you wish to be great in the Kingdom of Heaven, you should become a servant, but a servant cannot be of service to others for very long without maintaining the strength to serve. You can't help others when your own fire has grown cold.

Serving God and serving those in your community are actually inseparable parts of keeping your own altar fire strong. Since God created you to allow His love to flow out toward others, you will find that trying to tend your own fire for purely selfish reasons only brings more pain and grief. In His wisdom, God made the act of helping others a core part of keeping your own fire strong.

> If you have the tendency to define yourself partly by how much you help others, be watchful that you don't fall into the martyr complex: burning yourself out to help others and then playing the role of the martyr to gain the sympathy or admiration of others, or to make you feel better about yourself. You must take care to find a wise balance between caring for others and taking time to tend your own fire.

> God gives you those in your community of faith to help and support you in the times when your fire becomes dim. During the times when you are weak, accept the help of those you trust in your community. Don't allow prideful thoughts to keep you from accepting help when you are in need.

Week 8

The Third & Fourth Generations

Human nature is to focus only on the immediate, but this limited perspective can lead to thinking only of yourself and your desires for the present. Making it worse, the *now*-oriented messages of modern culture seem to reinforce the habit of thinking exclusively about the short-term. To counter this tendency, you must practice the spiritual discipline of meditating and praying about important decisions and carefully considering their long-term consequences.

God warns us that our sins today will affect our children and grandchildren, down to the third and fourth generations. The quality of the choices you make today can radically alter the path you end up following and the legacy you leave behind when you die, so when you make important decisions you should always ask whether they will bring peace for you and your community both now and into the future.

There are three areas you should prayerfully consider when determining how your actions will affect you and those you love today and for four generations hence:

First, and most importantly, think of what impact your decision will have on the relationship you, as well as those you influence, will have with God, both now and into the future.

Second, consider the impact on the relationships of everyone in your community and even beyond, and the possibility for healthy relationships in those who come behind you.

Third, think of the health and wellbeing of the land that supports you and your community, the Earth that God has given to provide your needs both now and into the future. Anything that damages or destroys the land will leave a poor inheritance for your great-grandchildren.

> *Compline*

> **Reading:** *John 14:27*

> **Reflection:** In what ways have your actions today come either from a place of peace or from negative emotions?

> **Prayer:** Ask God for the sensitivity to realize when you are acting or speaking out of a negative desire or emotion instead of from peace.

READING #1 - HEBREWS 12:14-15

The opening prayer for this week is drawn from the prayer of St. Francis on page 109.

Day 2

Preparation:

- Calm your mind and take a few deep breaths
- Start with a Prayer of Thanksgiving
- Continue with the prayer, *"Lord Jesus Christ, make me an instrument of your peace. Let me sow light where there is darkness and joy in the midst of sorrows."*

Lectio:

Make every effort to live in peace with all men and to be holy;
without holiness no one will see the Lord.
See to it that no one misses the grace of God
and that no bitter root grows up to cause trouble and defile many.

- Hebrews 12:14-15 (NIV)

Meditatio:

The bitter roots talked about in this passage often grow in your life because of an unwillingness to forgive, or because you have not received something you feel you deserve. Is there any root of bitterness growing in your heart because you are holding onto an old hurt or disappointment?

Oratio:

Release old hurts or unfulfilled desires to the Holy Spirit and ask for help in forgiving and letting go.

Remember to practice the Welcoming Prayer if you run into situations this week where negative emotions are provoked. If you don't have time to do the Welcoming Prayer immediately, use a Breath Prayer to calm down in the moment, and then return to the Welcoming Prayer later when you have time.

Contemplatio:

No matter the season, you can always see the patterns and cycles of life and death unfolding in the world around you. In Spring, new life is evident everywhere, as the trees put out new leaves and the birds build nests and begin to lay eggs. The Summer brings a time of growth, as the young plants reach upward and the young birds and animals begin to grow and learn to survive. Fall is a time of maturing and storing up for the cold weather to come. And even in the depth of winter, as the old passes away, the promise of new life to come is always present.

Sit in wide-angle vision today and simply observe the cycle of life and death at play around you. Think for a moment about how your journey through life fits into this cycle. God has appointed a time for you to be born, a time for you to live, and a time for you to die. He walks with you each step of the way, giving you His grace and peace to sustain you. As you let go of your thoughts today and turn your focus to God's presence, relax into the embrace of the One who never will leave you or forsake you, but will be with you always.

Benediction:

- Return slowly and peacefully from *Contemplatio*
- Take time to be thankful again
- Acknowledge that you have completed your time for today and ask God to go with you as you leave this time.

Compline

Reading: *James 3:13-18*

Reflection: Is your wish to act with wisdom and gentleness toward those around you? Are you sometimes tempted to push past others to get what you want?

Prayer: Be thankful for God's gentleness and grace toward you, and ask for wisdom to treat others with grace as well.

READING #2 - 2 TIMOTHY 2:22-26

Preparation:

- Calm your mind and take a few deep breaths
- Start with a Prayer of Thanksgiving
- Continue with the prayer, "*Lord Jesus Christ, make me an instrument of your peace. Let me sow light where there is darkness and joy in the midst of sorrows.*"

Lectio:

Day 3

Shun youthful passions and pursue righteousness, faith, love, and peace,
along with those who call on the Lord from a pure heart.
Have nothing to do with stupid and senseless controversies;
you know that they breed quarrels.
And the Lord's servant must not be quarrelsome but kindly to everyone,
an apt teacher, patient, correcting opponents with gentleness.
God may perhaps grant that they will repent and come to know the truth,
and that they may escape from the snare of the devil,
having been held captive by him to do his will.

- 2 Timothy 2:22-26 (NRSV)

Meditatio:

If you are not careful, you can easily get drawn into the middle of senseless arguments that do nothing but generate bad feelings between people. What kind of conversations do you find yourself caught up in that do nothing but create arguments between you and your friends or family? How could you manage these situations in a way that creates peace instead of strife?

Oratio:

> Talk to God about situations where you habitually find yourself in arguments or treating others with a lack of kindness. Ask that He will show you the root of the problem and replace the thoughts and motives that create the situation with His peace.

Contemplatio:

The topsoil beneath you forms a thin layer, usually no more than a few inches thick, that wraps the continents in a blanket of life. In many temperate landscapes, there is more life by weight living in and under the soil than on top of it. Even a teaspoon of healthy soil contains billions of microorganisms: bacteria, fungi, protozoa, and hundreds of other tiny life forms we are just beginning to understand. These organisms act as the major regenerative organ of our planet, breaking down the organic material from plants and animals that have died, making the nutrients available for new life.

Lay on the ground today with your eyes closed, letting your body relax into the soil beneath you. Reach out with your spiritual as well as your physical senses to feel the process of God at work, making something new out of the old and decaying. Surrender your spirit to God's work, allowing Him to regenerate the old, dead self and bring new life.

Benediction:

- Return slowly and peacefully from *Contemplatio*
- Take time to be thankful again
- Acknowledge that you have completed your time for today and ask God to go with you as you leave this time.

Compline

Reading: *Joshua 22:1-34*

Reflection: Do your thoughts ever look forward to the spiritual needs of those who will come after you?

Prayer: Pray for the generations that will follow you: your children and grandchildren. Commit to prepare the way for them by living a life of peace and integrity, following God's principles.

READING #3 - LUKE 12:51-53

Preparation:

- Calm your mind and take a few deep breaths
- Start with a Prayer of Thanksgiving
- Continue with the prayer, "*Lord Jesus Christ, make me an instrument of your peace. Let me sow light where there is darkness and joy in the midst of sorrows.*"

Lectio:

Day 4

The words of Jesus in this passage can be somewhat confusing at first. The Bible calls Jesus the *Prince of Peace*, but here He says that He did not come to bring peace to the Earth. The key to understanding what Jesus is saying is to realize that the division He is speaking about is between those who follow Him and those who don't. Jesus says that there will be cases where families will be divided because some choose to follow Him while others reject Him. We are to live in peace with other Believers, and do our best to live in peace with everyone else as well, although sometimes that may not be possible.

"Do you think that I have come to bring peace to the earth?
No, I tell you, but rather division!
From now on five in one household will be divided,
three against two and two against three; they will be divided:
father against son
and son against father,
mother against daughter
and daughter against mother,
mother-in-law against her daughter-in-law
and daughter-in-law against mother-in-law."

- Luke 12:51-53 (NRSV)

Meditatio:

Your responsibility is to live in harmony with all those who follow Christ, and to do your best to live in peace with all those who don't, even those who hate you or persecute you for your beliefs. You can't control other people's actions, but you can control your response.

Is there anyone with whom you have a division because of your faith? How do you handle living in peace with them? Are you ever tempted to compromise your faith just to keep difficulties from coming up? How should you handle keeping integrity in your faith while living with those who attack your beliefs?

Oratio:

Pray for anyone who you feel alienated from because of a difference in beliefs. Ask for wisdom in dealing with circumstances where others question or attack you because of your faith, so that your responses will flow from a place of peace and love instead of defensiveness or hurt.

Contemplatio:

Regardless of the time of year, the plants growing around you always paint a picture of God at work in the cycles of life and death. Even during the depth of winter, the frozen ground and barren branches of the trees hold the promise of new life just around the corner. As spring arrives, seeds germinate and new plants push up through the soil toward the sunlight. All through the summer, the new plants grow and build up strength to either survive through the winter or put out seeds so new life can come again next year. By fall, the plants are finishing the cycle of growth and begin to drop their leaves onto the soil below, where the soil life will make them available for fresh growth the next spring.

As you move into silence today, take with you the picture of the cycle of your own life, bringing forth fruit in season and preparing the way for future generations to come. Let go of your thoughts and turn your attention to the One who gives you peace in life and in death.

Benediction:

- Return slowly and peacefully from *Contemplatio*
- Take time to be thankful again
- Acknowledge that you have completed your time for today and ask God to go with you as you leave this time.

Compline

Reading: *Romans 12:18*

Reflection: Is there a person you have trouble living in peace with? You can't control their actions, but you can work to more clearly see the motivations and spiritual wounds that drive them, and to control the way you respond. In what specific ways could you attempt to better live in peace with them?

Prayer: Pray individually for someone you have a hard time getting along with.

READING #4 - MATTHEW 5:23-24

Day 5

Preparation:

- Calm your mind and take a few deep breaths
- Start with a Prayer of Thanksgiving
- Continue with the prayer, *"Lord Jesus Christ, make me an instrument of your peace. Let me sow light where there is darkness and joy in the midst of sorrows."*

Lectio:

"Therefore, if you are offering your gift at the altar
and there remember that your brother has something against you,
leave your gift there in front of the altar.
First go and be reconciled to your brother; then come and offer your gift."

- *Matthew 5:23-24 (NIV)*

Meditatio:

Have you done something to offend another person, but have not yet gone and made it right? What do you need to do in order to correct the situation?

Remember that you are only responsible for your own words and actions. If you try to make something right with a person and they refuse to talk it out and forgive you, then you have done what you are responsible for doing.

Oratio:

(blank lined writing space)

> If you have wronged someone but not yet made it right, commit to God that you will go to them and try to set it right. If someone has something against you but refuses to be reconciled to you, release the situation to the Holy Spirit and ask that He bring healing to both of you.

Contemplatio:

Look at the individual birds and animals in the landscape around you. Do they appear to be young or old? Do any appear especially vigorous and alive, or weak and perhaps closer to death? God has made us, in our sinful state, subject to the same pattern of birth, life, and death that we see in the birds and animals around us. The young are often vigorous, looking forward to a full life ahead, while age brings the knowledge that death draws nearer and that preparations for the next generation must be completed. If you watch the older birds for a while, you will realize they posses much wisdom of what it takes to survive, and they pass their wisdom to the younger birds who are paying attention.

Close your eyes for a moment and picture those people in your life who have shared wisdom with you. Then let go of these images and turn your attention and intention toward the presence of the Holy Spirit who uses these people to help you see the path He intends you to walk in life.

Benediction:

- Return slowly and peacefully from *Contemplatio*
- Take time to be thankful again
- Acknowledge that you have completed your time for today and ask God to go with you as you leave this time.

Compline

Reading: *Colossians 3:12-17*

Reflection: Is there anyone you need to forgive but keep holding onto how they wronged you? What is keeping you from forgiving them?

Prayer: Release anything you are holding against another person to God and ask Him to help you forgive and make peace.

READING #5 - JOB 5:6-11, 20-23, 26

Preparation:

- Calm your mind and take a few deep breaths
- Start with a Prayer of Thanksgiving
- Continue with the prayer, *"Lord Jesus Christ, make me an instrument of your peace. Let me sow light where there is darkness and joy in the midst of sorrows."*

Lectio:

Day 6

In this passage, Eliphaz, one of the three friends that came to comfort Job, speaks to Job of the wonders of God's work and of God's grace and mercy even in times of hardship. He points out that those who follow God will even have peace with the Earth itself.

> For hardship does not spring from the soil,
> nor does trouble sprout from the ground.
> Yet man is born to trouble
> as surely as sparks fly upward.
> But if it were I, I would appeal to God;
> I would lay my cause before him.
> He performs wonders that cannot be fathomed,
> miracles that cannot be counted.
> He bestows rain on the earth;
> he sends water upon the countryside.
> The lowly he sets on high,
> and those who mourn are lifted to safety....
> In famine he will ransom you from death,
> and in battle from the stroke of the sword.
> You will be protected from the lash of the tongue,
> and need not fear when destruction comes.
> You will laugh at destruction and famine,
> and need not fear the beasts of the earth.
> For you will have a covenant with the stones of the field,
> and the wild animals will be at peace with you....
> You will come to the grave in full vigor,
> like sheaves gathered in season.
>
> *- Job 5:6-11, 20-23, 26 (NIV)*

Meditatio:

God's design for us is to live in peace with each other, with Him, and with the Earth He made for us to inhabit. Is your goal to live fully each moment so that, when your time comes to die, you will come to your grave full of vigor, ready in your mind, body, and spirit to be gathered home to be with God?

Oratio:

Spend time today being thankful for the fullness of life, for the joy found in your relationships, and even for the pain and sorrow that causes you to deepen in faith as you journey along the path laid before you.

The fruit of silence is prayer;
the fruit of prayer is faith;
the fruit of faith is love;
the fruit of love is service;
the fruit of service is peace.

\- Mother Teresa

Contemplatio:

Sit today with your eyes closed and look inward to the cycles of birth, life, and death at work inside of you. Your physical body is the most obvious, with its one-way journey from birth through to physical death. Your spiritual journey began with you separated from God by your sinful nature. If you have entered into a covenant relationship with God, then He has caused you to be reborn spiritually into a new creation that will never perish.

The cycle of spiritual death and rebirth is not quite so simple, though. The Bible paints the picture of a daily cycle of the dying of the old self and the constant rebirth of your spirit into a new life that becomes more like Christ each day. Each day you must let go of the old self so God can make in you a new spiritual creation. As you move into the stillness today, consciously let go of the old self with the intention of letting God create a new heart and mind inside of you. Sit with Him in silence and allow the Holy Spirit to renew your mind and your spirit.

Benediction:

- Return slowly and peacefully from *Contemplatio*
- Take time to be thankful again
- Acknowledge that you have completed your time for today and ask God to go with you as you leave this time.

Compline

Reading: *Leviticus 6:8-13*

Reflection: How have you been tending the altar fire of your own heart? Are you able to offer your life as a daily sacrifice with joy, or is their some kind of grief or personal desire holding you back?

Prayer: Visualize offering yourself as a living sacrifice to God through your words and actions.

REFLECTION

Day 7

Revisit Your Favorite Passage

Reflections on the Week

Compline

Reading: *Isaiah 55:6-13*

Reflection: Simply reflect on the promises that God has given you in this passage.

Prayer: Be thankful for the blessings God has poured out on you this week.

WEEK 9 - HOLINESS

Consecrate yourselves therefore, and be holy;
for I am the LORD your God.
Keep my statutes, and observe them;
I am the LORD; I sanctify you.

-Leviticus 20:7-8 (NRSV)

FOR THOSE WHO ASSOCIATE THE WORD *Holy* only with God or a chosen few who have a special calling, the command to be holy just as God is holy can seem impossible. If God left us to our own devices, this requirement would indeed be impossible. To be holy means to be set apart from the world, to exist in the realm of the sacred, being pure and free from sin. The life of holiness is a life that is whole and without fault. Without the indwelling work of the Holy Spirit, the corrupting influence of our old nature would thwart our every attempt to think, act, or speak in a way that is sacred and holy.

During this life, you will never fully reach God's standard of holiness; doing so would require you to fully do away with your old nature and every vestige of your old ways of thinking. The transformation of your mind and soul into a new creation is the ongoing work of the Holy Spirit, but it is God's intention that you not be a passive recipient of this regenerative process. Since God's purpose is to transform your mind and spirit, He calls you to set your thoughts and will toward following His purposes. God calls you to strive toward holiness, and in response to your attempts to follow Him, He gives you the strength required to take the next step.

This process will continue for as long as you remain in this world, only being made complete when you see God face to face. As a Believer, it is enough that you are *being made* holy, that, through the Spirit's work, each part of your journey brings you closer to the mind of Christ.

The practical essence of holiness is the unfolding of sacred thoughts and deeds expressed out of God's love, acted out in the stream of everyday events. You don't obtain holiness by living in a cave to avoid sin; holiness is acting and speaking purely and without sin while surrounded by those whose sinful nature causes them to attack you because of how you live.

Holiness is also not a calling to sit in the corner and be boring; it is never fully expressed simply sitting in a room, even when praying or reading scripture. Its full expression comes in the moments of engagement with the world that cause you to stretch and grow as a person on the journey to know God.

We will use the patterns of growth and change this week as our focus for *Contemplatio* as a way to think about how God uses the experiences of life to cause us to grow and be formed into the image of Christ. The extraordinary life to which God called you is a journey of continual growth, as the Spirit purifies your heart and makes you a person called apart from the world and consecrated to God's purpose.

Extra Mile:

Wherever you have lunch each day this week, gather your friends, family, or coworkers who are Believers to share together in observing mid-day prayers before you eat. Pray together, giving thanks for the meal, and then sit together in silence for a minute or two and focus on God's presence as a community.

GROWING IN HOLINESS

THINK FOR A MOMENT BACK TO THE OLD ORDER AMISH communities we discussed the week before last. They choose to forgo modern technologies, travel by horse and buggy, dress plainly, and live a mostly agrarian lifestyle, often working the fields using animals and their own manual labor, all because they believe this is the best way to maintain the closeness of their community and avoid distractions that make it harder to hear God's voice. In this regard, the Amish provide a clear example of a community whose lifestyle holds integrity with its professed beliefs. They graciously accept the strange looks they often receive from outsiders because they place a much higher priority on God's approval than the approval of others.

You do not have to adopt the Amish lifestyle to understand their example of setting yourself apart from the world, and instead pursuing things of more lasting value. Most likely, your life travels at the much faster pace of the modern world, but you are still called to set yourself apart and develop patterns of thought that dwell on the sacred. It can be tricky trying to walk the path of holiness among the tangled web of distractions pushed on you by today's culture. Followers of Christ are commanded to be in fellowship with other Believers precisely so they can support each other when this path becomes difficult.

The practice of personal holiness is foundational for creating *shalom* between any group of people, whether a family or an entire community. Lasting peace in interpersonal relationships can never take root if those involved focus first on personal desires, or consistently fail to make wise decisions. God's command that we be holy is not just for us as individuals; we are to pursue holiness together as a community, allowing God to create among us a sacred space that communicates His presence to the world beyond.

Set Apart From the World

The pursuit of holiness, of being set apart from the world and consecrated to God's purpose, does not consist of a bunch of mystic rituals practiced in remote mountain temples. The practices that create personal holiness are much more immediate and practical, involving what you choose to do, where you choose to spend your time, and what you allow to occupy your mind.

You should first practice developing holiness in your thoughts, since this is the source from which your actions spring. God made you to think and relate to stories, and storytelling is one of the deepest sources of human connection. Stories communicate desires and motives in an almost subconscious way, and you should be careful to guard your mind to control which stories you allow to slip in unexamined.

It is no surprise that television and movies, being storytelling mediums, are so powerful at programming patterns of thoughts into a culture. The problem is that these mediums are best suited to telling stories about conflict and violence. A movie that showed a community dealing with each other from a place of peace would never sell as many tickets as the latest blockbuster in which people fight, stab each other in the back, and use violence to solve their problems. Don't underestimate the influence that watching this kind of story over and over has on your mind and way of perceiving the world.

Video games and the Internet also act as storytelling mediums, but in very different ways. Today's games actually put you in the middle of the story, often a story in which violence or deceit is the only way to win. The pull of these technologies can be very strong, and they reinforce the difficulty of pulling yourself away from their influence by feeding you yet another story: that anyone who warns you to be careful is simply old-fashioned or out of touch. It takes courage to examine these technologies in the light of scripture and decide how to handle them properly.

Day 1

Even though we are using the Amish as an example of a community of people who are willing to give up much in their pursuit of God, this does not mean they, or any other community of Believers, are perfect. As an example, the Amish have often been questioned over their practice of *shunning*, which many times neglects aspects of God's mercy and forgiveness in its effort to maintain church discipline.

As a follower of Jesus, you do not pursue holiness in an attempt to make yourself acceptable to God. The blood of Jesus already covers all your sins if you have received His gift of forgiveness and salvation. Those who have a covenant relationship with God are already counted as *righteous* due to Jesus' sacrifice on the cross. The desire to be *holy*, set apart from the world and consecrated to God's purpose, comes from love of the One who has already saved you. It is through the work of the Holy Spirit that your journey through this life becomes a journey of *being made holy*.

The word *world* is used here in the sense of the Greek word *kosmos*, which is used numerous time in the New Testament to refer to the moral and spiritual order created by humanity's sinful nature. To be *set apart from the world* therefore means to reject the viewpoint and priorities created by mankind's sinful nature.

Stories have a power that runs so deep that they drive much more than just your surface thoughts and reactions; they subconsciously create the narratives you use to determine the shape and goals of your entire life's journey. The stories you tell yourself about who you are and what defines success will help determine the choices you make when faced with major decisions.

If you look forward in your life and imagine a story dominated by nice houses, fancy cars, and all the other trappings of worldly success, these things will begin to dominate your thinking. Without realizing it, you will start leaning toward decisions you feel will help make this story come true. Your rational mind may know what you should do to follow God's commands, and you may make a conscious effort or do so, but you will find that the story of the world's priorities you are holding in your heart constantly sabotages your efforts to do what is right.

On the other hand, if the story you envision for yourself is one of a journey to follow Jesus, and of expressing His love to those around you, then the desires of your heart will grow from His purpose. This story turns your priorities on their head, as you redefine success in terms of how much you can bless and help others, of how much you can give instead of how much you can receive, and of how well you reflect God's love to the world. The priorities held by the world, such as a good education or a nice job, become tools in your journey instead of ends unto themselves.

The serene, silent beauty of a holy life is the most powerful influence in the world, next to the might of the Spirit of God.

- Blaise Pascal

Just trying to push the world's stories out of your head won't work unless you replace them with something more powerful and more fulfilling. *Philippians 4:8* gives the prescription for healing your patterns of thought by saying you should focus your mind only on what is true, just, honorable, and pure. As you fill your mind with stories that resonate with eternal purpose, the trivial distractions of modern culture—gadgets, status symbols, celebrities, movies and television, fashion trends, the latest gossip—will all come to seem increasingly shallow.

Focusing on God's priorities in this way will also transform how you relate to money. When you shift your purpose away from the world's definition of success, you will soon learn to be content with living simply and within your means. Many people today seem to be addicted to collecting stuff they don't need. Many gather possessions out of habits instilled in them by the consumer culture in which they grew up. Some are seeking the symbols of social status, while others try frantically to build up wealth out of fear for the future. Seeing money through God's perspective takes away the fear and allows you to handle your finances wisely. In God's economy, you learn to avoid debt, save wisely, and invest your resources in what really matters.

God will provide what you need for the journey He designed for you. If God chooses to bless you with material wealth, be thankful and seek to use it wisely. Money should be a tool you use to meet your own basic needs; when you realize God has given you in abundance, ask how you can use it to bless others. If you ever realize that your possessions are keeping you from God's path, ask yourself if it is time to start giving them away to those who are in need.

Be mindful also of who you choose to spend the most time with. Those who you hang out with, eat meals with, and share your thoughts and dreams with, will help shape the subconscious stories that determine your priorities. Your closest friends should be members of your community of faith, and should all be followers of Christ who also seek after holiness. This does not mean you are to avoid having friends who are not Christians; God put you into the world to be an example of His love, and you should reach out to those who are searching for the truth. Just make sure your core group of friends all seek to travel the same road you wish to follow.

Ultimately, if you and your community of faith are to be set apart in holiness, your hearts and minds must be set on following a story much different from the stories of the culture that surrounds you, a story that reflects God's holiness and love.

Most people in Western cultures like to think that their decisions are based on logic and reason, but in many cases this is simply not true. A great deal of the time, people actually make their decisions based upon emotions, feelings, and desires that flow out of the narratives they use to define who they are. Few people, for example, actually need an expensive sports car or luxury sedan to get them where they need to go, but they end up buying them anyway, even when they have to go into debt to do so. They make decisions like this from emotions and desires arising from their own internal story about themselves, and then rationalize their decisions so they can tell themselves that they were arrived at logically and rationally.

Set Apart in Purity

The best way to deal with the temptation to sin is to intercept the thoughts that lead you into the sin while they are still forming. This is the practice that Paul refers to in *2 Corinthians 10:5* when he says you should *take every thought captive* and bring it into obedience to Christ's will.

As you have learned from practicing *Contemplatio*, wrestling with impure thoughts usually just gives them more space and energy, as you go through cycles of self-blame and frustration that seem to keep pulling the thoughts back into your head. Whenever you try to wrestle with an impure thought, you are most likely going to end up pulling yourself down into the mud with it. Instead of trying to fight with the thought directly, try using the two-step process of *release and replace.*

As we discussed last week, the first step when you notice an impure thought arising is to release the thought just as you would release any thought during *Contemplatio*. Don't give the thought any more time or space in your mind by reflecting on it or getting angry at yourself over it. Just gently let go of the thought, using your sacred word if this helps.

The second step is to replace the thought with something positive. The most powerful thought to focus on as a replacement is one that centers on God's truth about the situation. If the negative thought arises from anger, then replace it with a thought about God's forgiveness. If it involves lust, replace it with a thought about God's presence.

Releasing and replacing just once or twice won't fix the problem. As in *Contemplatio*, you must repeat the process until it creates a new pattern of thought. Each time you make the choice to return your mind to the sacred, you agree inwardly with the Spirit's call to holiness and purity.

> Addiction problems such as those that occur around pornography, sexual sins, and substance abuse can be particularly difficult to overcome alone. Seek out the help of an organized support group, Christian counselor or other professional if you find yourself trapped in an addictive pattern you can't seem to break.

Choosing What Is Wise

Whenever you are faced with a decision, ask yourself what is wise, not merely what is permissible. Often, situations present you with a number of options, several of which might be within the bounds of God's commandments. If you listen to the voice of your old, sinful nature, you will tend to make selfish choices, but when you listen to the Spirit, you will be drawn toward the choices that are wise and that best express God's love.

When you try to find out how close to the line you can come without crossing over to the wrong side, you are willingly walking yourself right into temptation. Instead, seek to walk in the middle of God's will in every situation by asking yourself "*What is wise?*"

> Saint Augustine made the observation that total abstinence is often easier than perfect moderation. Sometimes the wise choice is to totally avoid a situation that you find brings you temptation. When you try to control something you find tempting through moderation, you will end up drawing a line in the middle somewhere in an effort to define what is acceptable and what is not. Once you draw this line, however, you will be tempted to move it little by little until what was once moderation descends into a major problem. Many people who fall into substance abuse and sexual sins do so by this path.

Experiencing What Is Real

Focus your mind, body, and spirit on what is real, not on a fake version of reality that has been filtered and re-formed by the minds of men—such as is found in television, movies, video games, the Internet, and all the other mediating technologies that interpose themselves between you and the raw experience of what God is doing in the moment. Learn to use phones, computers, and other technology as tools, rather than as entertainment.

Seriously consider getting rid of your television and video games. They do nothing but waste your time, feeding you stories that hinder your relationship with God and that create friction between you and those in your community. Spend your time instead in direct contact with the people around you, and in unmediated communion with God. Stop wasting major chunks of your life staring at all those glowing screens; get up, go out, and experience what is real.

Going Apart into the Wilderness

A life of holiness requires a balance of time spent with others and time spent alone. Jesus demonstrated this principle in His own life and ministry: His times of teaching and healing were often followed by a period of going apart into the wilderness to pray and have fellowship with His Father (as in *Luke 5:16* and *Matthew 14:13*).

When you take the time to go apart from the world, you allow yourself the space required to renew and deepen your spirit so that you have something of worth to bring back to the time you spend with your family and friends. The wilderness, or any natural space, is ideal for those situations where you need a place to pray without the usual distractions of life. When you feel the call to fast and pray over a crisis or critical decision, try to go to the wilderness if you can. To pray and fast in the wilderness invites a special experience of God's presence that is difficult to find elsewhere.

Even if you cannot go to the wilderness, try to find a place apart when you need to spend time alone, even if it is just a nearby park or your own closet. A community will never function properly if its members neglect time apart to reflect and listen to the Spirit.

Healing the Land

One of the aspects of holiness rarely touched on in churches is the fact that the health of the Earth is influenced by the spiritual health of the people who live on it. In several place in the Bible (such as *Leviticus 25:18-23*, *Leviticus 26:3-6*, and *Isaiah 24:4-6*) God says that the sins of the people will cause a curse on the lands they live in, and that their obedience to His commands will cause the land to bear much fruit and bring forth a great harvest.

Genesis 1:26 shows that God intended for mankind to tend and care-take the Earth. How can we be in harmony with God when we destroy the Creation He intended us to steward? If we take His command to be stewards of His creation and twist it into an excuse to dominate, misuse, or degrade the Earth, or to feed our own selfish desires, then we betray the fact that we do not value His gift at all. God created the Earth and called it good. He sustains it moment by moment as a manifestation of His ceaseless love and provision for us. To destroy the Creation shows a manifest disregard for its Creator.

Some groups have tried to justify their exploitation of God's creation by arguing that caring for the Earth is some form of nature worship. This argument is simply a transparent attempt to excuse a lifestyle that damages the gifts God has given us. When you are a guest in someone's house, you show them respect by taking care of their home, but nobody would say this means you are worshiping their house. In the same way, taking care of the home that God has given us should flow from our love of the one who gave it. Those who mistreat the Earth will never know peace, and will never build *shalom* in their communities, because they are at war with the land God gave them to provide for their needs and the needs of their grandchildren.

2 Chronicles 7:14 tells us that one of the results of repentance is that God will heal the land and restore the blessings of the Earth to those who call on Him. The reason repentance heals the land is because it restores God's blessing upon us, and it restores our right relationship with the land itself. When we tend the land and bless it, the Earth will yield great bounty and bless us in return. Part of our testimony of God's love should be that we seek to restore the Earth in those places it has been damaged, and work to return it to the abundance God intended as a blessing for the people of all generations.

It would go a long way to caution and direct people in their use of the world, that they were better studied and known in the creation of it. For how could man find the confidence to abuse it, while they should see the Great Creator stare them in the face, in all and every part thereof?

\- William Penn

Compline

Reading: *2 Chronicles 7:12-14*

Reflection: Have your choices today been wise? How have they influenced your friends and community?

Prayer: Offer a prayer of repentance for any actions you realize were not in line with God's wisdom. Ask God to bless your community and heal the land that feeds and supports you.

READING #1 - 1 PETER 1:13-16

Preparation:

- Calm your mind and take a few deep breaths
- Start with a Prayer of Thanksgiving
- Continue with the prayer, *"Lord Jesus Christ, make me holy, even as you are holy. Allow me to abide in you, as a branch abiding in the true vine, bearing much fruit."*

Lectio:

Day 2

Therefore, prepare your minds for action; be self-controlled;
set your hope fully on the grace to be given you when Jesus Christ is revealed.
As obedient children, do not conform to the evil desires
you had when you lived in ignorance.
But just as he who called you is holy, so be holy in all you do;
for it is written: "Be holy, because I am holy."

- 1 Peter 1:13-16 (NIV)

Meditatio:

What would it look like for you to be set apart from the world so that your character was more like God's than like the world? What would have to change in your life? What would you have to give up? What desires would have to be replaced by new thoughts and motives? What new things would God have you bring into your life?

Oratio:

> Express your desire for holiness to God. Ask Him to give you the self-control and self-discipline to act as you know you should.

Contemplatio:

Most people want their world to be as predictably comfortable, static, and unchallenging as possible. As long as your environment is comfortable, predictable, and "safe," you can sleep-walk through your day without too much thought or effort. The design God used for His creation, however, is anything but static and unchallenging. God designed a world that is dynamic, always growing and changing. Much of what mankind has built—houses, cities, factory farms, air conditioning, hot water heaters—is simply an attempt to make the world into a comfortable and predictable place, to make an ever-changing world static and unchanging.

Look around you at the patterns of growth and change evident in creation. When you are outside, without the insulating layers of a building around you, the ever-changing nature of creation becomes obvious. As you sit outside today, surrounded by the dynamic change and growth of God's creation, let go of your need for comfort and control, releasing them into the silence.

Benediction:

- Return slowly and peacefully from *Contemplatio*
- Take time to be thankful again
- Acknowledge that you have completed your time for today and ask God to go with you as you leave this time.

> **Compline**
>
> **Reading:** *Colossians 3:1-17*
>
> **Reflection:** Have you shown kindness, humility, and patience this week? What desires or fears are causing you problems in living as you should?
>
> **Prayer:** Be thankful for all the ways the Holy Spirit causes you to change and grow toward holiness.

Week 9

READING #2 - 1 PETER 2:4-10

Preparation:

- Calm your mind and take a few deep breaths
- Start with a Prayer of Thanksgiving
- Continue with the prayer, *"Lord Jesus Christ, make me holy, even as you are holy. Allow me to abide in you, as a branch abiding in the true vine, bearing much fruit."*

Lectio:

Day 3

As you come to him, the living Stone—
rejected by men but chosen by God and precious to him—
you also, like living stones, are being built into a spiritual house
to be a holy priesthood, offering spiritual sacrifices acceptable to God
through Jesus Christ. For in Scripture it says:
"See, I lay a stone in Zion, a chosen and precious cornerstone,
and the one who trusts in him will never be put to shame."
Now to you who believe, this stone is precious.
But to those who do not believe,
"The stone the builders rejected has become the capstone,"
and, "A stone that causes men to stumble and a rock that makes them fall."
They stumble because they disobey the message—
which is also what they were destined for.
But you are a chosen people, a royal priesthood, a holy nation,
a people belonging to God, that you may declare the praises of him
who called you out of darkness into his wonderful light.
Once you were not a people, but now you are the people of God;
once you had not received mercy, but now you have received mercy.

- 1 Peter 2:4-10 (NIV)

Meditatio:

God says that He has called you to be a living stone in His temple, to be a priest and part of His holy nation. What does it mean that you are part of the holy priesthood ordained by God? Why is the concept of all followers of Christ being part of God's priesthood threatening to many organized churches?

Oratio:

> Say a prayer of acceptance to the calling God has placed on you to be part of His holy priesthood. Accept the responsibility to speak and act in God's name as you walk through the journey of life and touch the people around you.

Contemplatio:

The Earth has many different types of soils, some rocky and barren, others fertile and rich. Notice the places around you where the plants and trees are growing well, and the places where there is little plant life. Think for a moment about how the type of soil affects this pattern of growth. Do the plants grow where the soil is shallow or poor? What happens in the places the soil is deep and fertile?

In one of His parables, Jesus compared our hearts to the soil, some ready to support growth and produce a great harvest, others shallow, rocky, and unproductive. Close your eyes and look inward to the ground of your own heart. Visualize it as deep and fertile, ready for the Holy Spirit to grow something new and produce a great harvest. Hold this image for a moment as a symbol to God for how you are entering into His presence today. Then release this picture, along with all your other thoughts and images, turning your intention toward God alone.

Benediction:

- Return slowly and peacefully from *Contemplatio*
- Take time to be thankful again
- Acknowledge that you have completed your time for today and ask God to go with you as you leave this time.

> ### *Compline*
>
> **Reading:** *Ephesians 4:17-24*
>
> **Reflection:** Have you been consistently yielding to the Holy Spirit's renewing of your mind and spirit, allowing Him to create you anew in the likeness of God's holiness?
>
> **Prayer:** Praise God for His holiness, and for the work of Christ to restore you to a right relationship with Him.

READING #3 - 1 JOHN 2:15-17

Preparation:

- Calm your mind and take a few deep breaths
- Start with a Prayer of Thanksgiving
- Continue with the prayer, "*Lord Jesus Christ, make me holy, even as you are holy. Allow me to abide in you, as a branch abiding in the true vine, bearing much fruit.*"

Lectio:

Day 4

The *world*, as the word is used here, does not refer to God's creation, which He made and then declared to be good, but instead refers to all the things ungodly people find so important: ego, comfort, possessions, and the satisfying of the unclean desires of the flesh.

Do not love the world or the things in the world.
The love of the Father is not in those who love the world;
for all that is in the world—the desire of the flesh, the desire of the eyes,
the pride in riches—comes not from the Father but from the world.
And the world and its desire are passing away,
but those who do the will of God live forever.

- 1 John 2:15-17 (NRSV)

Meditatio:

What desires of the flesh are the most tempting for you? Possessions? Lust or sexual desires? Seeking physical comfort ahead of following where God leads? Seeking the approval and praise of the world? How should you handle these temptations?

Oratio:

> Be thankful for the blessings God has poured out on you, and with a thankful spirit, give your unhealthy desires to the Holy Spirit and ask Him to replace them with the love of the Father.

> *We ask that God would make us holy. It is a good request indeed. But are we prepared to be sanctified by any process that God in His wisdom may call on us to pass through? Are we ready to be purified by affliction, weaned from the world by bereavements, drawn nearer to God by losses, sicknesses and sorrow? Alas! these are hard questions. But if we are not, our Lord might well say to us, "You don't know what you are asking."*
>
> *- J. C. Ryle*

Contemplatio:

The presence or absence of water is another major factor in where and how life grows. Where water is abundant, life flourishes. Where there is no water, there is no life. Even in deserts that seem devoid of water, the presence of plants and insects lets you know that water is there, hidden under the ground. The lushest growth anywhere on Earth can be found in the rainforests, where the constant supply of water supports an amazing array of life.

Notice the patterns of growth in the landscape around you and think for a moment about how this is affected by the presence or lack of water. Notice how the dry ground that is sheltered from the rain differs from the ground which can receive and gather water from the rains. With this picture in your mind, close your eyes and remember that Jesus is the Living Water who brings new life and growth to the open soil of your heart. As you move into inner quietness today, open yourself to receive a fresh rain of mercy from His Spirit.

Benediction:

- Return slowly and peacefully from *Contemplatio*
- Take time to be thankful again
- Acknowledge that you have completed your time for today and ask God to go with you as you leave this time.

> ***Compline***
>
> **Reading:** *Hebrews 12:14*
>
> **Reflection:** Is it your true desire to see God? Have you set yourself apart from the world and pursued His holiness so that you may see His face?
>
> **Prayer:** Talk to God about those things you most want to hold onto, but that tend to keep your desires bound to this world.

READING #4 - 2 CORINTHIANS 6:16-7:1

Day 5

Preparation:

- Calm your mind and take a few deep breaths
- Start with a Prayer of Thanksgiving
- Continue with the prayer, *"Lord Jesus Christ, make me holy, even as you are holy. Allow me to abide in you, as a branch abiding in the true vine, bearing much fruit."*

Lectio:

What agreement is there between the temple of God and idols?
For we are the temple of the living God. As God has said:
"I will live with them and walk among them, and I will be their God,
and they will be my people."
"Therefore come out from them and be separate, says the Lord.
Touch no unclean thing, and I will receive you."
"I will be a Father to you, and you will be my sons and daughters,
says the Lord Almighty."
Since we have these promises, dear friends,
let us purify ourselves from everything that contaminates body and spirit,
perfecting holiness out of reverence for God.

- 2 Corinthians 6:16-7:1 (NIV)

Meditatio:

What things in your life have become idols that keep you from a full relationship with God and fellow Believers? Have you become addicted to your cell phone, computer, or video games, spending too much time with them instead of living life fully? Do you subconsciously worship money and possessions, along with the status they bring? Does your life look just like everyone else's, or is it set apart by how you spend your time and where you choose to focus your mind? In what ways do you need to purify yourself by getting rid of distractions or desires that contaminate your body and spirit?

Oratio:

> If it is the desire of your heart, ask God to purify you and make you holy. Let go of any idols that hold you back from a life committed to holiness.

Contemplatio:

Look closely at the trees and herbaceous plants close to you, noticing their structure and form. If you look down on a bush or small plant from above, you can see how it is designed to efficiently position all of its leaves in a pattern that allows it to catch the maximum amount of sunlight. Each plant has a slightly different pattern of growth, according to where it grows and the niche it occupies. Some grow with limbs and leaves branching off in opposite pairs, while others branch in an alternating pattern. In many cases, the leaves and branches spiral so that each is positioned so as not to be shaded by the one above it.

God's patterns of design create abundance and ever-changing diversity. Close your eyes and notice for a moment how God designed your mind, body, and spirit to work and grow together toward a holy life, moving ever closer in form to His image. As you let go of your own thoughts and move into silence today, take your whole being into God's presence and focus fully on Him.

Benediction:

- Return slowly and peacefully from *Contemplatio*
- Take time to be thankful again
- Acknowledge that you have completed your time for today and ask God to go with you as you leave this time.

Compline

Reading: *Romans 1:18-23*

Reflection: Have you set your mind upon things created by God or by man this week? Have you let gadgets and technology take up time you should have spent with God or with friends?

Prayer: Ask God to help you give up any addiction or dependence on gadgets or other technology so you can experience what is real in life, fully and without anything in the way.

READING #5 - PHILIPPIANS 4:8-9

Preparation:

- Calm your mind and take a few deep breaths
- Start with a Prayer of Thanksgiving
- Continue with the prayer, "*Lord Jesus Christ, make me holy, even as you are holy. Allow me to abide in you, as a branch abiding in the true vine, bearing much fruit.*"

Day 6

Lectio:

Finally, beloved, whatever is true, whatever is honorable, whatever is just,
whatever is pure, whatever is pleasing, whatever is commendable,
if there is any excellence and if there is anything worthy of praise,
think about these things.
Keep on doing the things that you have learned and received
and heard and seen in me, and the God of peace will be with you.

- Philippians 4:8-9 (NRSV)

Meditatio:

Ungodly thoughts can slip in from many sources, such as advertisements, music lyrics, video games, or friends. Does the way you choose to spend your time help you set your mind on things that are true, honorable, pure, and pleasing to God? What activities do you need to eliminate? How should you spend your time instead?

Oratio:

Ask God for wisdom and discernment in how you spend your time and where you choose to focus your mind.

The free man is the one whose choices have given him the power to stand on his own feet and determine his own life according to the higher light and spirit that are in him. The slave, in the spiritual order, is the man whose choices have destroyed all spontaneity in him and have delivered him over, bound hand and foot, to his own compulsions, idiosyncrasies and illusions, so that he never does what he really wants to do, but only what he has to do.

- Thomas Merton

Contemplatio:

Lay on your back and close your eyes, taking a moment to notice your own body. God designed your body to be powerful and adaptable: able to run, dance, work, play, write, play an instrument, sing, or even hold and comfort a person in pain. He gave you the physical senses to connect you to the world He created for you, and the senses of your spirit so that you could know Him. He equipped you with a mind that can ponder the universe around you, and even seek to understand the mysteries of the One who made you.

Pause for a moment to consider where you are in your personal cycle of birth, growth, maturation, and death. How have you grown and matured so far along your journey? What are your desires for the time you have ahead of you? Are you on the path of growing and maturing in holiness? Look inward today, to the place where God's Spirit dwells inside of you, and meet with Him there in perfect stillness. Turn your intention toward God today with the desire that He infuse every part of you, purifying your mind and spirit to His purpose.

Benediction:

- Return slowly and peacefully from *Contemplatio*
- Take time to be thankful again
- Acknowledge that you have completed your time for today and ask God to go with you as you leave this time.

Compline

Reading: *Isaiah 57:14-21*

Reflection: What is God teaching you this week about how to make wise decisions along the path He has laid before you?

Prayer: Ask God to help you consider what is wise, not merely what is permissible, as you make your decisions this coming week.

REFLECTION

Revisit Your Favorite Passage

Day 7

Reflections on the Week

Compline

Reading: *Psalm 24:1-10*

Reflection: Do you have clean hands and a pure heart tonight? Is there anything you are holding onto that you need to confess, repent of, and get out of your life?

Prayer: Say a prayer of confession and repentance for anything you need to set right before God.

Week 10 - Consolation

When I thought, "My foot is slipping,"
your steadfast love, O Lord, held me up.
When the cares of my heart are many,
your consolations cheer my soul.

-Psalm 94:18-19 (NRSV)

If you were asked to imagine someone who is grieving, you would probably picture a person who has just lost someone they love, or perhaps whose family is undergoing a painful divorce. Although the majority of churches reach out to people undergoing these types of traumas, this kind of extreme and obvious grief is only one part in the spectrum of pain and loss caused by mankind's disobedience to God's commands. Sin creates a variety of wounds, both great and small, that bring grief not only to those who commit the sin, but also to those who are wounded by the consequences of the sin as well.

What we many times miss are the less obvious forms of grief that arise from acting in ways contrary to God's purpose. Many communities face a rising wave of self-destructive behavior such as drug and alcohol abuse, suicide, and violence, much of which is not the result of obvious wounds created by a major trauma, but that instead grow from a constant stream of little injuries that occur over and over, often across the course of years. These repeated small scars can eventually build into gaping wounds buried deep within.

The result is that, in an increasing number of cases, a person who seems to have everything the world defines as success suddenly turns destructive, harming themselves or others out of bitterness and pain. The world does not know how to handle these situations, or even how to understand them, since their causes are rooted deep within the heart.

God, however, can heal even the deepest wounds. A fundamental part of the Spirit's transforming work is *consolation*: the taking away of grief. The consolation of God heals the sense of loss created by sin; it heals the heart's wounds and brings God's own peace to the innermost self.

As the Spirit's hands and feet here on Earth, we are to be instruments of God's peace, a tool He uses to carry His healing to those in pain. We are called to minister God's consolation first to each other, and then to carry the gift of God's healing and forgiveness out into the world beyond. As we consider consolation this week, you will see that it is not abstract or theoretical; it flows out from us in practical ways as we care for each other, pray for each other, and support each other.

The work of consolation that God brings to those undergoing pain and grief is a work of renewal and regeneration, taking the old and dying self that suffers the grief of sin and replacing it with the new self fashioned in the image of Christ. The regeneration of death and decay can be seen throughout God's creation and will be the focus of *Contemplatio* this week as we look at the ways in which God's healing and renewal play out both in the natural world and inside of us.

Extra Mile:

Meet with two or three Believers with whom you are close for an hour this week, outdoors if possible. As you each share your cares and concerns in turn, have the others lay hands on the one speaking and pray for the needs expressed. Remember that anything shared during this time is private and should not be repeated without permission of everyone in the group.

CONSOLATION & REPENTANCE

You may find it helpful to re-read pages 14-17 from Week One as you begin thinking about grief and consolation this week.

Day 1

12 Symptoms of Grief

1. Feeling no need or seeing no reason to be thankful.
2. Strong negative emotions, especially those that erupt uncontrollably. Alternatively, negative emotions can be internalized and cause you to pull away and isolate yourself.
3. Becoming cynical about relationships, or always putting down yourself and/or others.
4. A sensation of tightness from holding emotions in your body. Deeper grief can also create a tightness in the gut that may cause a loss of appetite.
5. Eyes and ears that are clouded by grief so that you do not see the good around you or take joy in God's creation.
6. An inability to talk about the source of your pain or grief. Losing the ability to laugh.
7. Seeing no purpose or meaning in life. Also, losing the ability to trust others, even family or friends.
8. Falling into a pattern of not taking care of yourself, your possessions, or your relationships.
9. Turning to harmful addictions in an attempt to deal with the pain caused by grief.
10. Your mind is stuck in the past or refuses to let go of attachments to people or events in the past.
11. An unwillingness to take on the responsibilities of someone you have lost because you are still holding onto the pain.
12. An unreasonable belief that people are conspiring to keep you unhappy.

THE MODERN WORLD DOESN'T KNOW WHAT TO DO WITH GRIEF. It teaches you to push your grief down deep and never deal with it. It distracts you with gadgets, entertainment, and endless activities so you never have time to let grief surface. By refusing to listen to the voice of the Holy Spirit, most people remain largely unaware of their own grief, and never realize what it is doing to them, or how it is driving their thoughts. If they never turn to God for help with their grief, their pain will end up being redirected into negative emotions, which will ultimately erupt into damaging words and actions aimed at everyone around them—resulting in yet more wounds that ripple outward through the community.

The noise and distraction of the modern world is part of what lets people push their pain and grief down deep inside in an attempt to not have to deal with it. Many people are afraid to be alone with themselves for any period of time simply because they don't want to face what they carry inside. But grief that is suppressed never really goes away; unprocessed grief simply builds up over time until it begins to overflow into all your thoughts and actions.

For this reason, a community of faith must create the space in which all its members are fully supported in the work of dealing with grief. If the ministry of consolation is neglected, the toxic by-products of grief will eventually pull apart the fabric of *shalom* in your community.

Recognizing Grief

Spiritual and emotional wounds often provoke strong reactions when they are touched, and the frictions that arise normally between people in the course of daily life are often enough to cause someone holding grief to act out in pain. A person who is affected by grief will find it almost impossible to act from a place of peace, or to live out the biblical precepts that create *shalom*. Unless consolation is consistently practiced in your community, the other seven precepts will never be given room to take root and grow.

For this reason, it is important that your community of faith watch for those among its members who are in grief and work to help them find peace and healing. Those who have a gift of discernment should be encouraged to actively watch for the negative impacts of sin so grief can be dealt with before it develops into a major problem.

Even if you don't feel you have a gift of discernment, you should still learn to keep an eye out for grief developing in those closest to you, so you can offer help when needed. Listed in the sidebar to the left are twelve symptoms that often signal grief, with the indicators of deeper grief occupying the last half of the list. Since each of these symptoms can show up across a spectrum of severity, you should look carefully at what the depth of the symptom is telling you. Someone simply having a hard time being thankful one morning is probably just being touched by the edges of grief, while a person consistently feeling as if they have nothing of worth in life for which to be thankful is almost certainly mired deep in grief.

In addition to watching for grief in its own members, a community of faith must also develop habits that guard against grief coming in from the outside. The members of your community will almost certainly have to deal with those outside whose grief comes flying in toward them. The best approach is for everyone to practice the Peace precepts discussed in Week Eight until they can handle hurtful words or actions without allowing themselves to be pulled out of peace.

Churches and other communities must also take the time to carefully discern what new members of the community are carrying in the door with them when they join. Part of welcoming new members is getting to know them and recognizing their spiritual and emotional needs well enough that the community can offer consolation and healing for the wounds they carry.

Dealing with the Sources of Pain & Grief

Real consolation results in much more than just the temporary relief of painful emotions; it works on the underlying spiritual condition of the soul so the heart can be fully restored. In order to accomplish this healing, the sources of pain and grief must be addressed.

The most obvious sources of grief are the major traumas of life—such as the death or illness of someone you love—which bring with them immediate and intense pain. If you focus only on these more visible causes of grief, however, you will often miss the more common small wounds that over time create pain that can be nearly as intense. If not dealt with, the grief that comes from such problems as feelings of inadequacy, from guilt or self-blame as a result of past experiences, or from dwelling on the hurts of lost or damaged relationships, can slowly build up until they become almost debilitating.

For someone trapped in grief, finding healing on their own is almost impossible. Whenever someone in your community exhibits the symptoms of grief or is not acting from a place of peace, the community should respond by consoling their grief through the leading of the Holy Spirit. The ministry of consolation requires an environment of trust and openness, so in order for your community to successfully deal with grief, its members must be intimately involved in each other's spiritual lives and feel free to actively reach out to help each other.

Although providing consolation to its own members must come first, the Church is also called to reach out with healing toward those who are lost. For those who have never met Christ, the first step in the journey of healing must be to receive Him. Trying to provide consolation for one who doesn't follow Christ can at best provide some temporary emotional relief, since no deeper spiritual healing is taking place. Often, in the moment that a person first calls out to God for forgiveness, some of the burden of grief will be lifted—but at this point the healing is just beginning. Even though Jesus' blood completely covers the sins of all who follow Him, the process of healing the wounds of grief is a work performed by the Holy Spirit over time.

The process of grieving and healing can be supported in three major ways: first, by allowing individuals the room to feel and process their grief; second, by providing consolation to help those who are grieving; and third, in those cases where the grief is caused by personal sin, by helping individuals address the root causes of sin through repentance and restoration so that the source of grief is removed.

The Process of Grieving & Healing

The most foundational way in which a community can support those in grief is by providing a safe space in which those who are grieving can feel supported in allowing themselves to experience and process their grief. Members of the community must understand that grieving is a normal and expected part of each person's spiritual journey and be willing to help carry each other's responsibilities when someone in the community needs time and space to heal.

Only when you feel safe and supported by your community will you be able to open yourself to the grieving process completely. Just as with negative emotions, pushing down grief and ignoring it will simply internalize the wounds and allow them to become toxic. In order to fully heal, you must allow yourself to fully experience the pain and grief; it is part of the cycle of life, death, and regeneration that God has created. For most people, the processing of deeper grief comes in waves and in stages, with periods of wanting to be alone alternating with periods of simply needing those in the community to sit with them and support them with their presence.

Dealing with pain and grief takes time. When you are experiencing grief, slow down and allow the process to unfold. A person going through grief may need to take some time off from responsibilities in order to allow themselves to grieve fully.

Any time a person is experiencing grief that is deep enough that it is causing suicidal thoughts, drug or alcohol abuse, acts of self-harm such as cutting, or that renders them unable to carry out daily responsibilities, the community needs to work together to make sure that person gets help from a professional counselor and is fully supported by those in the community who have a gift of consolation.

Be careful in how you use touch when consoling someone experiencing grief. For many people, a caring touch from a friend when they are in the middle of allowing grief to express itself through words, or even in weeping, can stop the outflow of expression exactly when it most needs to be allowed to happen. In most cases, you should allow a person to fully express pain and grief while simply watching and listening, and then offer the support of a healing touch once the outflow has stopped.

When you or someone in your community is going through the process of grieving, taking the time to wander quietly through a natural place can often help. Just walking through a garden or sitting beside a babbling creek for a few hours can help turn your mind and spirit back toward God's presence, and the healing that He brings.

Dealing with the more minor sources of grief is also important so that it does not build up over time. Regular times of personal and corporate liturgy are important to help you process the everyday grief that accompanies life. Being mindful to release your grief to the Spirit each day helps keep your mind and spirit clear and focused on God's presence.

God uses times of grieving—both great and small—and the subsequent periods of healing to grow you in ways you would never grow otherwise. Even in the deepest valleys of grief, remember to be thankful. Thankfulness will help you find your way out of the other side of the valley.

Consolation: Being a Witness to Grief

In communities where grief is never discussed openly, people learn to hide their pain and try to pretend everything is fine. Hiding grief from your family and friends creates a pattern that makes it more likely you will find yourself trying to hide your grief from God as well. When you try to handle your wounds alone, you are never able to completely heal. It is the nature of grief that you can't grieve fully all by yourself. God intended grief to be witnessed, and He created the community of the Church so that His children could support each other through their grief. The Holy Spirit uses us in the work of consolation so that we can carry others' burdens in those moments when they are most in need.

Being a witness to another's grief does not mean that you are responsible for bringing them healing; it means you are present and prayerfully watching as the Spirit ministers healing to the one who is hurting. When witnessing another's grief, your job is just to create a safe space and listen with your whole being. In many cases, simply letting someone tell their story while you listen helps bring them to the point of healing. At other times, no words are needed.

The deeper parts of grief have no words, and sometimes trying to address pain with words does more harm than good. When someone is grappling with deep grief, use wisdom and speak sparingly. Your presence is more important than what you say.

When you are helping someone whose grief comes directly from their own sin, try to see their spiritual needs without judgment. Be more interested in healing than with blame. Space for dealing with the sin through repentance will begin to open once the grieving has progressed to the place where the pain begins to subside.

When supporting someone through consolation, simply listening and praying with them is often enough, but you will occasionally encounter situations where an individual has deep-rooted grief that is more difficult to address. In such cases, you should seek the help of those in your community to whom the Spirit has given a special gift for consolation.

A person with a gift of consolation is able, through the Spirit, to discern how to help others deal with grief. They help others find the right path forward toward healing, sometimes through ceremony, actions, or prayer. Exercising the gift of consolation is often difficult and emotionally demanding, so those with this gift must be fully supported by the community in this work.

Repentance & Restoration

When the source of grief is the person's own sin, both the grief and the sin that caused it must be addressed before the person can find peace again. Just dealing with the grief in order to achieve some emotional relief alone is not enough, since the root cause is still present. The only effective way for the community to support the healing of a member's sin is to pray for them and encourage them to accept the Holy Spirit's call to repentance of the sin.

Don't try to hide grief from children in an attempt to "protect" them. They may not be ready to fully understand the circumstances, but they need to learn that it is normal for people to grieve and receive support. Young children are especially sensitive and can tell when adults are upset or grieving. Help them understand what is happening at whatever level they are able.

In many cases, it is more appropriate for the men to console the men and the women to console the women. Be especially sensitive to this situation when sexual sins are involved in creating the grief.

The effects of grief are not limited to just the mind and the spirit. Throughout this study, we have discussed the impacts that negative emotions such as anger or worry can have on the body. These are really just specific examples of the fact that the grief caused by sin affects the body and can be felt and held in the body. Those carrying grief will often find that they feel physically run down, are more prone to illness, and seem to feel unrested even after sleep. When these symptoms are caused by grief, the act of consoling the grief and dealing with the underlying sin will often help heal the physical symptoms as well.

Any time you help someone else work through their grief, always take time afterward to make sure you have cleared yourself of the heaviness that comes from witnessing and consoling grief. Go outside for a few minutes and find a spot to sit on the ground where you can pray and ask the Holy Spirit to refresh your spirit and give you peace.

Repentance is another aspect of the Holy Spirit's transforming work that involves a fundamental change in the desires and motives of the heart, replacing the desires that originally caused the sin with new desires that create Godly actions instead.

The process of repentance is not complete until there has also been restoration. To ensure that healing is complete, and to guard the fabric of *shalom*, the community should be actively involved in making sure relationships damaged by the sin are healed and that communion is restored.

Breaking Cycles of Abuse

Children learn patterns of thought and behavior, both good and bad, from their parents and the other adults around them. As a result, patterns of abuse are often handed down from one generation to the next unless the cycle is somehow intercepted and broken. People are prone to repeat the abusive patterns they experience if they never learn healthy patterns to replace the abusive ones they have learned.

Almost a third of those who experience sexual, physical or psychological abuse become abusers themselves later in life. The repeating of these patterns is not logical or rational, but its force can be powerful, with victims often finding themselves doing to others precisely what was done to them, and not being able to understand why. A major responsibility of the Church is to help break this cycle where possible, replacing destructive patterns with ones that reflect God's love.

Addressing Generational Grief

The patterns of sin that create grief and cycles of abuse can be passed down generation to generation unless they are addressed through repentance, consolation, and reconciliation. This generational grief compounds with each generation if it is not dealt with and corrected, leading to deep-seated patterns of sin which become increasingly widespread and difficult to dislodge.

Such cycles of sin, hatred, and abuse can eventually grow to the scale of nations or entire ethnic groups, creating violence that can span centuries. Only the Holy Spirit can begin to heal wounds on this scale; simply be faithful to minister consolation in your own community.

Being Prepared for Death

If those in your community avoid talking about death and loss, treating the subject as taboo, then an unhealthy attitude toward death will inevitably develop. Physical death is the natural consequence of man's sinful nature, and is ultimately a kindness granted by God to those whose spirit longs to be restored to full fellowship with Him. If you avoid looking death fully in the face, you will end up not knowing how to handle death when it comes, or understanding how to comfort those who are grieving the loss of someone they love.

No matter your age, you must come to terms with the fact that you will experience physical death at some point in the future. There will come a time when you are no longer here, and those you love will have to move forward without you.

Only when you come to terms with your own impending death can you begin to clearly see your role in your community, and begin to plan wisely so those who remain behind when you leave will be left with a strong legacy. In this way, when the time comes, you can move forward from this life with no regrets, and those who remain, instead of mourning, can celebrate the gifts that God poured out through you into the world.

God teaches the soul by pains and obstacles, not by ideas.

- Jean-Pierre de Caussade
From *Abandonment to Divine Providence*

Repentance is harder when there has been no consolation, since the mind stuck in grief dwells on the past.

In *Deuteronomy 5:9*, the Bible says that the sins of the unrighteous can bring grief to those three or four generations into the future. But in *Ezekiel 18*, God promises that this cycle of grief will not curse those who follow His principles and deal with sin through repentance.

Once you realize that God has given you an important role in your community, you should begin to pray that God will help you find those in the next generation that will take on this role once you are gone. Often, God will use the wisdom you have learned through experience to help teach and prepare those who will eventually replace you, so be open to mentoring and training those who are coming along behind you.

Compline

Reading: *Romans 8:18-30*

Reflection: Think back to how God has used the painful times in your life to teach you deep lessons or bring you closer to His will.

Prayer: Be thankful for God's promise to use even times of suffering and grief to build you into His image.

READING #1 - 2 CORINTHIANS 1:3-7

The opening prayer this week moves from being a personal prayer to a prayer offered for the community of Believers to which you belong. As you say this prayer, reach out and include all those with whom you share Christian fellowship.

Day 2

In this passage, Paul tells the church at Corinth that he has undergone much affliction in spreading the gospel of Christ, but that God has brought him comfort and consolation amid those afflictions. Paul sees this process of affliction and consolation as God's way of preparing us to console others in need. He tells the Corinthians that his suffering and his resultant dependence upon God is how the Holy Spirit makes him a tool fit to carry God's consolation to the world.

How has the Holy Spirit brought you consolation for the pain and grief caused by sin? How has He used you in His work of consoling others? Are you afraid of letting God use you to comfort people who are in grief? Afraid you won't know what to say or do? How does your own experience with receiving consolation prepare you to be used in the consolation of others?

Preparation:

- Calm your mind and take a few deep breaths
- Start with a Prayer of Thanksgiving
- Continue with the prayer, "*Lord Jesus Christ, make us a community who shares Your consolation and Your peace one with the other, bearing the burdens of those in need.*"

Lectio:

Blessed be the God and Father of our Lord Jesus Christ, the Father of mercies
and the God of all consolation, who consoles us in all our affliction,
so that we may be able to console those who are in any affliction
with the consolation with which we ourselves are consoled by God.
For just as the sufferings of Christ are abundant for us,
so also our consolation is abundant through Christ.
If we are being afflicted, it is for your consolation and salvation;
if we are being consoled, it is for your consolation, which you experience when you
patiently endure the same sufferings that we are also suffering.
Our hope for you is unshaken; for we know that as you share in our sufferings,
so also you share in our consolation.

- 2 Corinthians 1:3-7 (NRSV)

Meditatio:

Oratio:

Ask God to prepare you to be a fit tool that can be used by the Holy Spirit to minister comfort and consolation to those in pain.

Both Breath Prayers and Welcoming Prayer are powerful tools for dealing with grief or strong negative emotions. Always take the time to deal with grief or strong emotions as they arise, otherwise they simply build up and create an even deeper cycle of pain and grief in the future. And always remember that God has given you those in your community of faith to support you as well.

Contemplatio:

Most people are happy to think about growth and change, since that is the prevailing narrative of modern culture. Death and decay, however, are things many people avoid. To modern culture, the old is something to be done away with and replaced. In God's economy, on the other hand, the old and dying is regenerated into something new and productive. Every leaf that falls to the ground is returned to the soil, its nutrients to be used to create new growth. The bodies of the birds and animals as well are returned to the Earth to create fertility and participate in the birth of future generations.

Look around at the signs of death and decay in the landscape. This can usually be seen most easily where the leaf litter meets the earth and is returned to the soil. As you think back to the places you observed growth and new life last week, think about the ways that God renews the old and dying to create new life. Release your thoughts and relax into the presence of the God who creates something new out of the old, forever making the world fresh and anew.

Benediction:

- Return slowly and peacefully from *Contemplatio*
- Take time to be thankful again
- Acknowledge that you have completed your time for today and ask God to go with you as you leave this time.

Compline

Reading: *Psalm 13:1-6*

Reflection: Look back at events that have created grief or worry in your life over the past year. How did this affect the way you call out to God in prayer?

Prayer: Tell God about your pain and grief. Ask Him any questions you have been afraid to ask. God will honor your prayers when you are honest with Him.

Reading #2 - 2 Corinthians 7:9-11

Preparation:

- Calm your mind and take a few deep breaths
- Start with a Prayer of Thanksgiving
- Continue with the prayer, "*Lord Jesus Christ, make us a community who shares Your consolation and Your peace one with the other, bearing the burdens of those in need.*"

Day 3

Sins that were occurring in the church at Corinth had forced Paul to rebuke them for their behavior. Paul's rebuke and correction created the sorrow about which Paul speaks in this passage. Paul is happy that his correction has lead to repentance and a return to right action.

Lectio:

Yet now I am happy, not because you were made sorry,
but because your sorrow led you to repentance.
For you became sorrowful as God intended and so were not harmed in any way by us.
Godly sorrow brings repentance that leads to salvation and leaves no regret,
but worldly sorrow brings death. See what this godly sorrow has produced in you:
what earnestness, what eagerness to clear yourselves, what indignation, what alarm,
what longing, what concern, what readiness to see justice done.
At every point you have proved yourselves to be innocent in this matter.

- 2 Corinthians 7:9-11 (NIV)

Meditatio:

Has God ever used someone to point out a sin to you and call you to repentance? How did you react? Were you angry at the person, or thankful? Did it create Godly sorrow that lead to repentance, or worldly sorrow that caused you to hide what you were doing?

Oratio:

_____

Express your thanks to God that He uses grief and sorrow over sin to call you back to a right relationship with Him. Ask that He will help you always to react wisely when sin brings grief and pain into your life.

No one ever told me that grief felt so like fear.

- C. S. Lewis

Contemplatio:

If you can, go to a place where you can pick up and smell the mixture of soil and leaf debris that exists just at the surface of the soil where the decaying leaves are finishing the process of being broken down and returned to the Earth. If you have ever smelled the rotting of old food or a dead animal, you know the odor of ammonia released when organic material is not recycled into the earth through proper composting. If the soil you are smelling is healthy, however, you will detect a rich and earthy smell instead.

God has created millions of soil organisms that quickly and efficiently break down old organic material and release it's nutrients back into the soil where they can become a part of new growth. Close your eyes and smell the earth, allowing it to remind you that God can take the dead and decaying parts of your spirit and transform them into a new creation. As you release your thoughts today, release your old self to the Holy Spirit and allow Him to create something new.

Benediction:

- Return slowly and peacefully from *Contemplatio*
- Take time to be thankful again
- Acknowledge that you have completed your time for today and ask God to go with you as you leave this time.

Compline

Reading: *Psalm 23:1-6*

Reflection: Sometimes the dark valleys of grief exist inside where they cannot be seen by others. Is God leading you through such a valley now? Or is God blessing you with a time on the mountaintops at this point in your journey instead?

Prayer: Re-read *Psalm 23*, making it your own prayer.

READING #3 - JAMES 5:13-16

Preparation:

- Calm your mind and take a few deep breaths
- Start with a Prayer of Thanksgiving
- Continue with the prayer, *"Lord Jesus Christ, make us a community who shares Your consolation and Your peace one with the other, bearing the burdens of those in need."*

Lectio:

Day 4

Is any one of you in trouble? He should pray.
Is anyone happy? Let him sing songs of praise.
Is any one of you sick? He should call the elders of the church to pray over him
and anoint him with oil in the name of the Lord.
And the prayer offered in faith will make the sick person well;
the Lord will raise him up. If he has sinned, he will be forgiven.
Therefore confess your sins to each other and pray for each other
so that you may be healed.
The prayer of a righteous man is powerful and effective.

- James 5:13-16 (NIV)

Meditatio:

Consolation is a deep and powerful form of spiritual healing that God pours out on His children, especially in response to prayer. How do you take advantage of God's promise to provide healing in response to prayer? How does your own relationship with God affect the power of your prayers? What happens when the righteous pray together as a community?

Oratio:

Ask God to make the fellowship of Believers around you into a powerful community of prayer that can call down His healing and forgiveness to deal with sickness and sin.

Contemplatio:

Return today to the place where you smelled the soil yesterday, this time picking up the soil and leaf litter and feeling how the leaves and other organic material break down into smaller and smaller pieces, eventually returning completely to the soil. This organic material adds fertility and richness to the soil, creates a structure in the soil that supports life, and greatly increases the ability of the soil to hold water so plants can grow.

Without the amazing variety of life in the soil—from bacteria and fungi to earthworms and beetles—nothing that died would break down chemically in ways that would complete the cycles that God designed to provide for the constant regeneration of His creation. Close your eyes and feel the soil between your fingers. With an attitude of thankfulness, release yourself fully to the cycle of life, death, and rebirth that God has created for you. As you relax into God's presence, accept His work of making your old self pass away and making you a new creation.

Benediction:

- Return slowly and peacefully from *Contemplatio*
- Take time to be thankful again
- Acknowledge that you have completed your time for today and ask God to go with you as you leave this time.

Compline

Reading: *Deuteronomy 5:1-10*

Reflection: Are you allowing anything in your life to act as an idol that you value above God? What kind of grief is this causing in your life? What do you need to do to break this cycle so that your children and grandchildren will inherit a blessing instead of a curse?

Prayer: Confess any way you are tempted to put something or somebody ahead of God.

READING #4 - GALATIANS 6:1-5

Preparation:

- Calm your mind and take a few deep breaths
- Start with a Prayer of Thanksgiving
- Continue with the prayer, "*Lord Jesus Christ, make us a community who shares Your consolation and Your peace one with the other, bearing the burdens of those in need.*"

Lectio:

Day 5

Your load becomes a burden when your grief makes it too much to carry alone.

My friends, if anyone is detected in a transgression,
you who have received the Spirit should restore such a one in a spirit of gentleness.
Take care that you yourselves are not tempted.
Bear one another's burdens, and in this way you will fulfill the law of Christ.
For if those who are nothing think they are something, they deceive themselves.
All must test their own work; then that work, rather than their neighbor's work,
will become a cause for pride. For all must carry their own loads.

- Galatians 6:1-5 (NRSV)

Meditatio:

We must all carry our own share of the load during those times that God blesses us to be able, but we must also be willing to help others by carrying part of their burden when they are unable due to sin or grief. Are you available for God to use when those around you need help carrying their burdens? Or are you mostly focused on yourself and your own problems? When you are experiencing grief yourself, are you willing to let others help you? Or do you hold all your pain inside and refuse to let others bear the burden with you?

Oratio:

> Tell God of your willingness to be a full part of His community of faith, helping to bear the burdens of others when they are in need, and open to God using others in the community to help you when you are overwhelmed by sin or grief.

When you are in the dark, listen, and God will give you a very precious message.

\- Oswald Chambers

Contemplatio:

Lie on your back today with your eyes closed. Look inward to the soil of your own being and think for a moment about the work of regeneration and renewal that God is doing in your life. The Holy Spirit takes the old motives and desires and regenerates them into desires and motives that are in line with God's nature. In the process, He uses the pain and grief caused by sin to help in the work of purification, taking away those parts of you that are rotting and decaying and replacing them with life fresh and new. As this happens, the Spirit also somehow transforms the sorrow and grief, creating joy that grows from the rich, fertile soil of a soul re-made into the likeness of Christ.

As you move into silence today, simply observe the presence of the Holy Spirit inside of you, performing this work of regeneration and healing. Breathe deeply, as if breathing in the Spirit's presence. Open your hands, palms upward, as a symbol of your surrender to the Spirit's work.

Benediction:

- Return slowly and peacefully from *Contemplatio*
- Take time to be thankful again
- Acknowledge that you have completed your time for today and ask God to go with you as you leave this time.

Compline

Reading: *Ezekiel 18:1-32*

Reflection: The righteous are called to deal with sin so that it does not cause grief, both now and for future generations. Is there any habitual sin you need to set right before it creates a cycle of pain and grief?

Prayer: Say a prayer of repentance if the Holy Spirit so leads.

READING #5 - PHILIPPIANS 2:1-5

Preparation:

- Calm your mind and take a few deep breaths
- Start with a Prayer of Thanksgiving
- Continue with the prayer, *"Lord Jesus Christ, make us a community who shares Your consolation and Your peace one with the other, bearing the burdens of those in need."*

Lectio:

Day 6

If you have any encouragement from being united with Christ,
if any comfort from his love, if any fellowship with the Spirit,
if any tenderness and compassion,
then make my joy complete by being like-minded,
having the same love, being one in spirit and purpose.
Do nothing out of selfish ambition or vain conceit,
but in humility consider others better than yourselves.
Each of you should look not only to your own interests,
but also to the interests of others.
Your attitude should be the same as that of Christ Jesus…

- Philippians 2:1-5 (NIV)

Meditatio:

Comfort and consolation ultimately flow outward from the love of Christ. This love expresses itself through you in humility, selflessness, and compassion. Is it truly your desire to have the same attitude inside yourself that Jesus has: to put the needs of others before His own needs and be used as an instrument of God's will to bring comfort and salvation to all those in need?

Oratio:

> Surrender your own will to the will of Christ, so that God can use you to pour out His love and compassion on all those who need comfort and healing.

Contemplatio:

Salvation is the ultimate work of regeneration, the act of God renewing the dead and decaying, transforming it into the very image of His Son. In this process, God uses all the joys and sorrows of life, weaving them together as part of His transformational work. It is for this reason we have the promise of *Romans 8:28*, that God will work all things together for the good of those who love Him and who are called according to His purpose. Even the deepest periods of grief and hardship become part of God's work of redemption and restoration.

Lie on the ground and close your eyes again today, taking a moment to notice your whole being—mind, body, and spirit—as you come into your time of inner stillness, listening to God speak through the silence. If you have been holding anything back from God, any pain or grief you don't want to let go of, release your grip today and open yourself fully to the consoling presence of the One who created you and sacrificed Himself to restore you to His will.

Benediction:

- Return slowly and peacefully from *Contemplatio*
- Take time to be thankful again
- Acknowledge that you have completed your time for today and ask God to go with you as you leave this time.

Compline

Reading: *Isaiah 40:1-31*

Reflection: Has the Holy Spirit used you to comfort those around you? Is God calling you to minister consolation to anyone close to you who is hurting?

Prayer: Commit to God that you will be available to bring comfort and consolation to those who need it whenever He wishes to use you in this way.

REFLECTION

Revisit Your Favorite Passage

Day 7

Reflections on the Week

Compline

Reading: *Matthew 5:1-16*

Reflection: The blessings that flow from God result in inner peace, which the world cannot see and cannot take away. Therefore the world cannot understand how we can be the salt and light that God sends forth into the darkness.

Prayer: Sit in God's presence with a thankful heart for the blessings and peace that He provides in abundance.

WEEK 11 - INVOCATION

Reckless words pierce like a sword,
but the tongue of the wise brings healing.

-Proverbs 12:18 (NIV)

IN THE BEGINNING, GOD SPOKE THE HEAVENS AND THE EARTH INTO BEING, creating them simply through the strength of His divine intent channeled through the instrumentality of His spoken word. He said *Let there be light*, and light came forth from the nothingness.

From the story of creation, the ancient Hebrews gained an appreciation for the power that God invested in words and language. When the apostle John wrote his gospel, he began by describing Jesus as the *Logos*, a Greek word meaning *Word*. Today this title may seem confusing, but to the people of that time, the *Logos*—the *Word*—represented the instrument through which God's divine will and imagination are expressed. By calling Jesus by this title, John indicates that Jesus was the one through whom God called the Universe into being and through whose hands He shaped it for His purpose.

When God created mankind, He gave us the gift of words as well—a gift whose power carries with it a heavy responsibility. The capacity of the human tongue to bring both blessings and curses is shown repeatedly throughout the scriptures. Words can wound deeply, or they can be used to heal. They can express hatred as well as love. Just as the words of God can create or destroy, your own words also carry a certain echo of this power.

Even though your words cannot call worlds into being as can those of your Creator, they still carry with them the power of *invocation*: the ability to provoke thoughts and emotions in others, to call back to their minds that which was forgotten, and even to call forth into being new thoughts or possibilities which they have never considered before.

But the power of invocation carried by your words is not limited to affecting others only. The ability of your words to invoke either good or evil is often at work most strongly deep inside of yourself, as your own inner voice speaks into the quietness of your mind. The thoughts and actions called forth by this inner dialog in many ways direct the path you will choose to follow.

God gave you the power of words to use carefully and wisely. You should never allow your tongue to speak unguarded. God intended words to be a tool used when needed, not something you should allow to overrun your mind with constant internal chatter so you are unable to listen to His voice. To help you begin to carry the silence with you more deeply throughout the day, this week we will practice *Contemplatio* while walking. Eventually, as you learn to carry inner silence with you as you travel through the world, you will find within you the ability to sense the path of the Spirit laid out before you, calling you onward in your journey to follow Christ.

Extra Mile:

Take time to have one-on-one conversations with three people this week, each lasting at least an hour. Make the space between you sacred: choose words that honor and bless each person, give each person your full attention, pray together, and share with each other stories of your spiritual journey.

Invocation & the Power of the Tongue

Words carry the power of invocation no matter the form used to deliver them. Whether they are written or spoken, sung or chanted, you should always remain aware of the power hidden in words. In fact, you should be especially mindful of the power of words set to song, since they come embedded within the raw evocative power of music.

Day 1

The Bible uses the word *tongue* in four distinct connotations. It is used to refer to the physical organ of the body (as in *Luke 1:64*). It can also be used in reference to a spoken language of a specific group of people (*Acts 2:11*), or a spoken language that is unknown on Earth but that the Holy Spirit gives to people on certain occasions so that they can speak or pray directly from their spirits (as Paul discusses in *1 Corinthians 12-14*). The fourth connotation, of the tongue as the seat of discursive thought, is actually the most commonly used throughout the Old Testament with over a hundred occurrences. It is also used in the New Testament in the same sense in numerous passages (*James 3:5-8* being one of the most often quoted).

The Bible's use of the tongue to represent the seat of discursive thought is not the only example of the Bible using a part of the body to represent a broader aspect of human nature. A few others include:
The **heart** represents the inner self, the seat of feelings, the innermost thoughts and motives.
The **eyes and ears** represent the ability to perceive, both physically and spiritually.
The **lips and mouth** represent the part of the self that speaks aloud so that others can hear.
The **hands and feet** represent the ability to carry out physical actions in this world.
The **bones** are sometimes used to represent the physical body that experiences the physical reality of life here on Earth.

History contains innumerable examples of the power words hold to express and shape the products of human will and imagination, calling them forth into being. Much of the mid-twentieth century was defined by the actions of Adolph Hitler, who used the power of words to tell a story whose message of hatred was so compelling that it convinced an entire nation of ordinary people to follow him, plunging the world into a war that ultimately killed millions of people. Just a few decades later, Martin Luther King Jr. used the power of words to call people to peacefully resist injustice and inequality, thereby helping to begin the healing of centuries-old prejudices and bringing about major advances in civil rights.

As Jesus says in *Luke 6:45*, it is from the overflow of the heart that the mouth speaks. And the words you speak have the power to invoke thoughts and actions in those around you. Therefore you must guard your heart and mind in Christ Jesus so that your words create blessings for those around you, calling them to thoughts and actions that reflect the mind of God. The way in which words are used in your community are critical. Words can either help knit together the fabric of peace among people, or they can violently rip it apart.

The Power of the Tongue

Anyone who has spent time reading the scriptures will be familiar with its use of the word *heart* to represent a person's seat of emotion, empathy, and feeling. Throughout scripture, the heart is used to symbolize the interior self: the place where the spirit and the mind meet to create the emotions, will, and imagination. In much the same way, the word *tongue* is used in many passages to represent a person's seat of discursive thought: the place in which the mind engages in thinking via analytical reasoning, often using words in an internal dialog. In the passages that use it in this sense, the *tongue* symbolizes the power of words as one of the main tools the mind uses to express the thoughts arising either out of the internal workings of the heart or in response to external events.

The modern concept of the brain as the seat of consciousness developed centuries after the Bible was written, as our understanding of the human body increased. Neither the New or Old Testaments have a specific word for *brain*, and the Old Testament actually has no word that directly translates as *mind*. As a result, a number of human attributes we now think of as functions of the brain or the mind are, in many places in scripture, instead shared between the concepts of the heart and the tongue.

A number of occult practices revolve around the power of the tongue. The word *incantation* comes from the Latin word *incantatio*, meaning to speak, chant or sing into being—a concept from which we also get our word *enchantment*. The original meanings of these words are lost to most people today, whose perceptions have been formed by modern books and movies. In reality, most occult practices involving incantations were not trying to achieve anything "supernatural," but instead simply used the power of words and stories to create thoughts and images in the minds of other people in order to achieve a specific purpose. The occult practice of using incantations is actually a corruption of the Biblical practice of invocation that we practice every day as we pray and speak through the authority and leading of the Holy Spirit.

Always remember that your words can call into being thoughts and images in the minds of those who hear or read them. These thoughts can create actions, changing the course of events for good or ill, sometimes for decades to come. Always consider what your words might conjure into being before you release them. Words come quickly, and the damage they can create can be instantaneous, while knitting back together the wounds they cause can take years.

Let Your Words Arise from Stillness

God gave you the power of the tongue to be used wisely and only when needed. The baseline of your life should be standing in the silence and listening to God, following His presence, not letting empty words consume your attention. When you need to use words to communicate with others or as a tool for your own inner thoughts, allow them to arise out of the inner silence where you live in God's presence. When you have said what is needed, return to listening in silence. Don't let a stream of words and images of your own making continually clutter your head.

The things you choose to allow your inner words to invoke in your mind will soon start showing up in your interactions with the outside world. An important spiritual discipline is learning to watch your inner dialog to notice when it begins to turn negative. If you find your inner dialog turning toward negative thoughts, simply release the words moving through your mind just as you have learned to release thoughts during *Contemplatio*, and replace the dialog with something that arises from your awareness of God's presence.

If you find it difficult to shift your inner dialog away from an unhelpful line of thought, then you can use the power of your own words to assist you. Say to yourself, aloud if needed, "*With the help of the Holy Spirit, I choose to focus my mind on...*" and then name what you choose to think about instead.

Avoid idle chatter. Don't talk simply to fill up the silence. Idle talk leads to the diluting of the spiritual power of your words. God's Spirit chooses to use the words of those who are wise to accomplish His will, not those who chatter on endlessly.

You should also avoid getting entangled in meaningless arguments. Let your words arise from a place of calm deliberation, considering the impact of your words before you release them. Once spoken, words can never be called back or unspoken. A few words thoughtlessly spoken can wound deeply and undo trust that has taken years to build.

Strive to find the sacred balance between the stillness of listening and the powerful moving force of the tongue. Inner silence and reflection give your words a deep well from which to draw.

The Sacred Space of Conversation

Many people today are so overscheduled and overcommitted that they rarely make the time or space required to have a real conversation, instead settling for brief exchanges that convey little more than logistical information or social window-dressing. Others seem to use idle chit-chat as a tool for keeping people at a comfortable distance so they can avoid the scary terrain of opening themselves in real conversation. A critical dimension of any community of faith is the creation of the safe and open space in which everyone can share with and support each other. God intended conversation between His people to be an act of communion: a sacred space in which two or more souls meet.

In every conversation, whether with those who follow Christ or not, start with the intent of making the space between you sacred. Choose your words with care, speaking words that benefit and bless those who hear them.

Give higher priority on your schedule to the needs of others than to the world's eye-catching time traps. Be fully present in your conversations, paying complete attention and not being distracted by things going on elsewhere.

Sacred conversation may at times move through deep and challenging waters, but among God's people it is more often filled with laughter and play, overflowing from joy.

Words of thanks and encouragement can be healing, especially to those in leadership positions or who carry responsibilities. Don't assume people know that you are thankful for what they do; make sure you tell them. Especially when a person is a strong leader, many people don't think of them as needing encouragement, but they are often exactly the ones who need to hear your words of thanks and encouragement because they receive them so rarely.

If you dwell on something negative, even just to think about why you hate it or how destructive it is, you will soon find it infecting you in ways you didn't expect. Whatever you meditate upon, whether good or bad, will drive the pattern of your thoughts, and you will soon find yourself repeating those patterns in some way. Therefore, you should be careful to give no space to negative thoughts. Release any negative thoughts as they arise, and choose instead to meditate upon that which is true, honorable, and pure (*Philippians 4:8*).

Be careful not to let cell phones, text messages, computers, or other distractions take your attention away from the sacred space of an important conversation. You should, of course, uphold your responsibilities and commitments, but in general you should give your attention to the people who you are actually with. Whenever possible, let the text messages, emails and calls wait until the conversation is over.

Some churches call the prayer used to open a service the *Invocation Prayer*, which is often a prayer calling on God to be present and asking that He use the service to accomplish His will. The privilege of invoking God's presence is a reminder of the power your words carry when you speak in accordance with the Spirit's leading.

Everyday Language & Humor

Be careful of self-deprecating humor. It can be used in certain situations to indicate that you don't take yourself too seriously, but if overused, this form of humor can grow into a pattern of self-defeating language. You should be careful not to think too highly of yourself, but on the other hand you should not get into the habit of putting yourself down or minimizing the gifts and talents God has given you.

The ways in which you choose to use words in the everyday exchanges of life—in the passing conversations and interactions that occur throughout your day—help set the underlying tone for your community. As cynicism has become more fashionable in post-modern culture, the habit of using cynical and negative language in order to appear more sophisticated or savvy has become increasingly common. Learn to pay attention to the passing comments you make, always considering the impact they will create. If the people around you are in the habit of being negative or discouraging, it is easy to fall into the same pattern yourself.

Words can become self-fulfilling, especially words you say to yourself. Since words form the backbone of discursive thought, words that are repeated often enough begin to create patterns of thought and thus eventually create patterns of action. If you constantly spread negative words to those around you, allow negative words to run through your mind, or continually listen to negative words coming at you from outside, the result can be profoundly destructive.

Try to make the words you speak as you go about the day encouraging and helpful, a blessing to those who hear them. Words can carry a tremendous power of encouragement, and a few words spoken in love can be a transformational experience. Many people have stories of how a simple thing said at the right time made a huge difference in their life.

Music, even when it has no words, carries with it another form of the power of invocation. It can directly invoke feelings and emotions, sometimes quite powerfully. This is part of the reason that movies have sound tracks. Try watching an emotional scene from a movie both with and without the sound track and notice the difference. Even though these emotions don't come packaged in words, they can end up provoking words, thoughts, and actions through the feelings they stir up. For this reason, you should give some care to the choice of music you listen to, noticing what it tends to invoke inside of you.

Humor can be a particularly powerful use of the tongue and, like any powerful tool, can be used either wisely or destructively. When used properly, humor can help lighten the mood, break the tension in a difficult situation, or bring laughter to a gathering of friends. But, because it is supposed to be so "harmless," humor can also be made to hide a variety of toxic payloads.

Be careful to never use humor that tries to be funny by making a person the target, whether that person is yourself or someone else. The kind of "put-down" humor that is common today is not funny; it is demeaning and belittling, and can create real damage.

The practice of disguising insults or put-downs as humor is particularly insidious, because it is a form of verbal aggression designed to make the target look bad if they get upset about being attacked. They are often told that it is all *just a joke* or that they need to *learn to take a joke*. When you see this sort of attack happening, engage the power of your own words and—speaking from a place of peace—help turn the situation into something more positive.

The Black Magic of Gossip

Human language is limited, and some things of the Spirit are well beyond the conceptualizing power of human words. For this reason, Paul tells us in *Romans 8:26-27*, the Holy Spirit assists us in praying when our words are not able to express our needs. The Holy Spirit speaks directly with the innermost parts of your spirit in communication not intermediated by words but which is instead expressed in the sacred language of inner silence.

Given what the Bible says about gossip, it is somewhat stunning to find so many cases of churches whose members consistently engage in some of the most malicious gossip to be found anywhere. Take a juicy rumor, add a twist of holier-than-thou judgment, and you have the recipe for some of the most damaging words you could ever speak.

It is no accident that *Romans 1:28-32* lists people who gossip alongside murderers and those who are ruthless and who hate God. Gossip is a form of spiritual, psychological, and emotional assault. It can destroy a person's reputation and permanently damage their friendships, their family, their self-image, and even their relationship with God.

A good number of traditional cultures clearly labeled gossip as a form of black magic: a use of words and incantations to speak into existence negative thoughts and images about the target of the gossip. These thoughts and images become lodged in the minds of those who hear those words, and then get spread throughout the community. This black magic is so potent that it can create deeply-held negative feelings against people that last for decades.

In general, anything that involves talking behind a person's back or sharing information about them that is personal or intimate without their explicit permission should be considered gossip, regardless of whether it is fact or rumor. Discussions of personal or family problems in the community should remain between those who are directly involved.

While there is plenty of room for open discussion and debate in any healthy community, any serious disagreements should be handled by the parties sitting down and talking to each other directly; complaining to those not involved only creates more strife and division.

Gossip is so common in modern media and culture that you will probably have to make a conscious effort to avoid it. Monitor what you say about others to make sure you are not letting gossip slip in. Also make it a policy to refuse to listen to gossip coming from others. This even includes those who try to use a time of prayer requests as an excuse to gossip about somebody in the guise of praying for them. If you are among other Believers, gently remind them of what the Bible says about gossip. If they will not stop, you should simply leave.

Avoid talking about another person's character when he or she is not present, except in cases where it is required to fulfill a legitimate responsibility, such as parents talking about their children or leaders discussing how to solve a problem in the community. When you must speak about someone's character with them absent, make sure you do so in a sacred manner. In cases where you must discuss the character of someone who is not present, you should talk to that person afterward, letting him or her know what you discussed and why.

A community of Believers should have no tolerance for gossip, and should actively root it out and expose it when it happens. Once gossipers begin to be brought before the entire community to account for their words, those with no interest in following the Bible's commands against gossiping will most likely decide to go elsewhere.

Blessing Those Who Curse You

One of the most powerful uses of invocation, and one of the hardest to put into practice, is to learn to speak blessings to those who throw hateful and intentionally damaging words in your face. The natural reaction of your sinful nature is to respond in kind, returning hateful words in response.

Jesus teaches in *Luke 6:27-36* that you are to instead speak blessings back to those who curse you, that you should pray for those who cast hatred and abuse on you. In this way, you demonstrate to them the mercy and love God has shown to you and defuse the power of their words so they can no longer harm you.

The Power of Listening

The act of truly listening contains a kind of power that complements and balances the power of the tongue. Listening forms the other half of the sacred space of conversation. Try to listen to others with a depth and intensity that makes them feel as if they are being fully heard. When another person is speaking, concentrate first on being present with their words and understanding them; don't think about what you will say in reply until they have finished speaking.

Listening in this way creates the kind of space that allows people to open up and share what they have been needing to get out into words, both the good and the bad. Allowing people to tell their stories can produce deep healing, but this can only happen when you provide a welcoming space for these stories to be heard so that people will feel safe to tell them.

If you listen to how a person talks about other people to you, soon you will get an excellent idea of how they talk about you to others when you aren't there.

Social media acts as an amplifier for whatever you choose to invoke with your words, spreading it widely in a short time. Anything posted online can be almost impossible to totally erase, and can follow a person for years. Some people have used this power to intentionally attack others, spreading malicious gossip or rumors, or posting embarrassing materials intended to destroy their reputation. In a number of cases, these attacks have been so powerful that they have driven people to kill themselves because they could see no other way out of the situation. In a very literal sense, this is an example of one person casting black magic incantations so powerful and damaging that they drive their target to suicide.

Although you should be careful to not engage in gossip, it is appropriate to warn members of your community of someone who poses a legitimate danger. Just be sure you are dealing with facts and not speculation. Never accuse anyone in your community unless you take the time to be absolutely certain of the facts. Once you are certain, bring the problem to the attention of the elders in the community so that it can be handled properly.

Compline

Reading: *Proverbs 10:11-21*

Reflection: Have you used the power of your tongue wisely today? Has it been a blessing or a curse to those around you?

Prayer: Use your finest words to praise God for what He has done and for who He is. Give Him thanks for all He has given you.

READING #1 - MATTHEW 12:33-37

Preparation:

- Calm your mind and take a few deep breaths
- Start with a Prayer of Thanksgiving
- Continue with the prayer, *"Lord Jesus Christ, may my words today call forth Your love and grace into a world in need of peace."*

Lectio:

Day 2

Try reading the scripture aloud each day this week and notice the power of God's Word when spoken.

"Make a tree good and its fruit will be good,
or make a tree bad and its fruit will be bad,
for a tree is recognized by its fruit.
You brood of vipers, how can you who are evil say anything good?
For out of the overflow of the heart the mouth speaks.
The good man brings good things out of the good stored up in him,
and the evil man brings evil things out of the evil stored up in him.
But I tell you that men will have to give account on the day of judgment
for every careless word they have spoken.
For by your words you will be acquitted, and by your words you will be condemned."

- *Matthew 12:33-37 (NIV)*

Meditatio:

Have your words this week called forth that which is good or that which is evil? Do you speak carelessly, letting words issue forth without considering their consequences? Or do you guard your tongue with care so that everything that comes out of your mouth will be a blessing? When you give an account of your words, will you be condemned by them, or acquitted of wrongdoing?

Oratio:

Pray that you will have wisdom to guard your tongue, using the power of your thoughts and words to bring forth that which is good and holy.

Contemplatio:

This week we begin to think about how to practice _Contemplatio_ while walking. Most people move through the world accompanied by a constant interior dialog, their thoughts always chattering away as a continuous steam of words and images in their heads. As you move always closer to living with an unbroken sense of God's presence, you must learn to spend more and more of your time in the silence that is God's first language. In this way, you learn to listen to God in all things. When you need them, words arise within you, but you then return to the silence once the need is over.

Spend your time of _Contemplatio_ today experimenting with walking while you let go of your thoughts and focus your intention on God's presence in silence. Open up your physical senses and let the world around you bring your attention to the Creator. Don't get discouraged if you find this hard on your first attempt. Simply relax and take a stroll, enjoying God's presence in the world He created.

Benediction:

- Return slowly and peacefully from _Contemplatio_
- Take time to be thankful again
- Acknowledge that you have completed your time for today and ask God to go with you as you leave this time.

If weather and safety permit, try walking barefoot during Contemplatio _this week. Going without shoes opens up your feet and lets them touch the earth, sensing the landscape as you walk over it._

Also try to walk through your neighborhood each day this week instead of simply sticking to the area around your personal spot. You will find the practice more rewarding if you are actually going someplace instead of just walking around in a small space.

Compline

Reading: _2 Timothy 2:14-17_

Reflection: Did you use your words today to make idle chatter or engage in arguments that really don't matter? Or did you use your words wisely, to speak the truth with kindness?

Prayer: Confess those ways in which you have not used your tongue wisely today.

Week 11

READING #2 - JAMES 3:1-12

Preparation:

- Calm your mind and take a few deep breaths
- Start with a Prayer of Thanksgiving
- Continue with the prayer, *"Lord Jesus Christ, may my words today call forth Your love and grace into a world in need of peace."*

Lectio:

Day 3

This passage is an example of the word *tongue* being used to mean the seat of discursive thought. It would be difficult to understand how to interpret this passage if you tried to use *tongue* to simply mean spoken words. If spoken words were the source of the problem, then it could be addressed simply by taking a vow of silence. Resorting to not speaking, however, will not fix the words and images that rage through your mind and that ultimately become the source for what you say aloud.

Not many of you should become teachers, my brothers and sisters, for you know that we who teach will be judged with greater strictness. For all of us make many mistakes. Anyone who makes no mistakes in speaking is perfect, able to keep the whole body in check with a bridle. If we put bits into the mouths of horses to make them obey us, we guide their whole bodies. Or look at ships: though they are so large that it takes strong winds to drive them, yet they are guided by a very small rudder wherever the will of the pilot directs. So also the tongue is a small member, yet it boasts of great exploits. How great a forest is set ablaze by a small fire! And the tongue is a fire. The tongue is placed among our members as a world of iniquity; it stains the whole body, sets on fire the cycle of nature, and is itself set on fire by hell. For every species of beast and bird, of reptile and sea creature, can be tamed and has been tamed by the human species, but no one can tame the tongue—a restless evil, full of deadly poison. With it we bless the Lord and Father, and with it we curse those who are made in the likeness of God. From the same mouth come blessing and cursing. My brothers and sisters, this ought not to be so. Does a spring pour forth from the same opening both fresh and brackish water? Can a fig tree, my brothers and sisters, yield olives, or a grapevine figs? No more can salt water yield fresh.

- James 3:1-12 (NRSV)

Meditatio:

The tongue can only be tamed through submission to the Holy Spirit. In what situations do you have the most difficultly controlling your tongue? What emotion or desire creates the urge to use your tongue in an unfit way? How can you break the cycle of misusing your words in this situation?

Oratio:

Give the power of your tongue to the Holy Spirit in a prayer of submission. Confess any way that you have been using the power of your words in a way that creates hurt or division.

Contemplatio:

Take a walk again today during your Contemplatio time. If you watch and listen to the created order, you will soon discover a pace of walking that seems to match the natural pace of nature. If you walk too fast, you seem to send out ripples of disturbance that get reflected back to you by the behavior of the birds and animals. If you slow down to a more natural pace, these ripples of disturbance disappear.

Walking barefoot will encourage you to slow down and open up your senses. If possible, walk in an area where your feet can touch the grass or the bare earth instead of asphalt or concrete.

As you walk, try not to carry an agenda with you. You aren't trying to get someplace on a schedule; you are wandering gently through God's creation and enjoying His presence. Don't set out trying to walk around the block or to get to some place in particular. Let your route unfold as you go, always following the sense of God's presence. In each moment, let the wordless inner pull of the Holy Spirit guide your next steps. Remember to breathe deeply as you walk. With each breath, let go of your own thoughts and any agenda you might be carrying. For these few moments, walk with God in the timeless silence of His presence.

Benediction:

- Return slowly and peacefully from *Contemplatio*
- Take time to be thankful again
- Acknowledge that you have completed your time for today and ask God to go with you as you leave this time.

Compline

Reading: *James 1:19-27*

Reflection: Have you been using your words with integrity? Do the things you say and the things you do match up? Would those around you ever say you have acted like a hypocrite, saying one thing but doing another?

Prayer: Express your desire to God to have integrity in your words and actions, always acting in accordance with what you profess to believe.

READING #3 - 1 TIMOTHY 5:13

Preparation:

- Calm your mind and take a few deep breaths
- Start with a Prayer of Thanksgiving
- Continue with the prayer, *"Lord Jesus Christ, may my words today call forth Your love and grace into a world in need of peace."*

Lectio:

Day 4

In this passage, Paul is addressing the problem of younger women who have become widowed and are being supported by the church. He notes that many of them use this support as an excuse to go from house to house spreading gossip. Even though this passage is specifically speaking about widows, the principal of avoiding being a gossip or busybody applies to all Believers equally.

Besides that, they learn to be idle, gadding about from house to house;
and they are not merely idle, but also gossips and busybodies,
saying what they should not say.

- 1 Timothy 5:13 (NRSV)

Meditatio:

Are you ever guilty of spreading gossip about others? Do you ever find yourself using your spare time to talk about people behind their backs, or to speculate about other people's lives, even when it is none of your business? Why is this sometimes tempting? What could you do instead that would use your words to call forth good? When would it be better simply to remain silent?

Oratio:

Tell God about any habits you have of talking about others in a way that does not honor them or call forth what is sacred. Make a commitment to not talk about others behind their backs, and to not listen to those who do.

Contemplatio:

Most people who wear modern footwear learn the habit of walking with the heel striking the ground first, instead of landing on the ball of the foot as is more natural. This way of walking also leads to the habit of looking down at the ground as you walk so that you won't lose your balance. You will find it difficult to remain in the silence if you walk heavily on your heels and look down as you go.

Start today by standing with your eyes looking out at the horizon in wide-angle vision, taking in the landscape around you. When you begin to walk, you may find your eyes want to drop back down to the ground. Gently resist this urge and keep your eyes looking out at the horizon. Starting very slowly, reach out with the ball of your foot and find the ground ahead of you, letting you foot sense where to let your weight rest. Softly place each foot down as you go, trusting your body to find a safe place for each step as you walk silently before God.

Walking with your eyes up and using your foot to sense the ground may seem awkward at first, but this way of moving makes it much easier to keep your mind attuned to God's presence instead of collapsing inward toward its own thoughts. If you find this difficult, try practicing barefoot in the grass.

Benediction:

- Return slowly and peacefully from *Contemplatio*
- Take time to be thankful again
- Acknowledge that you have completed your time for today and ask God to go with you as you leave this time.

Compline

Reading: *Proverbs 16:27-28*

Reflection: Has your speech today brought people together or created strife and separation?

Prayer: Be thankful that God has given you the gift of speech so that you can bring healing and peace instead of pain and strife.

READING #4 - MATTHEW 18:15-20

Preparation:

- Calm your mind and take a few deep breaths
- Start with a Prayer of Thanksgiving
- Continue with the prayer, "*Lord Jesus Christ, may my words today call forth Your love and grace into a world in need of peace.*"

Lectio:

Day 5

"If another member of the church sins against you, go and point out the fault when the
two of you are alone. If the member listens to you, you have regained that one.
But if you are not listened to, take one or two others along with you, so that every
word may be confirmed by the evidence of two or three witnesses.
If the member refuses to listen to them, tell it to the church;
and if the offender refuses to listen even to the church,
let such a one be to you as a Gentile and a tax collector.
Truly I tell you, whatever you bind on earth will be bound in heaven,
and whatever you loose on earth will be loosed in heaven.
Again, truly I tell you, if two of you agree on earth about anything you ask,
it will be done for you by my Father in heaven.
For where two or three are gathered in my name, I am there among them."

- Matthew 18:15-20 (NRSV)

In this context, when Jesus says that you are to treat someone who refuses to accept correction like *a Gentile or tax collector*, He means that they should be treated as one who refuses to accept God Himself. Anyone who refuses to repent once a sin has been made known to them is disobeying God's direct command.

Meditatio:

Do you go and talk to a person directly when you have been wronged, or do you complain about it to others? How should you handle such a situation? How should the community of Believers react when one of its members falls into sin? What is the spiritual authority we have when we come together to deal with sin and call others to repentance?

Oratio:

Pray that God would give you an open heart to receive correction when you have sinned or wronged another person. Pray also that you would be able to act with wisdom and gentleness when you must deal with someone who has wronged you.

What a sinner needs is life, not some sublime thought. A believer needs whatever can nourish his spiritual life, not mere Bible knowledge. If all we communicate are excellent sermonic divisions, wonderful parables, transcendent abstractions, clever words, or logical arguments, we are but supplying additional thoughts to the people's minds, arousing their emotions once again, or activating their will to make one more decision. A sinner needs to have his spirit resurrected, not to be able to argue better, shed profuse tears, or make a firmer resolve.

- Watchman Nee

Contemplatio:

As you walk with the Lord today, reach out with your ears and listen to the sounds of Creation that surround you. Remember to keep your eyes up on the horizon in wide-angle vision and use your feet to sense where you are stepping. Once you have established your pattern of walking so that you can comfortably step without looking down, shift your focus for a moment to the world of sound and notice what God is doing in the landscape you are moving through.

Listen to the response of the birds as you move past them. Do they calmly accept your presence, or do they complain as you come close? If the birds show alarm at your presence, try slowing down even more. Make sure to keep your wide-angle vision and remember to breathe in your slow, deep pattern. Each time a thought arises, use your sacred word to let it go and move back into the silence. Be gentle with yourself if you find this difficult. Learning to carry a quiet inner attention on God's presence with you as you walk takes time.

Benediction:

- Return slowly and peacefully from *Contemplatio*
- Take time to be thankful again
- Acknowledge that you have completed your time for today and ask God to go with you as you leave this time.

Compline

Reading: *1 Peter 1:22-25*

Reflection: As a follower of Christ, you carry with you God's words of truth that will endure forever. Have you used the power of these words wisely today? Have you shared them with those who need them?

Prayer: Be thankful for the words of truth you have been given to share with those in need.

READING #5 - 1 PETER 4:11

Preparation:

- Calm your mind and take a few deep breaths
- Start with a Prayer of Thanksgiving
- Continue with the prayer, "*Lord Jesus Christ, may my words today call forth Your love and grace into a world in need of peace.*"

Day 6

Lectio:

If anyone speaks, he should do it as one speaking the very words of God.
If anyone serves, he should do it with the strength God provides,
so that in all things God may be praised through Jesus Christ.
To him be the glory and the power for ever and ever. Amen.

- 1 Peter 4:11 (NIV)

Meditatio:

How would your use of your tongue change if you made sure that every time you spoke, you spoke as if it were the very words of God being spoken through you? How would your words change? What sort of things would you no longer say? In what situations would you speak where you now remain silent?

Oratio:

> Give yourself to the Holy Spirit to be a vessel through which He can speak words of love and peace into the world.

> *The mark of solitude is silence, as speech is the mark of community. Silence and speech have the same inner correspondence and difference as do solitude and community. One does not exist without the other. Right speech comes out of silence, and right silence comes out of speech.*
>
> - Dietrich Bonhoeffer

Contemplatio:

Begin today's time of *Contemplatio* by re-establishing your pattern of walking slowly and gently on the balls of your feet while keeping your eyes up in wide-angle vision. Once you are comfortable with this, reach out with your ears again to listen to the world of sound surrounding you. Finally, when you have your eyes and ears fully engaged, add your other senses until you are fully present with what is happening in God's Creation.

Notice the feel of the air moving past your skin as you walk. Notice the temperature and humidity, along with any breeze or wind moving the air around you. Smell and taste the air as well, noticing any scent the wind is carrying to you. Reach out with your spiritual sense and feel the rhythm of God's hand at work, guiding and holding all things together. Return to your sacred word when needed to help you release words or images that come into your mind. As you breathe, allow each exhale to relax you further into the dynamic stillness of walking with God.

> As you walk, open your senses by taking off your shoes and removing unneeded layers of clothes that keep you isolated from experiencing Creation. Even if it is a little bit cold or wet, challenge yourself not to hide behind many layers of clothes that cut you off from the Earth.

> ### Compline
>
> **Reading**: *Acts 19:11-20*
>
> **Reflection**: How have you been using the authority that comes with bearing the name of Christ? Do your words flow from the power of the Holy Spirit within you or from your own thoughts and desires?
>
> **Prayer**: Ask that the word of God might flow forth from you and be a blessing to the world.

Benediction:

- Return slowly and peacefully from *Contemplatio*
- Take time to be thankful again
- Acknowledge that you have completed your time for today and ask God to go with you as you leave this time.

REFLECTION

Revisit Your Favorite Passage

Day 7

Reflections on the Week

We first read *Psalm 66* during *Compline* for Week 6. Each time you revisit a passage, you will find that the Spirit teaches you something new. As you read back over this psalm, notice particularly the ways in which we are called to use the power of the spoken word.

Compline

Reading: *Psalm 66:1-20*

Reflection: Have you used your tongue as an instrument of peace this week? Have the words of your lips blessed God and provided light to those in darkness?

Prayer: Address your words to God tonight in a prayer of blessing and thanksgiving.

WEEK 12 - COMMUNION

This is the message we have heard from him and proclaim to you, that God is light and in him there is no darkness at all.
If we say that we have fellowship with him while we are walking in darkness, we lie and do not do what is true;
but if we walk in the light as he himself is in the light, we have fellowship with one another,
and the blood of Jesus his Son cleanses us from all sin.

-1 John 1:5-7 (NRSV)

ALTHOUGH THE WORD *COMMUNION* IS MOST OFTEN USED in the Christian church to refer to the sacrament of sharing a meal together, the broader meaning of the word is actually a concept about which the Bible has much to say. *Communion* is another word which comes from Latin and literally means "a oneness created out of mutual participation." The sacrament of sharing together the bread and the wine reminds us of the larger things we share as Believers: the forgiveness of sin through Christ's sacrifice and a call to return to a whole relationship with our Creator. Christian communion is the fellowship of those who share in the Holy Spirit because they have participated in the covenant of the body and blood of Christ Jesus.

The Church is one body with Jesus Himself as the head. The Church is the communion of all those who follow Christ living together in this world, supporting each other, working together, eating together, and praying together. What most people think of as "church" is actually just the weekly gathering of their one small part of that community to worship, encourage each other, and participate in a time designed to celebrate the experiences of the rest of the week when the real life of the community happens.

When we live together as the Bible intends, this communion of Believers grows and is enriched through both phases of the daily cycle of life and liturgy: as we walk together each day through the joys and challenges of life, and as we meet together corporately in times of worship and reflection. Many people today are searching for this promise of Biblical community but finding it hard to realize. Those who have grown up lacking communion have never experienced a model of what community looks like or feels like, and thus don't know how to achieve it.

Simply pushing together a group of people who like the idea of having community will only create conflict and division if they do not work together through the leading of the Spirit and follow the Bible's principles for how to walk together on the spiritual journey. To again find the communion that God called us to have, we must first relearn the patterns of community and learn to live selflessly with each other. The precepts we study throughout the last eight weeks of this book are an important part of God's blueprint for building *shalom* among His children.

As we think about carrying the communion of Christ into the world with us, it is appropriate that we continue to work on walking during *Contemplatio* this week. We are called to take the peace and healing we find in our times alone with God and carry them with us as we go into the world, sharing them with those in our community of faith, and with those who have yet to hear the call of the Holy Spirit and follow.

Extra Mile:

Do a "technology fast" this week by not using computers, televisions, cell phones, video games or other modern devices unless required by school or work. Spend all the time you would have spent with technology with a family member, mentor, or friend.

THE COMMUNION OF BELIEVERS

The first few precepts we studied, such as integrity and peace, spoke mostly to what we must each do individually to support peace in our community. As we continue to move forward through the precepts, they shift increasingly toward those things that God has commanded us to do together as the body of Christ.

Day 1

The sacrament that Jesus shared with His disciples just before His death has been called a variety of names by different denominations and groups over the years, even as they have argued about what exactly it means to share in the body and blood of Christ. In addition to being called *Holy Communion*, the name *Eucharist* is often used, which arises from the Greek word meaning *thanksgiving* used in *Matthew 26:27*. The name *Lord's Supper*, from *1 Corinthians 11:20*, is also common.

The followers of Christ in the first century often endured hardships as a result of their faith—many times meeting together secretly to avoid persecution or even death—but, as the stories throughout the book of *Acts* show, the result of these hardships was that they banded together as a community to support each other in a way that is almost unheard of in modern churches today. They sold their possessions and shared all things in common, making sure that everyone in the community was fed and provided for. They met together in each other's houses and shared meals together. They prayed together daily, seeking to know God intimately.

Today, we have invested in mega-churches, multi-million dollar buildings, and luxury resort-style church camps, yet many who come to these churches feel more isolated and alone than ever before. Often, the fancy buildings and cutting-edge programming don't serve to build community, but instead threaten to distract us from the simple, quiet spaces that are created between people when the community focuses first on the fellowship of daily life lived together in God's presence. Through the shared journey of walking the world's byways together in search of God's kingdom, the Spirit builds the bonds of family between God's children.

The communion of Believers creates a safe space in which you can share the innermost parts of your spiritual journey with those who God has made your brothers and sisters. Whenever God's children begin to live together in this way, the Spirit responds by teaching them to minister peace one to the other, so the wounds and fears that they each carry may be healed.

Living in Communion

God designed us such that our inner selves are satisfied with nothing less than searching to know Him in all His mystery, and to seek Him in the company of others who feel the same longing. Psychologists have observed for decades that modern cities are increasingly suffering from an epidemic of loneliness, as more and more individuals find themselves unable to connect or feel accepted, even when surrounded by throngs of people.

Many of the stories found in television and movies teach the idea that those who are strong practice a kind of rugged individualism, going it alone and never showing weakness. Those who try to live out this image find themselves afraid to ask anyone for anything, pushing down and hiding their own feelings until they are cut off from the possibility of real friendships. They become surrounded by acquaintances with whom they exchange safe but shallow chatter, instead of making lasting friendships which provide the mutual support God intended.

God calls for you to find a wise balance between taking personal responsibility for your own spiritual journey and seeking the support of your community of faith to walk with you along the way. The problem is that Christian communion only happens when there is no separation between those in your community during daily life. Communion can't happen between people who only see each other an hour or two each week, or between those who don't develop enough trust to be open and vulnerable with each other.

Those in your community must work together, eat together, and prepare food for each other as an act of spiritual service if the community is to function as God designed. In a healthy community, members naturally extend hospitality to each other, sharing their homes and possessions freely. The love of Christ teaches us to see past our differences to care deeply for each other and to care for each other's needs. In this way, we learn to accept each other, warts and all. A group that calls itself a church where this isn't happening or where members are locked into cycles of pain and loneliness, feeling unable to reach out for help, is lacking in communion. A church where people feel judged or unwanted instead of loved is not a real church.

The practice of the community meeting together for times of liturgy and worship are the other part of the cycle of communion that balances the experience of living everyday life together. Gathering together with other Believers for times of corporate worship is important, but going to a service once a week will not, by itself, create community; it can only reinforce the community that is being formed elsewhere. Imagine trying to keep a family healthy if the members only saw each other for an hour a week, and then only to sit together silently and listen to someone else speak. The relationships that knit together a community of faith are the same: they require intentional time spent together to form and weave together into something strong and lasting.

It doesn't help that most church buildings are designed with an architecture that encourages non-participation, where everyone sits quietly in rows and watches what happens up on the stage. With most of the time spent listening passively, many people attend church services for years and never really talk to anybody other than to exchange a few pleasantries.

Bible studies and other church-based activities with groups small enough to allow everyone to be involved and get to know each other can be better at supporting and building the community, but even these smaller groups can fall short if they do not foster relationships that carry forward into everyday life. An hour or two a week is no substitute for day-by-day.

A Shared Story of Grace

The communion of all those who follow Jesus comes, at its root, from the story we all share of receiving God's gift of forgiveness through Christ's sacrifice on our behalf, through our sharing in the grace bought for us by the body and blood of Christ. The fact that we share the experience of receiving God's forgiveness binds us together and gives us a common story, even if we come from very different backgrounds. Just as the people of Israel shared the story of the Passover and of being delivered from slavery in Egypt, and were bound together as a people and a nation by this experience, we who follow Christ share the story of being delivered from sin and are bound together by the indwelling of the Holy Spirit, who leads us out of our blindness and into all truth.

This shared story of grace is what binds us as Believers together as one family, regardless of differences in age, race, denomination, or any of the other artificial divisions created by the human mind. Even as different parts of the family practice the rituals and ceremonies of our faith in different ways, this shared story allows us to all find common ground and common purpose.

God's faithfulness and provision weaves over time a unique story of grace particular to each community of faith—a story that grows and deepens with each passing generation, creating a legacy that becomes part of the spiritual heritage of the community. *Psalms 145:4* tells us that each generation carries the responsibility of sharing their stories of God's mercy and grace with the next. The elders must take the time to tell the stories of place and community—of how God has blessed and provided for them and their forefathers—to the younger generations, so that each generation learns and carries forward these stories to share with their own children.

Hospitality & Sharing Meals

A common complaint among modern Christians in the developed world is that a sense of community seems somehow elusive, that the kind of meaningful connections to other Believers that they seek seems difficult or impossible to form. The problem is that relationships that grow only out of casual social contact rarely form ties strong enough to withstand the pressures the world uses to try to tear them apart. A community of faith must meet real needs—physical, emotional,

Larger church congregations must be even more careful about welcoming those new to the community and helping them become connected and involved. Individuals can easily feel lost when walking into a big building with lots of people. In a smaller group, visitors are easier to recognize and welcome, but in a larger group they can easily go unnoticed. Those who come to visit should find people who want to sit and have a real conversation with them, not just shake their hand and say hello in passing.

For Jewish families around Jesus' time, the sharing together of dinner was an important aspect of family and community life. The father would pray and lead songs around the dinner table, and would share teachings from the scripture after the meal. The early Christians carried forward this understanding of the importance of sharing meals as an act of hospitality and spiritual fellowship. In the early church, the Lord's Supper would have often been a full meal during which the elements of the bread and the cup were included, thus bringing the remembrance of Christ's sacrifice into the daily life of the community.

Although many translations of *Acts 2:46* say *they broke bread at home*, the original Greek literally says that *they broke bread from house to house*. The picture is of the families of the first-century Church opening their homes to each other, inviting each other to come and eat as a common practice, using the opportunity of making and serving meals for each other as an act of spiritual fellowship and service.

The way the term *elder* is used here does not simply mean any person of advanced age. An elder is someone who has been on the spiritual journey for many years and has learned through personal experience to hear the voice of the Spirit, and through listening to this voice has received wisdom that God intends to be shared with the entire community. Don't simply label anyone over a certain age as an elder; look for those whose words and actions reflect the wisdom gained through a life spent seeking to hear and follow God's calling.

Larger communities need to allow for people to feel connected to a small cross-generational group in which they can invest themselves. A community group of more than about 50 people starts to feel too spread apart. People don't feel safe sharing deeply with each other if the group is so large they can't get to know and trust everyone.

spiritual and practical—in order to create something that weaves deep connections between its members. A community that doesn't address the physical and practical needs first will have a hard time dealing with the emotional and spiritual dimensions which are often thought of as the primary focus of the Church. If a community doesn't have structures to allow its members to support each other with such fundamental needs such as food, water, and shelter, then it will almost certainly fail in its spiritual mission as well.

The model for this kind of fellowship is seen in the description of the first-century Church found in passages such as *Acts 2:42-47*. The members of this early community of Believers shared their homes and possessions freely, living and working together, supporting each other both through prayer and physical means to ensure that everyone's needs were met.

This depth of sharing and mutual support grew out of a spiritual desire to be like Christ, not from an imposed political or social structure. For those who follow Christ, eating together becomes an act of spiritual fellowship, the making and serving of meals becomes an act of spiritual service, and the hospitality of opening your home to others becomes a picture of Christ's love made practical and visible.

Communion Across Generations

Many churches, in an effort to break down their members into age and demographic groups that can be more effectively targeted with programs and activities, tend to overlook the importance of the inter-generational web of relationships that God intends to exist in a healthy community. These connections across generations allow people of every age and life situation to be in service to each other, to share together their diversity of life experiences, and to bring to the community the unique gifts and abilities that come with each stage of life.

When space is created for these relationships to be nurtured and honored, the entire community of faith is strengthened. The elders build meaningful relationships with the children and youth, so their wisdom is passed on. The youth and college students find mentoring relationships with adults who act as an extended family of aunts and uncles. The children develop big brother and big sister relationships with the youth from other families.

It is important that these communities are set up on a human scale so that people don't get lost in the crowd. Every community of more than a few dozen people should help its members get together into smaller cross-generational groups comprised of people who live physically close together, encouraging them to meet together and support each other day by day.

Looking Inward & Reaching Outward

There is a wise balance between a community of faith looking inward to grow its own members and reaching outward to share the gospel with the world. When a community becomes overly focused on being evangelistic, it almost always fails to spend enough energy ministering to its own members, mentoring them, and helping them heal. If you get the community right, the evangelism will follow naturally.

The most effective testimony is the life of a person who is walking a path in search of knowing God intimately. As the Holy Spirit allows those who follow God to see the spiritual needs of others through His eyes, they will almost automatically begin to minister to those around them, both within their community of faith and in the world beyond. God's love should flow organically outward from the entire community, not just from those few called as professional ministers.

Judging & Discerning

One of the major challenges of living together in communion with other Believers is learning how to handle each other's faults and shortcomings wisely. Everyone who seeks to follow Christ needs, from time to time, the council and correction of others who also listen to the voice of the Holy Spirit. A critical dimension of communion is allowing space for this kind of sacred responsibility one toward the other, creating a space in which we deal with each other's sinfulness in a gentle but firm way that is a concrete expression of Jesus' love.

Communities often try to gloss over this need for mutual accountability among its members by using passages such as *Matthew 7:1-5*, in which Jesus warns about judging others, to discourage the practice of discernment and spiritual correction. This hesitancy to encourage Believers to become involved in each other's spiritual journey is partly caused by the degree of wisdom and sensitivity that it requires, but also grows out of a confusion between what it means to judge versus discern when dealing with other people.

To judge is to look down upon or pass sentence on a person because of their actions or social position. Discerning, in contrast, is the process of the Spirit allowing you to see God's perspective on a situation or to clearly see another person's spiritual needs so that you know best how to pray for or minister to them. Jesus taught that we are not to judge others, but instead to use the discernment provided by the Holy Spirit to deal with each other's burdens from a place of wisdom and gentleness.

God provided many passages in scripture (such as nearly all of the book of 1 John) that clearly outline the differences between those who truly follow Christ and those who merely claim to believe. These passages, plus the insights provided by the Spirit, are designed to allow you to discern between those who are your spiritual brothers and sisters, and those who are not. This ability to discern who is truly part of your spiritual family is given by the Spirit so you can use wisdom in protecting yourself from the influence of those who falsely claim to speak for Christ, so you can minister God's love to those who have not yet found a relationship with Him, and so you can have confidence in building communion with those around you who also follow Christ.

Those Who Carry Christ's Name in Vain

The Bible warns in several places (such as *Matthew 18:15-20, 1 Corinthians 5:9-13*, and *2 Thessalonians 3:6-14*) that a community of Believers should not have fellowship with someone who claims to follow Christ but who refuses to follow His commands. Many churches today are weak because they tolerate members who claim to be followers of Christ, but who live in willful, habitual sin.

A community of Believers will be pulled apart and rendered ineffective if hypocrisy is allowed to go unaddressed. Handling these situations is one of the more difficult challenges a community of faith must address. It must be done with careful thought and much prayer, but it must not be ignored or the communion of the local church will be weakened.

Most communities don't have the stomach for the kind of spiritual discipline required to cut off fellowship with those who carry Christ's name in vain, since it involves dealing with sin in a real and personal way. This type of discipline can only happen in groups small enough that people can get to know each other and can be accountable to each other. If you do not have a formal church that is willing to practice accountability, try to find a small group of Believers who can covenant together to practice mutual accountability.

Family & Community

One of the most important roles of a community of faith is to provide support for the families of its members. Families with no supporting community are isolated and will struggle to survive. Without this support, conflict and stress can build inside of families, which will struggle to provide everything that God intended them to find through the extended family of their community of faith. Families whose church congregations function more as social outlets than as real communities will not have the support needed to overcome adversity and will risk falling prey to the world's attacks.

Our individual families are each part of the larger family of the Church. Since we as Believers are bound together through the communion of the Spirit, we should act like family, loving one another and caring for each other's needs. No member of the family should go hungry or lack any basic necessity when others in the community have all they need and more to spare.

Compline

Reading: *Proverbs 13:20*

Reflection: Who have you spent the most time with in the last week? Are you spending your time with those who are wise, or those who act foolishly?

Prayer: Be thankful for those who serve as examples of wisdom for you.

Reading #1 - Acts 2:42-47

As you think this week about the communion of those who follow Christ, offer your opening prayer on behalf of all those in your community, asking for oneness of spirit.

Day 2

Preparation:

- Calm your mind and take a few deep breaths
- Start with a Prayer of Thanksgiving
- Continue with the prayer, *"Lord Jesus Christ, may we be one in communion with You. Cleanse us of our unrighteousness so we may become one in fellowship with each other."*

Lectio:

They devoted themselves to the apostles' teaching and fellowship,
to the breaking of bread and the prayers.
Awe came upon everyone, because many wonders and signs were being done by the
apostles. All who believed were together and had all things in common;
they would sell their possessions and goods and distribute the proceeds to all,
as any had need.
Day by day, as they spent much time together in the temple,
they broke bread at home and ate their food with glad and generous hearts,
praising God and having the goodwill of all the people.
And day by day the Lord added to their number those who were being saved.

- Acts 2:42-47 (NRSV)

Meditatio:

How does the communion shared by the early Christians differ from how churches operate today? How often does your family share meals with other families in the church? How often do you share your possessions with those in the church who are in need? What does the world think about the modern Christian church? Why?

Oratio:

Pray for those in your community of faith, that they would become ever more sensitive to the call of the Holy Spirit to share with each other in the love of Christ.

Contemplatio:

As you continue the practice of walking during *Contemplatio* this week, remember to begin each day by establishing a slow walking rhythm that you can easily maintain while keeping your eyes up on the horizon in wide-angle vision. Relax your feet and ankles, letting them feel their way into each step as you land on the forward part of your foot and then smoothly transfer your weight once your foot is fully in contact with the ground.

If practical, go barefoot again this week as you practice walking during Contemplatio.

If you are having trouble slowing down your breathing while you walk, you might want to try linking your breathing to your walking rhythm by breathing in as you take three or four steps, and then breathing out on the next three or four steps. Make sure you keep your breathing soft and deep, taking the same amount of time on the inhale and exhale. If thoughts try to grab your attention, you may find it helpful to release them as you begin each exhalation. Set out today with no particular destination in mind. In each moment, simply follow the direction that seems to invite you deeper into the silence.

Benediction:

- Return slowly and peacefully from *Contemplatio*
- Take time to be thankful again
- Acknowledge that you have completed your time for today and ask God to go with you as you leave this time.

Compline

Reading: *1 Corinthians 5:1-13*

Reflection: Are you spending time with anyone who claims to be a follower of Christ, but who continues to live with willful sin? How would God have you handle this situation?

Prayer: Ask for wisdom in dealing with friends or family who are living hypocritically.

READING #2 - ROMANS 12:9-18

Preparation:

- Calm your mind and take a few deep breaths
- Start with a Prayer of Thanksgiving
- Continue with the prayer, "*Lord Jesus Christ, may we be one in communion with You. Cleanse us of our unrighteousness so we may become one in fellowship with each other.*"

Lectio:

Day 3

Love must be sincere. Hate what is evil; cling to what is good.
Be devoted to one another in brotherly love. Honor one another above yourselves.
Never be lacking in zeal, but keep your spiritual fervor, serving the Lord.
Be joyful in hope, patient in affliction, faithful in prayer.
Share with God's people who are in need. Practice hospitality.
Bless those who persecute you; bless and do not curse. Rejoice with those who rejoice;
mourn with those who mourn. Live in harmony with one another.
Do not be proud, but be willing to associate with people of low position.
Do not be conceited.
Do not repay anyone evil for evil.
Be careful to do what is right in the eyes of everybody.
If it is possible, as far as it depends on you, live at peace with everyone.

- Romans 12:9-18 (NIV)

Meditatio:

How well do you follow Paul's instructions from this passage in *Romans*? What would it look like today if a group of people actually lived together in a community that practiced all these principles?

Oratio:

> Be thankful that God has called us to live together in such a way as to support each other and carry each other's burdens. Ask for the courage to live as God calls you to live in today's scripture.

> *The full flowering of our relationship with God is somewhat like that of an elderly couple who have lived together for a long time, brought up the children, suffered together the ups and downs of daily life, and who really love each other. They don't have to talk all the time. They chat as they pour coffee in the morning, but they can also sit together and look at a sunset and just enjoy each other's company. They might hold hands or look at each other's eyes to maintain the sense of union. They have moved beyond conversation to communion.*
>
> - Father Thomas Keating

Contemplatio:

As you begin your walk today, choose a direction that will take you through a grove of trees if possible. A group of older trees is ideal, but even a single tree will be fine if that is all you have available. As you approach the trees and walk through them, use your wide-angle vision to watch any movement of the leaves created by the wind. Notice the changing patterns of light and shadow created by the play of the sunlight on the leaves, the movement caused by the wind, and your own motion as you walk.

Feel free to pause as you walk and simply stand in silence. Let the trees remind you that God created a time for everything: a time for moving and a time for standing still. Remember that the roots of the trees reach out in all directions under the earth and interlock with the roots of the other trees nearby. In this way, the trees support and stabilize each other. Let this image remind you of the support God designed for us to give each other as we live in His communion.

Benediction:

- Return slowly and peacefully from *Contemplatio*
- Take time to be thankful again
- Acknowledge that you have completed your time for today and ask God to go with you as you leave this time.

Compline

Reading: *Hebrews 13:1-5*

Reflection: Have your actions this week shown that you are more committed to your community, or to your own possessions and comfort?

Prayer: Confess to God any way in which you have put yourself first today when you knew that God was calling you to serve others in your community instead.

READING #3 - 2 THESSALONIANS 3:6-13

Preparation:

- Calm your mind and take a few deep breaths
- Start with a Prayer of Thanksgiving
- Continue with the prayer, "*Lord Jesus Christ, may we be one in communion with You. Cleanse us of our unrighteousness so we may become one in fellowship with each other.*"

Lectio:

Now we command you, beloved, in the name of our Lord Jesus Christ,
to keep away from believers who are living in idleness and not
according to the tradition that they received from us.
For you yourselves know how you ought to imitate us;
we were not idle when we were with you,
and we did not eat anyone's bread without paying for it;
but with toil and labor we worked night and day,
so that we might not burden any of you.
This was not because we do not have that right,
but in order to give you an example to imitate.
For even when we were with you, we gave you this command:
Anyone unwilling to work should not eat.
For we hear that some of you are living in idleness, mere busybodies, not doing any
work. Now such persons we command and exhort in the Lord Jesus Christ
to do their work quietly and to earn their own living.
Brothers and sisters, do not be weary in doing what is right.

- 2 Thessalonians 3:6-13 (NRSV)

Meditatio:

Day 4

Does the community of Believers to which you belong tolerate those who refuse to follow the teachings of Christ or who are idle and refuse to work to support themselves or the community? What should your community do with those people who willfully continue to sin even after they are called to repentance by the community? What happens to a community of faith when it tolerates those who claim to follow Christ but who refuse to do as He commanded?

Oratio:

If you are hanging onto relationships with people who claim to be Christians but who habitually refuse to follow Christ's commandments, release these relationships and pray that the Holy Spirit would help you step away from these people with gentleness and humility.

Contemplatio:

The practice of walking while carrying an immediate sense of God's presence is an important step toward carrying peace and stillness with you out of your morning prayer time and into your community. As you go through the day, take those times when you are walking somewhere alone as an opportunity to return to the silence of *Contemplatio*, bringing your attention back to the working of the Holy Spirit in the world around you.

During your walk this morning, watch the birds as they move through the bushes and trees. Listen to their songs and calls as they communicate with each other. God has made all the creatures of the Earth to fit into the ecosystems for which He designed them. Even if you do not fully understand God's purposes, He has made all the pieces of His creation to fit together into His perfect plan. As you walk today, let go of your need to control or even fully understand what God is doing. It is enough that God walks with you.

Benediction:

- Return slowly and peacefully from *Contemplatio*
- Take time to be thankful again
- Acknowledge that you have completed your time for today and ask God to go with you as you leave this time.

Compline

Reading: *1 Corinthians 12:12-31*

Reflection: Are you ever guilty of being jealous of the gifts God has given to others? Are you using the gifts God has given you in the way that God intended?

Prayer: Release any jealousy of others to the Holy Spirit and ask that He would give you clarity as to how best to use your gifts.

READING #4 - HEBREWS 10:24-25

Day 5

Preparation:

- Calm your mind and take a few deep breaths
- Start with a Prayer of Thanksgiving
- Continue with the prayer, "*Lord Jesus Christ, may we be one in communion with You. Cleanse us of our unrighteousness so we may become one in fellowship with each other.*"

Lectio:

And let us consider how we may spur one another on toward love and good deeds.
Let us not give up meeting together, as some are in the habit of doing,
but let us encourage one another—and all the more as you see the Day approaching.

- Hebrews 10:24-25 (NIV)

Meditatio:

The practice of meeting together spoken of here is not simply the practice of going to church a couple of times a week. We are to make the meeting together with fellow Believers a practice that is integrated into our daily lives. Is your spiritual life limited only to the church building, or do you spend time with other Christians each day, encouraging each other and praying together when needed?

Oratio:

> Pray for those in your community with whom you are closest, that God would bless your friendships and use all of you to encourage each other as you travel together in your spiritual journeys.

> *I think I speak not too strongly when I say that a church in the land without the Spirit of God is rather a curse than a blessing. If you have not the Spirit of God, Christian worker, remember you stand in somebody else's way; you are a tree bearing no fruit, standing where another fruitful tree might grow.*
>
> - Charles Spurgeon

Contemplatio:

As you start your walk through your neighborhood today, think for a moment about how many of the people who live near you are part of your community of faith. If you are fortunate, you may be part of a community of people who live close enough together that you can support each other easily in dealing with the everyday issues of life. If you live in a more typical neighborhood, however, you may realize that you only have one or two families as part of your community who live within easy walking distance. God designed us to live together with our brothers and sisters in Christ, but the modern world seems to be designed to make this difficult.

As you walk, open up your skin to feel the touch of the sun and the wind. Let them remind you of God's unseen presence with you wherever you go, whether surrounded by other Believers or seemingly alone. Release your thoughts and bring your intention to being fully in God's timeless presence, which deepens the fellowship of all Believers, regardless of distance.

Benediction:

- Return slowly and peacefully from *Contemplatio*
- Take time to be thankful again
- Acknowledge that you have completed your time for today and ask God to go with you as you leave this time.

Compline

Reading: *1 Peter 4:7-10*

Reflection: Have you disciplined yourself to move past your own comfort zones to serve others in your community this week? Have you been a good steward of the grace of God?

Prayer: Bless God for the grace and mercy He has shown to you and allows you to show towards others.

READING #5 - DEUTERONOMY 6:20-25

Preparation:

- Calm your mind and take a few deep breaths
- Start with a Prayer of Thanksgiving
- Continue with the prayer, "*Lord Jesus Christ, may we be one in communion with You. Cleanse us of our unrighteousness so we may become one in fellowship with each other.*"

Lectio:

Day 6

When your children ask you in time to come,
"What is the meaning of the decrees and the statutes
and the ordinances that the LORD our God has commanded you?"
then you shall say to your children,
"We were Pharaoh's slaves in Egypt,
but the LORD brought us out of Egypt with a mighty hand.
The LORD displayed before our eyes great and awesome signs and wonders
against Egypt, against Pharaoh and all his household.
He brought us out from there in order to bring us in,
to give us the land that he promised on oath to our ancestors.
Then the LORD commanded us to observe all these statutes,
to fear the LORD our God, for our lasting good,
so as to keep us alive, as is now the case.
If we diligently observe this entire commandment before the LORD our God,
as he has commanded us, we will be in the right."

- Deuteronomy 6:20-25 (NRSV)

Meditatio:

What stories do you share with those who ask what God's promises mean to you? Can you tell the stories of God's love and grace in your life clearly and openly? Do you know the spiritual stories of your ancestors and of those who shared their faith with you so you could know Christ?

Oratio:

_____

Be thankful for the unbroken story of God's grace and mercy poured out to each generation, through which the message of salvation has been handed down to you. Accept God's calling for you to live out your own story of faith, through which He can bless generations yet to come.

Contemplatio:

Begin today by re-establishing your slow and relaxed rhythm of breathing and walking, keeping your eyes up in wide-angle vision and landing on the balls of your feet. Take a few moments as you begin your walk to notice the sensation of your body moving. Notice those places that are tight or where you are holding tension in your muscles or joints. Try to release any tension as you exhale on each breath. As you let go of tightness in your body, you will find your walking becomes more fluid and flowing.

Take time to pause during your walk today to close your eyes and be fully present in your body. A time of _Contemplatio_ is not defined by just sitting or walking; it is a dynamic process whereby you focus your full attention on God's presence and respond as His Spirit leads. You may find that you need to stand still or sit down, lie on the ground or dance with joy, run with all your might or walk quietly. As you meet with God today, let your body join with your mind and spirit in listening with your whole being and responding with nothing held back.

Benediction:

- Return slowly and peacefully from _Contemplatio_
- Take time to be thankful again
- Acknowledge that you have completed your time for today and ask God to go with you as you leave this time.

Week 12

Compline

Reading: _John 17:1-26_

Reflection: Does a sense of oneness exist in your community of Believers? Why or why not?

Prayer: Ask the Holy Spirit to surround you with a community of those who follow Christ with their whole hearts so that you might know the fellowship of those who share the body and blood of Christ.

REFLECTION

Revisit Your Favorite Passage

Day 7

Reflections on the Week

Compline

Reading: *Psalm 145:1-21*

Reflection: Have you spent any time this week learning from those who are elders in the faith? Have you spent any time sharing with those younger than you who are coming along the path of faith behind you?

Prayer: Pray that you would find ways to connect with those in the generations ahead of you and behind you so the legacy of your faith may remain unbroken.

WEEK 13 - UNITY

Therefore, as God's chosen people, holy and dearly loved,
clothe yourselves with compassion, kindness, humility, gentleness and patience.
Bear with each other and forgive whatever grievances you may have against one another.
Forgive as the Lord forgave you. And over all these virtues put on love, which binds them all together in perfect unity.

-Colossians 3:12-14 (NIV)

MODERN CULTURE TRAINS YOU TO SEE THE WORLD THROUGH STORIES where you yourself are the central focus, the chief protagonist around which everything else revolves. Your own personal wants and desires take center stage, and you begin to subconsciously cast everyone else as secondary characters in your own story. Soon, you find yourself interpreting events in terms of *I* instead of *We*. If you allow this kind of narrative to dominate your thinking, you will end up focused on what you want instead of what is best for your community.

Self-centered thought patterns are destructive not just to the community, but to the individuals who carry them, since in a community where everybody thinks of themselves first, nobody can get the spiritual, physical, and emotional support they need. The biblical picture of Christ's followers tells a much different story: of a people who love each other so much that they each make the welfare of the others in their community a central concern of their life. In such a community, each individual is fully cared for, their needs met, since the other members of the community provide them with constant support and love.

People often talk of wanting to regain the sense of community that they know has faded over the last few decades, as the technology that was promised to make life easier, give us more free time, and allow us to communicate more easily has instead left most of us more busy and disconnected than ever before, more self-absorbed, and more divided. Instead of looking at the root cause—the lack of the unifying story of Christ as a common ground for understanding the world and making group decisions—many communities of faith have wasted time experimenting with new programs and organizational gimmicks in an effort to solve these problems.

But unity cannot be created simply by fiddling around with outward forms. Unity in a fellowship of Believers comes from traveling the same path, led by the same Spirit, in search of the same God who awaits us at journey's end.

This communion of purpose, almost paradoxically, grows deepest and strongest as we each spend time alone daily, individually seeking to be one with Christ, just as He said that the Father and He were one. To set our intent even more firmly on finding unity with Christ, we will shift our attention inward this week during *Contemplatio*, turning down our physical senses and focusing exclusively on the spiritual sense of God with us and within us. When we find a unity of mind and purpose with Christ, we will then find a unity of purpose with each other, allowing God's love to move through us as a community of faith and bringing with it healing and peace.

Extra Mile:

Take time to visit an elder this week. Choose someone who is over sixty years old who has been on the journey of following Christ for many years. Go and spend time talking and sharing stories. Ask the elder to pray with you during your time together. If you are an elder yourself, go and visit a younger person, taking time to talk and pray with them.

UNITY

Day 1

God's call for unity among His children does not mean that we are to compromise on the core teachings of the Bible. We should certainly stand against groups that claim to carry the name of Christ but that distort or pervert the Bible's message. However, the sad truth is that many churches and denominations that seek to faithfully follow the scriptures, and who agree on practically all of the core elements of the faith, remain divided because of the human tendency to get stuck on the interpretation of details that are far less important than the core teachings of salvation through Christ. When it comes to these differences over minor issues of theology, we should accept that no one group has all the answers and get on with the work that God has called us to perform as His representatives here in this world, working together as one community instead of fighting among ourselves.

As the Roman Empire began to collapse during the fourth and fifth centuries, and the institutions that maintained the cultural and intellectual core of civilization fell apart with it, the newly emerging monastic orders slowly grew into the last refuges of order and stability throughout much of Europe. These monasteries helped sustain the Church through the Dark Ages and were ultimately responsible for saving and passing down the texts of the Bible, along with a great deal of other scientific and literary writings, through a period when little else survived. How was it that these monks, living together simply, growing their own food, and working with their hands, could hold together through such difficult times when everything was falling apart around them?

The answer seems to lie in the unity that these communities found through the shared story of God's purpose at work in them, both individually and collectively. History suggests that this kind of shared purpose is one of the only things that can sustain a community through such hardships. It also serves as a reminder that unity is often most difficult exactly when circumstances are the easiest, when we are not forced to depend so closely on each other and have the option of placing our own wants and desires above those of the community.

Building the communion that God intends requires that we work together in unity to follow Him, first through the valleys and trials of hardship and persecution, and then onward through an even greater test: along the easy paths lined with prosperity and abundance.

The Divisiveness of Denominations

Perhaps one of the biggest obstacles to the unity of the Church is the tendency of many people to put small matters of theology ahead of God's command that we love each other and care for each other. In many cases, denominations that agree on the essentials of the faith remain divided because they focus more on their differences than on the common story they share.

No church or denomination has a monopoly on God, and no human mind is capable of fully comprehending the truth of God's nature. What do we gain if we argue over fine points of theology but fail to follow God's plain and unmistakable commands to love each other? It is often easier to distract ourselves from the work God set before us by debating endlessly than it is to let go of our need for certainty and admit that our minds will never create a theology that fully wraps itself around the mysteries of the Spirit.

Chief Joseph, one of the leaders of the Nez Perce tribe during the nineteenth century, after watching the European settlers, said, "We do not want churches because they will teach us to quarrel about God, as the Catholics and Protestants do." Those of us who follow Christ should strive instead to be known to the world by the unity we find through the Spirit, putting this ahead of man-made distinctions of denomination or church membership.

The Unity of a Shared Story

Whenever Believers come together in an organized fashion to form a formal group such as a church or community, one of the most important practical questions that must be answered is how the group will govern itself. One solution that has been tried in recent years is to have leaders or committees make recommendations for the whole body to vote on in a democratic process. Another has been to invest the leadership with almost all the decision-making authority and ask the members to simply respect and follow the leadership's planning and guidance for the community.

Both of these approaches create major problems with building unity in a community of faith, and neither is reflective of the examples shown in the New Testament of how Believers should live together. Nowhere does scripture show a church or body of Believers being run as a democracy where everyone votes and a majority rules. This arrangement often creates division and friction among people as they pick sides and dig in to defend their positions instead of working together to understand everyone's concerns. The idea of running a church by majority vote comes from secular culture, not the Bible, and has resulted in many churches pulling themselves apart.

Similarly, the idea of a community being governed by a single individual or a small group is nowhere seen in the Bible. The scriptural picture of a leader in the church is of a servant and teacher who helps others along their spiritual journey, not that of a CEO running a business. There should be elders and leaders in the community whose voices carry weight in every major decision, but that should not replace the process of all members discussing and praying together to clearly discern the voice of the Spirit.

A community of Believers should instead strive to operate on the principle of unity. All members should be included whenever any major decision must be made, working through the question together until a consensus has been reached. The major challenge of working with the principal of unity is that it only works in a community where all members are committed followers of Jesus. If factions of non-Believers are allowed to participate in the decision-making processes of a community, they will destroy the ability of the community to come to unity.

Without the unity that comes from a shared story, people will almost always fail at consistently building a consensus, especially on difficult issues. In the late 1960's, many groups from the Hippie culture decided to form communes which would be governed by full consensus. Most estimates are that over 95% of these communes failed, due in part to the fact that the members were not ready to give up their own personal agendas. Once a few selfish people realized they could gain power by blocking all decisions until their demands were met, the process would become stuck and held hostage by a handful of individuals. The tyranny of the majority created by a democratic system was replaced by an effective tyranny of the minority.

Unity requires carefully considering who will be allowed to enter the fellowship of the community. Simply letting people join the community without getting to know them and understanding their commitment to the Faith means people will end up joining who do not have a covenant relationship with Christ, thus ensuring that consensus is not possible. Most Christian groups are unwilling to guard themselves in this way, thus opening themselves to non-Believers becoming members and destroying the possibility of creating unity in the community.

Listening to All Voices

Another important dimension of creating unity is the practice of listening to all voices. God chooses to speak to the community through different voices at different times, so no one person can become prideful. God sometimes uses the quiet, unassuming person to bring a message of importance to His people. The community of faith should create an environment in which all members feel safe speaking and making their voices heard. Listening to all voices slows things down and derails attempts by a few people to push through their own agendas.

A church in which the pastors and ministers meet behind closed doors or with committees and then tell the members what is to be done, or present finished programs for rubber-stamp approval will never create unity. Taking time to listen and build unity also allows time for the community to build a shared vision in which everyone feels included.

If a member of the community is not in a place of peace or is undergoing a period of traumatic grief, they should not participate in the decision-making process for the community until they can be restored. Meetings where the community must make important decisions are not the place to work out personal issues, seek attention, or process grief. The community should minister consolation and healing privately to those who need it, so they can be restored to peace.

Joining a church or other Christian community should, in principle, be the same as accepting the precepts we are discussing in this book, since all these precepts are based on commandments from the Bible. In practice, however, this is often not true. In many cases, communities are allowing people to join before the community has fully established their commitment to live according to Christ's teachings. If a community wishes to work toward unity in its decision-making, then everyone included in the process must have made a firm commitment to God's precepts for community, otherwise they will bring division into the process and destroy the unity of the group.

Achieving unity in a body requires more than just responding to the concerns of those who are brave enough to speak up in front of a large group. Unity is the active presence of agreement between everyone included, not just a lack of overt opposition. Building unity in this way requires that larger groups have some way to break down into smaller gatherings that are each small enough so that everyone feels free to join the conversation. Each small group can then choose a representative to bring their concerns to the larger body. When meetings grow larger than human scale, unity will not be possible.

One Body, Many Gifts

Don't worry too much about figuring out exactly which spiritual gifts God has given you; focus instead on what God is calling you to do. The Spirit will give you the gifts and abilities needed to accomplish whatever He intends for you to accomplish, many times developing new gifts and talents you never suspected you had. God will equip you to take on whatever task He sets before you, and will bless those who are faithful in using their gifts by pouring out even more gifts on them as a reward.

In his first letter to the church at Corinth, Paul addressed a problem that they were having with people becoming jealous of each other's gifts and talents. In explaining how to deal with this issue, Paul uses the image of the Church as one body with Jesus as the head and His followers making up the other parts. The Holy Spirit gives each member a unique collection of spiritual gifts with which to serve the rest of the body. Just as the body must have all its parts in order to operate correctly, all members of the community play a vital role. Paul tells them that, as they love each other, they will learn to celebrate each other's gifts instead of envy them.

For there to be peace in a community of faith, all members must be free to operate in the gifts the Spirit has given them. If a church is only organized to provide opportunities for service inside the structure of the church programs, it will not have places of service for many of its members since many of the gifts of the Spirit are meant to support the community in the context of everyday life.

God also gives you the capability to see and encourage the gifts of others. As the Spirit shows you the gifts of those in your community, pray for them and encourage them so that these gifts will develop as God intends.

Unity and Diversity

Because they are so emotionally involved, parents are often not the best qualified to identify and develop the gifts of their own children. Some parents become angry when it is suggested that the Holy Spirit might use other adults in the community to encourage and mentor their children, but this simply indicates that they are in danger of becoming so possessive of their children that they lose objectivity. In a healthy community, parents are supported by many other adults who use their discernment to help identify and encourage the gifts of the younger generation so that they grow and mature as God intends.

If you stop to consider the great diversity that God created when making the Earth, the amazing range of beautiful landscapes, the abundance of different cultures, you will quickly realize that God expresses His love and creativity in many varied ways. God also paints with a wide and expressive palette when it comes to how He teaches each of us to know Him and to express our unique relationship with Him while on our journey through this world.

Unity is a oneness of mind given by the Spirit that is often expressed in great diversity. God does not intend for us all to look the same, worship in the same way, or experience life in exactly the same way. We should embrace differences and diversity in the tastes, styles, and expressions of the members of our community, as well as those of other communities of faith, provided they flow from a deep desire to follow Christ.

Handling Disputes & Accusations

The next three sections address how to handle problems in a community that will threaten unity if not dealt with properly. *Handling Disputes & Accusations* talks about what to do if somebody in the community is accused of wronging somebody else. *Calling Another to Repentance* discusses how to handle a member of the community who is knowingly engaging in habitual sin. *Reconciliation* deals with how to restore unity between individuals or groups who have developed hostility towards each other.

Whenever one person in a community of faith has a dispute with another member, or accuses another of wrongdoing, care must be taken to follow the Bible's instructions on how to deal with the situation. First, no anonymous accusations should be allowed, since this encourages gossip and slander. As *Proverbs 18:17* points out, an accusation can seem convincing until both sides have been required to answer questions about what happened. If an accuser will not stand behind an accusation publicly, then the accusation should not be accepted.

According to *Deuteronomy 19:15-21* and *2 Corinthians 13:1*, accusations of wrongdoing require two or three witnesses to be considered proven, unless independent evidence is available. Accusations should be taken before the elders of the church so they can determine what has happened and how peace can be restored in the community. The evidence they hear must be based on first-hand knowledge of what happened, not on suspicions or gossip.

Disputes should not be made public until the truth is fully established and the elders have determined how best to involve the larger community in the process of healing.

Calling Another to Repentance

If another Believer in your community of faith is engaged in a pattern of habitual sin, then it is your responsibility, along with the other Believers in your community, to privately approach that person and call them to repentance. *Galatians 6:1* says that if anyone in a group of Believers is found to be in sin, then those who are spiritually mature in the community should go to them and work to restore them in a spirit of gentleness.

The responsibility we have of helping call each other to repentance must be handled with great humility and careful discernment. If you are part of a community that actually practices this level of accountability, then any time you are involved in helping another through their sin, simply remember that it may be your turn next. We are to bear each other's burdens, praying with each other and for each other, so that any sinfulness that would bring discord into the community of faith is addressed and all those involved are restored to a place of peace.

Reconciliation

If there is division between you and another person or group in your community of faith, it is your responsibility to try working it out so that fellowship can be restored. Follow the pattern that Jesus outlined in *Matthew 18:15-20* and go talk to those involved directly instead of complaining to other people behind their back.

Go to the person or group and pray about the situation until it is resolved. If you need someone to act as a moderator, bring in an elder who is respected by both sides. If the person or group will not be reconciled to you, then you must forgive them and let go of any bitterness so you can be clear and deal with them out of love regardless of how they treat you.

The fact that God expects you to forgive, however, does not remove the fact that any division in the community must be resolved if the peace of the community is to be maintained. If a matter cannot be worked out in any other way, then it must be brought to the attention of the entire community. According to Jesus' instructions, those who refuse to listen to the correction of the entire community should be removed from the fellowship so that the fabric of the community can remain strong.

Seeking Divine Union

The two times of greatest testing for a community of faith are periods of great hardship and periods of great prosperity. During the times of hardship and tribulation, the community must learn to depend upon each other and upon the provision of God's hand. In those times of prosperity, when the temptation is for people to look inward toward their own selfish desires, the members of the community must keep their eyes first on Christ and allow His love to cast aside their old, selfish nature.

One of the best indicators that the precepts of *shalom* are working in a community is that times of testing, whether it be a trial of disaster or of prosperity, makes the unity of the group grow stronger instead of weaker. The unity of the Church grows out of the union that each of God's children finds with their Heavenly Father through the leading of the Spirit. Unity in the body of Believers can only exist when each member first seeks oneness with God individually. As the Spirit teaches each of us to be more like Christ, to think and love more like Him, then we will find that a sense of unity among Believers is a natural side-effect of oneness with Him.

In almost every case, trying to call a non-Believer to repentance for a specific sin is the wrong approach. They will usually just shut you off and not listen. Our first responsibility toward those who do not follow Christ is to love them, just as God does, As we share with them the reality of God's presence, the Holy Spirit will handle calling them to turn back toward God and away from their sinful nature. God's love pouring out through you is the strongest call to repentance you can offer to one who does not know Christ.

There may occasionally be people in your community who you simply find irritating, or who seem to rub you the wrong way, even though they are doing nothing that is wrong or contrary to God's principles. When this happens, you should first look to yourself to see why their actions provoke this reaction from you. Sometimes the fact that certain words or actions push your buttons is a good indicator of something you need to examine inside your own self.

In any community, divisions or ill-feelings will sometimes arise that people find difficult to acknowledge or address. When this happens, the elders have the responsibility to gently help those involved bring the problem into the open, either by discussing it with those affected directly, or through storytelling that indirectly starts a healing dialog.

Compline

Reading: *Ephesians 4:1-16*

Reflection: What part has God called you to play in the body of Christ? Do you feel united with or disconnected from the body?

Prayer: Visualize the friends and family with which you feel unity of mind and purpose in following the spiritual path. Pray that God would knit you together in love and fellowship.

READING #1 - 1 CORINTHIANS 1:10-17

Preparation:

- Calm your mind and take a few deep breaths
- Start with a Prayer of Thanksgiving
- Continue with the prayer, "*Lord Jesus Christ, make me to dwell always in your presence. May all those who bear your name be one, even as the Father and You are one.*"

Lectio:

Day 2

Now I appeal to you, brothers and sisters, by the name of our Lord Jesus Christ,
that all of you be in agreement and that there be no divisions among you,
but that you be united in the same mind and the same purpose.
For it has been reported to me by Chloe's people that there are quarrels among you,
my brothers and sisters. What I mean is that each of you says, "I belong to Paul," or
"I belong to Apollos," or "I belong to Cephas," or "I belong to Christ."
Has Christ been divided? Was Paul crucified for you?
Or were you baptized in the name of Paul?
I thank God that I baptized none of you except Crispus and Gaius, so that no one can
say that you were baptized in my name. (I did baptize also the household of Stephanas;
beyond that, I do not know whether I baptized anyone else.)
For Christ did not send me to baptize but to proclaim the gospel,
and not with eloquent wisdom,
so that the cross of Christ might not be emptied of its power.

- 1 Corinthians 1:10-17 (NRSV)

The modern version of what Paul is warning about here is the division between denominations. Today he would probably write: "each of you says, 'I am a Catholic,' or 'I am a Baptist,' or 'I am a Methodist.'" We should never let the "eloquent wisdom" of the theologians empty the cross of Christ of its power. We are to follow Jesus Himself, not some second-hand version debated about between the denominations.

Meditatio:

Do you ever find yourself building walls of separation between yourself and other followers of Jesus simply because you go to different buildings on Sunday morning, or because you belong to different denominations? How should you handle differences of opinion on minor matters of theology? What matters are so important that they indicate that a person who claims to be a Christian really isn't?

Oratio:

Pray by name for the people who God has placed in your life at this time to be part of your community of faith. Ask that God would grant you all oneness of mind through the leading of His Spirit.

Even in the apostles' days, Christians were too apt to strive after a wrong unity and uniformity in outward practices and observations, and to judge one another unrighteously in these things.
It is not the different practice from one another that breaks the peace and unity, but the judging of one another because of different practices.

- Isaac Penington

Contemplatio:

The highest form of unity is found in the innermost part of your being, where your soul meets the Spirit of the Most High God in divine union. Throughout this week, you will move past the external senses and focus only on the spiritual sense of God's presence in you and around you. Start each day by using your physical senses to check in with what God is doing around you just long enough to help your mind slow down and become quiet. Then close your eyes and slowly let go of your physical senses, focusing instead on the spiritual sense by which you feel God's presence.

As you begin, you may find it easiest to focus on the sense of divine presence in the space immediately surrounding your body. Remember, this is not the same as using your skin to feel something physical. Let go of your sense of touch and simply focus on the sense of presence. You may find this challenging in the beginning, so be gentle with yourself and use your sacred word if you find thoughts wanting to intrude.

Benediction:

- Return slowly and peacefully from *Contemplatio*
- Take time to be thankful again
- Acknowledge that you have completed your time for today and ask God to go with you as you leave this time.

Week 13

Compline

Reading: *1 Corinthians 3:1-15*

Reflection: If your works this week were tested by fire, what would be lost and what would prove of enduring worth?

Prayer: Be thankful for the ways in which the Spirit has used you to build upon the foundation laid by Christ.

READING #2 - ROMANS 15:1-7

Day 3

The passage quoted here is from the Old Testament and can be found in *Psalm 69:9*. This Psalm was written by David and reflected his suffering by being wrongly persecuted. Here, this passage is shown as a foreshadowing of the deeper suffering Jesus endured on our behalf.

Is there anyone in your community of faith who you dislike for purely personal reasons? How do you treat this person? Do you avoid them or speak poorly about them to others? How should you handle your relationship with this person? What could you do to bring healing to the situation?

Preparation:

- Calm your mind and take a few deep breaths
- Start with a Prayer of Thanksgiving
- Continue with the prayer, *"Lord Jesus Christ, make me to dwell always in your presence. May all those who bear your name be one, even as the Father and You are one."*

Lectio:

We who are strong ought to bear with the failings of the weak and not to please ourselves. Each of us should please his neighbor for his good, to build him up.
For even Christ did not please himself but, as it is written:
"The insults of those who insult you have fallen on me."
For everything that was written in the past was written to teach us, so that through endurance and the encouragement of the Scriptures we might have hope.
May the God who gives endurance and encouragement give you a spirit of unity among yourselves as you follow Christ Jesus, so that with one heart and mouth you may glorify the God and Father of our Lord Jesus Christ.
Accept one another, then, just as Christ accepted you, in order to bring praise to God.

- Romans 15:1-7 (NIV)

Meditatio:

Oratio:

> Ask that God would allow you to see all those in your community through His eyes, so you can love them even as He loves them. Ask that your mind and spirit be made one with the mind and heart of God so you may find unity with all those who carry the name of Jesus in the world.

Contemplatio:

Start today by reaching out with your physical senses for a minute or so in order to ground yourself in your place, and then close your eyes and slowly let go of your physical senses. Move your focus toward your spiritual sense and re-establish the feeling of God's presence in the space around your body. Remember to breathe slowly and deeply, using your sacred word to help you let go of any thoughts. You may find that the sense of presence is very vague at first, but it will deepen over time.

Once you have moved out of your physical senses and into your spiritual sense, notice the place where God's presence in the world around you meets your skin and penetrates into your being. As you deepen the sense of God's presence both around you and filling you, your spirit will begin to understand that the divisions you have always imagined between yourself and your Creator are dissolving as you abandon yourself to His love.

> The fact that the indwelling of the Holy Spirit moves you toward unity with God should not be confused with the false teaching of some religions that suggest you are somehow yourself divine or part of God. You are a distinct spiritual creation of God who is adopted as His child when your enter into a covenant relationship with Him. This covenant moves you toward unity with God, but in no way makes you somehow part God yourself.

Benediction:

- Return slowly and peacefully from *Contemplatio*
- Take time to be thankful again
- Acknowledge that you have completed your time for today and ask God to go with you as you leave this time.

> ### *Compline*
>
> **Reading:** *Romans 16:17-18*
>
> **Reflection:** Who around you claims to be a Christian but often brings division into the fellowship of Believers? How should you handle such people?
>
> **Prayer:** Ask for wisdom and courage in dealing with those who cause dissension among Believers.

Week 13

READING #3 - JAMES 2:1-9

Preparation:

- Calm your mind and take a few deep breaths
- Start with a Prayer of Thanksgiving
- Continue with the prayer, "*Lord Jesus Christ, make me to dwell always in your presence. May all those who bear your name be one, even as the Father and You are one.*"

Lectio:

Day 4

My brothers and sisters, do you with your acts of favoritism really believe in our glorious Lord Jesus Christ? For if a person with gold rings and in fine clothes comes into your assembly, and if a poor person in dirty clothes also comes in, and if you take notice of the one wearing the fine clothes and say, "Have a seat here, please," while to the one who is poor you say, "Stand there," or, "Sit at my feet," have you not made distinctions among yourselves, and become judges with evil thoughts?
Listen, my beloved brothers and sisters. Has not God chosen the poor in the world to be rich in faith and to be heirs of the kingdom that he has promised to those who love him? But you have dishonored the poor. Is it not the rich who oppress you?
Is it not they who drag you into court?
Is it not they who blaspheme the excellent name that was invoked over you?
You do well if you really fulfill the royal law according to the scripture,
"You shall love your neighbor as yourself." But if you show partiality,
you commit sin and are convicted by the law as transgressors.

- James 2:1-9 (NRSV)

Meditatio:

With the emphasis our culture places on wealth and status, it is difficult not to fall into the habit of subconsciously favoring those who are wealthy or in positions of power. Are you ever guilty of this? Is there anyone you have looked down on or ignored simply because they don't have as much or are considered by the world to be of little importance? What happens to the unity of the body when Believers act this way?

196

Oratio:

Pray that God would allow you to look beyond the things the world considers important to see the true beauty in all His children.

The Holy Spirit moves in our spirit, producing in us a spiritual sense; afterwards we exercise our brain to study and to understand the meaning of this sense. It requires the cooperation of both spirit and mind to comprehend fully the will of God. The spirit enables our inner self to know, while the mind causes our outer self to understand.

- Watchman Nee

Contemplatio:

Begin today by again using your physical senses for a few moments to quiet your mind and get you settled in your place. Then close your eyes and turn down the intensity of your hearing and sense of touch. Move your focus to the inward parts of yourself, where your spirit dwells in communion with the Holy Spirit. If it helps in the beginning, you may use the image of going into the innermost chamber of your being to meet with God in silence. When you close the door of this chamber, the sensations of the world become dull and far away, and your sense of God's presence becomes more intense, growing to fill your whole attention.

Go into your chamber and close the door. In this place, fix your spiritual eyes fully upon the one who created you and who dwells with you in this innermost place of your being. You will find that the thoughts of the world sound hollow and distant in this place. When the noise of the world tries to intrude, simply breathe out your sacred word and let it carry away all thought.

Benediction:

- Return slowly and peacefully from *Contemplatio*
- Take time to be thankful again
- Acknowledge that you have completed your time for today and ask God to go with you as you leave this time.

Compline

Reading: *1 Peter 3:8-17*

Reflection: Has your pride or ego caused you to be a hindrance to unity this week? If so, how should you correct this problem?

Prayer: Ask for humility and an understanding spirit so you can see the spiritual needs of those around you without judgment.

READING #4 - ACTS 15:36-41

Preparation:

- Calm your mind and take a few deep breaths
- Start with a Prayer of Thanksgiving
- Continue with the prayer, *"Lord Jesus Christ, make me to dwell always in your presence. May all those who bear your name be one, even as the Father and You are one."*

Day 5

The disagreement between Paul and Barnabas caused the two to split into two missionary teams instead of continuing to travel together. The end result was actually a wider spreading of the gospel throughout the world.

Lectio:

Some time later Paul said to Barnabas, "Let us go back and visit the brothers in all the towns where we preached the word of the Lord and see how they are doing."
Barnabas wanted to take John, also called Mark, with them, but Paul did not think it wise to take him, because he had deserted them in Pamphylia and had not continued with them in the work. They had such a sharp disagreement that they parted company.
Barnabas took Mark and sailed for Cyprus, but Paul chose Silas and left, commended by the brothers to the grace of the Lord.
He went through Syria and Cilicia, strengthening the churches.

- Acts 15:36-41 (NIV)

Meditatio:

Sometimes disagreements arise between Believers. Is this always a bad thing, or does God sometimes use divisions to accomplish His intent? Does God want for these divisions to happen, or does He simply use them to accomplish His will in spite of the fact they come from our own immaturity?

Oratio:

If you have differences with a fellow Believer, ask God to show you how to heal this problem. If you are holding onto any bitterness caused by the division, let go of it in prayer.

Contemplatio:

Close your eyes, quiet your mind, and move into the inner chamber of your being again today. If your physical senses pull at you, relax and let go of them. With your spiritual sense, begin to listen for the silent echo of God's presence that surrounds you and fills you, like a chord whose harmonies resonate with a spiritual instead of an audible sound.

Your spiritual sense may come to you at first in subtle and indistinct impressions. For some, the sense of God's nearness comes as a feeling of warmth and presence that is felt with the spirit instead of by the physical senses. For others, it comes almost like a soundless resonating note that fills the ears of the soul. People experience the sense of God's presence in very personal and individual ways. Sit quietly and patiently with the Holy Spirit, silently inviting Him to reveal His presence to you more deeply, remaining open to whichever way your spiritual sense opens within you.

Benediction:

- Return slowly and peacefully from *Contemplatio*
- Take time to be thankful again
- Acknowledge that you have completed your time for today and ask God to go with you as you leave this time.

Compline

Reading: *Ecclesiastes 4:9-12*

Reflection: Do you have faithful companions on your spiritual journey who can help you when you are having trouble?

Prayer: Express your thanks for those who God has given you to help and encourage you when you are weak.

READING #5 - GALATIANS 5:13-15, 22-26

Preparation:

- Calm your mind and take a few deep breaths
- Start with a Prayer of Thanksgiving
- Continue with the prayer, *"Lord Jesus Christ, make me to dwell always in your presence. May all those who bear your name be one, even as the Father and You are one."*

Lectio:

Day 6

For you were called to freedom, brothers and sisters;
only do not use your freedom as an opportunity for self-indulgence,
but through love become slaves to one another.
For the whole law is summed up in a single commandment,
"You shall love your neighbor as yourself."
If, however, you bite and devour one another,
take care that you are not consumed by one another....
By contrast, the fruit of the Spirit is love, joy, peace, patience, kindness, generosity,
faithfulness, gentleness, and self-control. There is no law against such things.
And those who belong to Christ Jesus have crucified the flesh with its passions and
desires. If we live by the Spirit, let us also be guided by the Spirit.
Let us not become conceited, competing against one another, envying one another.

- Galatians 5:13-15, 22-26 (NRSV)

Meditatio:

Does your life show the fruits of the Spirit? Do you find it easy to love your neighbor, or is it sometimes a struggle? Are there those in your community of faith who continually bite and devour each other out of pride or envy? What does this do to the unity of the community, including those who are not directly involved?

Oratio:

Go through the fruits of the Spirit one at a time and say a prayer of thanksgiving that God is creating in you each of these gifts. Express your thanks that, through these gifts, He brings you into union with Himself and all those who are His children.

True evangelical faith cannot lie dormant. It clothes the naked, it feeds the hungry, it comforts the sorrowful, it shelters the destitute, it serves those that harm it, it binds up that which is wounded, it has become all things to all people.

\- Menno Simons

Contemplatio:

As you begin today, move your attention for a moment to your breath. Breathe deeply for a few cycles, gently letting go of the tension in your body. Each time you exhale, allow yourself to release anything you are holding physically or emotionally, relaxing ever deeper into complete rest in God's hand. Once you feel ready, close your eyes and move inward to the place where your spirit and God's Spirit meet.

Enter this space with no expectation except to sit for a while enjoying the healing presence of the Holy Spirit, allowing Him to do whatever work within your spirit that He wills. Turn your attention away from your physical senses and toward the subtle ways in which your soul can sense the Spirit's presence with you and within you. The outer world will begin to feel distant and dim as the nearness of Holy Spirit fills you. Let go fully and rest in the timeless place of being enveloped by the warm embrace of God's presence.

Benediction:

- Return slowly and peacefully from *Contemplatio*
- Take time to be thankful again
- Acknowledge that you have completed your time for today and ask God to go with you as you leave this time.

Compline

Reading: *John 15:1-11*

Reflection: Do the patterns of your thoughts and actions reveal that you are rooted in the ways of the world, or in the true vine of Christ?

Prayer: Meditate upon what it means to abide in Christ and to have Him abide in you.

REFLECTION

Revisit Your Favorite Passage

Day 7

Reflections on the Week

Compline

Reading: *Psalm 133*

Reflection: As you traveled through the world today, with whom did you feel unity, and with whom did you feel separation? Why?

Prayer: Release to the Holy Spirit anything you found this week that holds you back from unity with Christ or those who follow Him.

WEEK 14 - LOVE

> "I give you a new commandment, that you love one another.
> Just as I have loved you, you also should love one another.
> By this everyone will know that you are my disciples,
> if you have love for one another."

> *-John 13:34-35 (NRSV)*

NEAR THE END OF JESUS' TIME ON EARTH, as He taught and ministered in Jerusalem, preparing for His imminent journey to the cross, the Pharisees and Sadducees came to Him attempting to trap Him with questions. They hoped to provoke Jesus into giving an answer that would either turn the crowd against Him or for which they could charge Him with heresy. After several failed attempts, one of the Pharisees finally asked Jesus which of God's commandments was the greatest.

Jesus responded that the first and greatest commandment is to love God with every part of your being: with all the strength of your mind, all the passion of your heart, and all the depths of your soul. The second commandment is to love those around you with the same intensity that you love yourself. Jesus said that all of the other precepts and instructions God had given us hung from these first two commandments.

Part of the problem we have with understanding these commandments today is that people throw the word *love* around so casually that they have diluted its power. In God's definition, love is neither an abstract ideal nor a vague expression of enjoyment. Such ideas as *loving pizza* or *loving a good movie* are not really found in scripture. The Biblical concept of love is better captured in the Hebrew word *hesed*, which is sometimes translated as *loving-kindness*. *Hesed* refers to a deep caring and nurturing spirit that expresses itself as mercy, compassion, and profound love.

To fully understand love, you must realize that it is an attitude of the soul instead of simply another emotion among the many others. While emotions are temporary and prone to change, love is steadfast and unfailing because it is an act of the will and an abiding desire of the heart.

You were designed in the image of God to love in the same way that God loves you. God's love flows out from Him freely to all, even when they don't deserve it. God's desire is for you to learn to love freely and extravagantly, even as He loves you.

The root of your sinful nature is love turned inward, preferring yourself over others. When you let love turn inward in an unhealthy way, it produces pride and selfishness; letting the Spirit teach you to turn your love outward cleanses you of self-centeredness. When you love as God has commanded, the Spirit begins to breathe in and out through you, transforming your life into a walking prayer traveling along the byways of this world.

Extra Mile:

Get together with your group one night this week and build a campfire. You can talk and tell stories part of the time, but make sure you spend at least 30 minutes in silence together around the fire. If possible, arrange for everyone to sleep around the fire for the night, each person taking a turn sitting up to tend the fire, then all getting up together just before dawn to share a time of Vigil. If you have been doing the program independently, ask a group of other Believers to join you at the fire so you can share with them the stories of what you have learned through *Vigil*.

LOVE

Day 1

There are actually four different words in ancient Greek that can be translated as *love*, but only two of them are used in the Bible.

Éros refers to intimate love that includes sexual passion, such as between a man and a woman, while *Storge* is used to refer to the kind of natural love and affection felt between members of a family, such as by parents for their children. Neither of these terms is found in the New Testament.

Philia refers to the kind of affectionate, non-passionate love felt between friends or siblings. This was the most common word for love in ancient Greek, and is used in the New Testament with a variety of shades of meaning, including that of affection and concern between friends.

The fourth word for love, *agápe*, was actually a fairly generic word in Greek before the New Testament took and suffused it with an entirely new meaning: that of God's unconditional love for His children. The Bible uses this word when it is exploring the depths of God's care for us, and in this sense it is probably the closest in meaning to the Hebrew word *hesed* in referring to the loving-kindness God shows toward us and that He expects us to show toward each other. In this sense, *agápe* and *hesed* are the words used in scripture to capture the idea of the selfless love that is at the core of this week's precept for creating peace in a community of faith.

G OD'S COVENANT WITH US, HIS CHILDREN, IS A COVENANT BORN OF LOVE. In love He created us in His own image, and in love He sent His only Son to rescue us from our sin when we had disobeyed Him and brought grief and death upon ourselves. It was because of His unceasing love that He made provision for those of us who call upon Him to be adopted as His own children and be made members of His eternal spiritual family.

Since God has made all of His children a part of the same covenant, and thus all members of the same family, we have a responsibility of love one toward the other. As we sit with the Spirit and allow Him to change the innermost desires of our hearts, He teaches us to care for each other as brothers and sisters, treating each other with mercy, compassion, and loving-kindness.

During this final week of our study we come to reflect on love as the last and highest of the precepts that God has given us for creating peace among Believers. Without love as our primary motivation, all of the other principles we have studied turn out to be nothing but empty, hollow rules. Love is the quality that binds together a community so its members can live together with *Shalom,* becoming a visible reflection of God's own peace here in this world.

Love Is the Fulfillment of the Law

In *Romans 13:8-10*, Paul expands on what Jesus said about all of God's law hanging from the commandments to love God and to love others. The reason all the other aspects of God's law flow from the commandment to love others even as God has loved you, Paul says, is that following this single commandment will naturally result in you fulfilling all of the other requirements of God's law.

When you are motivated by love, the things that God instructs you to avoid—such as envy, gossip, and sexual immorality—will simply never arise as temptations for you, and the things that God has commanded you to do—care for the poor, bring hope to those in despair, help bear your neighbors' burdens—will automatically flow from you as a natural consequence of the way you see the world.

Your actions will inevitably reveal the true motives of your heart, because what you do ultimately arises from your innermost desires. If you try to follow God's commands out of a sense of duty or guilt, but do not have love, you will inevitably fail because you are trying to act contrary to what is in your own heart and mind. When you allow God's love to express itself in you through the leading of the Holy Spirit, you will find that God's commands bring you deep joy because they are the practical expressions of love made visible and real.

It is in this context that we must see the other precepts that we have considered over the past few weeks. These other seven precepts are actually the concrete expressions of love at work in a community of faith, and must all be motivated by love if they are to work the way God intends.

When a group tries to impose God's precepts on its members out of a sense of fear or guilt, the end result is only more fear and guilt, because people are destined to fail at keeping God's commandments unless they are motivated by love. The only way to have the precepts really work in a community is to first cultivate the kind of love that will make the precepts an outward reflection of the inner landscape of the heart.

Without love guiding a community, the rest of God's commandments can become legalistic weapons with which people attack each other, inflicting deep spiritual and emotional wounds. When we become fixated on the rule itself, instead of God's love that is the reason behind the rule, we risk becoming like the Pharisees, focused on pointing out to others where they have failed instead of helping them find the mercy and grace they need to move forward with love.

Love That Is Visible

When you love someone deeply, you can't hide it. Who and what you love shows itself concretely in how you choose to spend your time, energy, attention, and resources. If you say you love someone, whether it be another person or God Himself, but don't value them enough to spend time with them, then you are just deceiving yourself. Love that is true and deep expresses itself in ways that are clearly visible.

If your community is healthy, those who visit should immediately be struck by the atmosphere of loving-kindness that fills the spaces between members of the community and reaches out to envelop and include them as well. In a community where the Biblical precept of love is operating properly, a guest should feel welcomed and included, fully embraced, and invited into the conversation. If not, something is fundamentally wrong. If people feel more accepted and valued in a non-Christian community than at a church, then that congregation is bearing a false witness of Christ.

In any group where loving-kindness is present, the other seven precepts of *shalom* will naturally begin to arise and become evident. The members will begin to hold integrity, peace, and holiness inside of themselves. They will be careful of what they invoke with their words, always seeking communion and unity with others in the community. And they will come together to provide support and offer consolation for those who get trapped in the mire of sin and grief, even when simply ignoring the problem would cause less fuss. God's love at work in a people is transformative in a way that can be clearly seen even by those outside of the community.

> Some churches end up organizing official greeters to stand at the door and greet people as they arrive. This can be a good thing if it is done well, but can in no way make up for a lack of welcome from the people who are inside those doors. The real test of whether a church, or any community, is truly welcoming comes in the ways that guests are offered love that is practical and visible during every moment of the time they spend with the community.

Love One Another

Because God's command that we love one another is such a central theme of scripture, and one that so deeply challenges our old, sinful nature, it is not surprising that people have come up with many ways to twist this command around to make it less threatening to their own self-centered desires. For people who have not allowed the Spirit to transform their innermost self so that they begin to naturally express God's love, a common tactic is to try to redefine love into terms they find more comfortable.

One of the more toxic ways this happens is the case of the person who intellectually decides that God is calling them to show concern for the spiritual wellbeing of others, who then tries to force that concern out of a sense of duty rather than out of a genuine love for them given by the Spirit. Guided by their own mind instead of by God's love, they begin to chatter on about other people's spiritual issues—both directly to them and behind their backs—using their knowledge of scripture to condemn instead of call to repentance, often times in terms that are discouraging and hurtful, all the while claiming that everything they say is motivated by God's love.

When you hear somebody who calls themselves a Christian talking in self-righteous tones about how important it is to be loving and non-judgmental, get ready, because what follows will almost always be some of the most hateful and judgmental words you will ever encounter. People who hand out their own judgment in the name of God's love are some of the most dangerous to the health of a community because they will poison it from within.

Those who carry a loving spirit are usually too focused on God's mercy and forgiveness to make an issue of how much others should be impressed by their own holiness. The people who genuinely exhibit unconditional love and a non-judgmental attitude are usually the ones who don't seem so driven to talk about it all the time; they just quietly go about doing it.

> In order for a community of faith to be healthy, it must avoid the two extremes of ignoring sin on the one hand, and attacking and destroying those who have fallen into sin on the other. Beware of people who twist God's commandments around and weaponize them, using them to attack others in the community with guilt and condemnation when they fail. Likewise, be on the lookout for those who use the idea of not judging to excuse the community from dealing with problems. Our responsibility toward each other as brothers and sisters in Christ is to help each other in a way that expresses God's loving-kindness, including helping each other deal with the problems and temptations of sin when they arise.

Week 14

A *thought-stopper* is something that people say in order to stop a line of thought they find uncomfortable or wish to avoid. When it comes to helping others in the community through their sin and grief, most people find it easier to block such unpleasant topics by throwing out words that are designed to stop the conversation rather than do the hard work of addressing the situation through the Spirit's guidance.

The modern news industry has realized that fear is a great hook for grabbing attention and thereby making lots of money. News outlets from TV to print media to the Internet use fear to drive a sense of urgency and draw in their audience. We as Believers must use good discernment to understand and deal with the dangers that are real while not becoming trapped in the fear machine created by the media. When we let our fear get ahead of us, it quickly creates suspicion and hatred that can form prejudices that take years to overcome.

When the members of a community of faith follow God's precepts out of love, they provide the perfect role model that allows the families in the community to function as God intends. When parents show love and respect to their children, the children learn to show love and respect in return. Where you find families who love each other in this way, you have the foundations for a strong community in which God's love is felt and seen.

In thinking about obedience coming from love, you must remember that love is not an emotion, but an attitude of the soul. Since love will provoke you to actions that place God's priorities ahead of your own, it can sometimes be challenging and uncomfortable. That, however, is something very different that being driven to obey by fear or guilt.

Other people reflexively say *but we are supposed to be loving and non-judgmental* as a thought-stopper or excuse to not deal with problems in the community of faith. Godly love means helping other members of the extended faith family through their problems, even when this is not easy or comfortable.

You wouldn't tell members of a family that being loving and non-judgmental meant ignoring each other's problems or not helping each other when needed. The same is true for your brothers and sisters in Christ, although the dynamics of those relationships mean that you offer love and support in a different way than family members do for each other. Godly love cares enough to get involved in a gentle and kind way, being quietly supportive and understanding.

Perfect Love Casts Out All Fear

Fear is a powerfully disconnecting and isolating force in any community. Whenever fear is present—fear of rejection, fear of judgment, fear of being hurt—it creates an environment in which people don't feel safe to reach out toward each other and connect. The shadow of fear instead encourages them to pull back within themselves and keep others at an arm's distance, often due to painful experiences from the past.

The kind of love that God wants us to show toward one another is the most powerful tool we have for tearing down the walls of separation built by fear. Being surrounded by the loving-kindness of God's people creates precisely the kind of safe space that those trapped in fear and uncertainty need in order to find healing. As it says in *1 John 4:18*, God's love is the antidote for fear because perfect love casts out all fear and replaces it with mercy and acceptance.

A community of people who spend time alone with God each day, seeking to know Him and to be like Him, will naturally radiate this kind of love and create a space in which they weave the fabric of peace among themselves and open the possibility of healing to others.

This tapestry of loving-kindness also creates the kind of space in which individuals feel safe accepting the consolation and support of their community so that they can be returned to a place of peace when they find themselves lost in sin and grief.

Obedience Flows From Love

God's commandments for us are a reflection of His perfect love, and they can only be lived out as He intends by those who abide in that love. For those who have not been transformed by the Spirit, the commandments found in the Bible create a standard that is impossible to meet. The requirements of God's law hold up a mirror to your innermost self that clearly shows you how far short of perfect love you come when you try to follow God's commandments on your own.

Obedience flows from only one of two places: either out of love and respect, or out of fear. For those who were taught to follow God's commands out of fear, the Bible feels like a trap. Everything they are told to do in scripture is at odds with their sinful nature, so all their efforts to do what it says simply end in failure. Trying to live up to God's requirements on your own will only drive you deeper into fear and guilt. God gave us His law to show us we are not capable of choosing to do what is right on our own, and to illustrate the need for letting the Spirit transform us completely.

When you let the Holy Spirit heal you, He will transform the motives and desires of your heart, teaching you to love God in the same way that He loves you. As you learn to let God love through you, obedience to God's precepts will flow out of you naturally and automatically.

Love Your Enemies

The true test of love is not in how you treat your friends, but in how you treat those who are unkind to you, who take advantage of you, or who even try to destroy your reputation. The natural reaction of most people is to repay their enemies in kind, lashing out to hurt those who have hurt them. But the response of those who are led by the Spirit is altogether different; they look beyond the hurtful words and actions of those who attack them to see the spiritual need that lies hidden underneath.

Unkind words and actions coming at you from others arise from their own internal issues and often have nothing to do with you—in most cases you are just a convenient target. When you learn to see the spiritual pain and self-destructive motives behind these attacks, it becomes much easier to respond from a place of love. As *Romans 12:14-21* instructs, you should respond to those who curse you by blessing them in return. In this way, you will not repay evil with evil, but will overcome evil with good.

When you encounter a person who treats you unfairly or attacks you in some way, try setting an intention to pray for them at least twice each day. Instead of praying that you will be vindicated or that they will receive the judgment you think they deserve, ask God that their spiritual, emotional, and physical needs will be met and that they will receive healing.

The Bible's command that we love our enemies, praying for them and forgiving them, contains great wisdom. When you respond to attacks by getting angry or trying to get even, you trap yourself in a cycle of negative thoughts and emotions that will destroy your inner peace. By forgiving and showing love in the face of evil, you completely defuse its power over you. By loving even your enemies, you take away their ability to pull you down into hatred and bitterness. In God's economy of love, forgiving your enemies is the ultimate form of self-defense.

Forgiveness & Mercy

The strength to walk through this world, with all the negativity and hate it can sometimes throw at you, while responding only out of love does not come from yourself. The ability to love others just as God has loved you comes from the quiet moments you spend sitting with the Spirit, letting Him teach you to see others as God sees them.

When you learn to see through the eyes of God, mercy and forgiveness will begin to overflow in your spirit and slowly change the way you perceive the world, replacing the tendency of your old self to judge and condemn. The kind of mercy that comes from the Spirit is not one that tolerates or excuses sin, but one that sees its root cause and seeks to address it with gentleness and love.

I have found the paradox, that if you love until it hurts, there can be no more hurt, only more love.

- Mother Teresa

Be Known for Your Love

In the end, it is our loving-kindness toward each other that is the ultimate testament to whether we truly follow Christ. If a group of people come together and do all the things that a church normally does—build nice buildings, have Bible studies and worship times each week, do missions, and even offer service to the poor—but do not love each other, then they are not really part of the Church. If they belonged to Jesus, they would love each other first, and the fruits would follow organically as a result.

In *John 13:34-35*, Jesus says that the world will know we belong to Him first and foremost by our love one for another. People will identify us with Christ not because of our clever theology, our beautiful buildings, or great worship music, or even because our of good deeds, but by the way we love each other and love the world.

To find peace within ourselves, within our community of faith, and ultimately with *Yahweh Shalom*— the God of Peace Himself—we must follow the instructions in *Colossians 3:12-14* and, before all else, clothe ourselves in His love, which will bind us all together in perfect unity.

Compline

Reading: *John 15:12-17*

Reflection: How did you pour out your life today for your friends? Were you more centered on your own needs, or on the needs of your friends?

Prayer: Pick a close friend and pray for him or her this evening, asking that God would use you to pour blessings into their life.

READING #1 - MATTHEW 22:34-40

Preparation:

- Calm your mind and take a few deep breaths
- Start with a Prayer of Thanksgiving
- Continue with the prayer, "*Lord Jesus Christ, may Your love flow out through me into the world. Make me a vessel of Your grace poured out as water on dry and thirsty ground.*"

Day 2

Lectio:

Hearing that Jesus had silenced the Sadducees, the Pharisees got together.
One of them, an expert in the law, tested him with this question:
"Teacher, which is the greatest commandment in the Law?"
Jesus replied: "'Love the Lord your God with all your heart
and with all your soul and with all your mind.'
This is the first and greatest commandment. And the second is like it:
'Love your neighbor as yourself.'
All the Law and the Prophets hang on these two commandments."

- Matthew 22:34-40 (NIV)

Meditatio:

The English word *love* is used with many different connotations. What kind of love does Jesus mean when He says that the greatest commandment is to love God with all your being? What kind of love are you to show to your neighbor? What does it look like in the practical terms of what you do each day?

Oratio:

Try using part of your time of *Oratio* today in breath prayers that express your love toward God.

Contemplatio:

In many ways, the beauty you see around you in Creation is the fingerprint of God's love at work in the world. Even the most harsh and bleak landscapes hold hidden beauty and hidden blessings. Just as Brother Lawrence was able to glimpse God's promise laying beneath the surface of the barren limbs of the trees even as the cold winds of winter blew around him, you should learn to look for God's love at work around you, especially in those places where it may not at first be obvious.

Take a few moments to look at the trees around you, trying to see them again as if for the first time. Whether they are in the full strength of summer or dormant and bare in the depths of winter, they serve as a reminder of God's faithfulness through the cycles and seasons of life. When you are ready, close your eyes and move inward, carrying this feeling of God's love and provision with you into the inner chamber of your being. As with last week, turn down your outward senses as you set your mind and intention on being in Christ's presence.

Continue this week the practice of moving inward during *Contemplatio*, turning your attention from your outward physical senses and toward your spiritual sense of God's presence exclusively. Begin each day by using your external senses to help slow down your thoughts and get you settled in place before you move inward and let the outside world become dim.

Compline

Reading: *Luke 11:37-44*

Reflection: Were you more focused today on just following God's rules, or on the freedom that comes from allowing God's love to flow through you?

Prayer: Ask for the freedom and boldness to act spontaneously out of love and grace as you go through the world tomorrow.

Benediction:

- Return slowly and peacefully from *Contemplatio*
- Take time to be thankful again
- Acknowledge that you have completed your time for today and ask God to go with you as you leave this time.

READING #2 - ROMANS 13:8-10

Preparation:

- Calm your mind and take a few deep breaths
- Start with a Prayer of Thanksgiving
- Continue with the prayer, "*Lord Jesus Christ, may Your love flow out through me into the world. Make me a vessel of Your grace poured out as water on dry and thirsty ground.*"

Lectio:

Day 3

Owe no one anything, except to love one another;
for the one who loves another has fulfilled the law.
The commandments, "You shall not commit adultery; You shall not murder;
You shall not steal; You shall not covet"; and any other commandment,
are summed up in this word, "Love your neighbor as yourself."
Love does no wrong to a neighbor; therefore, love is the fulfilling of the law.

- *Romans 13:8-10 (NRSV)*

Meditatio:

Why does the act of loving your neighbor automatically fulfill all the requirements of the law? Is it possible to love others in this way if you don't first love God with all your heart? What would happen if a non-Believer attempted to follow this commandment?

Oratio:

Spend your time of prayer today praying specifically for individuals in your community of faith for whom the Spirit has given you a sense of concern. Ask the Holy Spirit to allow you to see their needs through the eyes of God Himself.

Contemplatio:

As you settle into *Contemplatio* today, take a few moments to listen to the language of the birds around you. Think about how your understanding of the birds has changed over the weeks you have been coming outside each morning, and how the birds' reaction to your presence has changed. What do the birds tell you about your own thought patterns? About whether your own presence is peaceful or agitated? About how you fit into the flow of the natural world unfolding around you?

If there is a variety of bird sound in the area around you, try not to focus on just one or two of the loudest or closest sounds. Try instead to make your attention diffuse so that you take in even the quieter sounds coming in from all directions. Close your eyes and let your ears take in the canvas of sounds surrounding you. Then, when you are ready, slowly shift your focus inward toward the sound of the Spirit's voice echoing through the silence.

Benediction:

- Return slowly and peacefully from *Contemplatio*
- Take time to be thankful again
- Acknowledge that you have completed your time for today and ask God to go with you as you leave this time.

Compline

Reading: *Romans 8:31-39*

Reflection: Did you feel connected to Christ's love today, or separated from it? Why?

Prayer: Say a prayer of thanksgiving for the faithfulness of God in loving and caring for you, even when you don't deserve it.

Week 14

Reading #3 - Matthew 5:43-48

Preparation:

- Calm your mind and take a few deep breaths
- Start with a Prayer of Thanksgiving
- Continue with the prayer, "*Lord Jesus Christ, may Your love flow out through me into the world. Make me a vessel of Your grace poured out as water on dry and thirsty ground.*"

Day 4

Lectio:

"You have heard that it was said, 'You shall love your neighbor and hate your enemy.'
But I say to you, Love your enemies and pray for those who persecute you,
so that you may be children of your Father in heaven;
for he makes his sun rise on the evil and on the good,
and sends rain on the righteous and on the unrighteous.
For if you love those who love you, what reward do you have?
Do not even the tax collectors do the same?
And if you greet only your brothers and sisters, what more are you doing than others?
Do not even the Gentiles do the same?
Be perfect, therefore, as your heavenly Father is perfect."

- Matthew 5:43-48 (NRSV)

Meditatio:

Is there a person or group of people with whom you have some enmity or division? How are you handling the situation? Do you pray for them each day and treat them with love and kindness? If not, what should you be doing differently?

Oratio:

> Ask the Spirit to help you let go of any bitterness or other hurtful parts of your ego that keep you from loving those who treat you poorly or with whom you have differences. Ask for assistance from the Spirit in praying for them with wisdom and sincerity.

Contemplatio:

If you think back to the first time we practiced *Contemplatio* at the beginning of the first book, you will remember that we used the weeds as our focus, reflecting on how God uses them to repair disturbed or damaged soil and prepare it for new growth. Take a moment to bring the full attention of all your senses back to the weeds growing around you, feeling and smelling them as you examine their various patterns and structures. As you do this, look inward also, to the fertile soil of your own spirit, from which the Holy Spirit has also been preparing to bring forth a harvest in due season.

Notice what your own spirit feels like as it sits inside your body, how the ground of your inward self has been planted and prepared to bear spiritual fruit. As you begin to move out of your physical senses and toward the place where you meet quietly with God, remember that often the unwanted experiences of life are there to prepare the soil for something new.

Benediction:

- Return slowly and peacefully from *Contemplatio*
- Take time to be thankful again
- Acknowledge that you have completed your time for today and ask God to go with you as you leave this time.

> *Compline*
>
> **Reading:** *Psalm 36*
>
> **Reflection:** How did you do today in dealing with those you don't like or with whom you have division? What should you have done differently?
>
> **Prayer:** Pray by name for those who have treated you unfairly or with whom you have some disagreement.

Reading #4 - 1 John 2:3-11

Preparation:

- Calm your mind and take a few deep breaths
- Start with a Prayer of Thanksgiving
- Continue with the prayer, "*Lord Jesus Christ, may Your love flow out through me into the world. Make me a vessel of Your grace poured out as water on dry and thirsty ground.*"

Day 5

Lectio:

We know that we have come to know him if we obey his commands.
The man who says, "I know him," but does not do what he commands is a liar,
and the truth is not in him. But if anyone obeys his word, God's love is truly made
complete in him. This is how we know we are in him:
Whoever claims to live in him must walk as Jesus did.
Dear friends, I am not writing you a new command but an old one, which you have
had since the beginning. This old command is the message you have heard.
Yet I am writing you a new command; its truth is seen in him and you,
because the darkness is passing and the true light is already shining.
Anyone who claims to be in the light but hates his brother is still in the darkness.
Whoever loves his brother lives in the light,
and there is nothing in him to make him stumble.
But whoever hates his brother is in the darkness and walks around in the darkness;
he does not know where he is going, because the darkness has blinded him.

- 1 John 2:3-11 (NIV)

Meditatio:

Why is obedience so closely tied to love of God? This passage says that the ultimate test of whether you have a relationship with God is whether or not you walk as Jesus did. How are you doing with this test? Is it the desire of your heart to follow Jesus, even if you fall short from time to time?

Oratio:

> Release any motive or desire that holds you back from walking as Jesus did, giving it to the Holy Spirit and asking that your heart be purified and made open to the love that God wants to pour out through you.

> *Our Lord told His disciples that love and obedience were organically united. The final test of love is obedience.*
>
> - A. W. Tozer

Contemplatio:

Love can sometimes inspire the most dramatic and selfless of actions, while at other times it can be so subtle that the full breadth of its power is almost below the threshold of conscious perception. Just as your ear is often drawn to the loudest and most obvious of sounds, your mind can often be drawn toward the hustle and urgency of daily events, missing the almost silent foundation of love with which God undergirds you.

Begin your time of inner stillness today by bringing your attention back to the quietest sounds of the natural world surrounding you. Close your eyes and listen first to the North, taking in the softest and farthest sounds your ears can perceive. Then slowly listen to the East, the South, and the West each in turn, finding the quietest messages coming to you on the wind. Finally, turn your spiritual ears inward toward the voice of the Spirit speaking through the silence, listening for the quiet, almost imperceptible, moving of God's healing love at work within you.

Benediction:

- Return slowly and peacefully from *Contemplatio*
- Take time to be thankful again
- Acknowledge that you have completed your time for today and ask God to go with you as you leave this time.

Compline

Reading: *1 John 3:11-24*

Reflection: How well did your actions reflect love today? Where were you strong? Where were you weak?

Prayer: Pray aloud this evening, talking to God about your day, confessing where you fell short, and giving thanks for the blessings you received.

Week 14

READING #5 - 1 JOHN 4:7-19

Preparation:

- Calm your mind and take a few deep breaths
- Start with a Prayer of Thanksgiving
- Continue with the prayer, "*Lord Jesus Christ, may Your love flow out through me into the world. Make me a vessel of Your grace poured out as water on dry and thirsty ground.*"

Lectio:

Day 6

Dear friends, let us love one another, for love comes from God.
Everyone who loves has been born of God and knows God.
Whoever does not love does not know God, because God is love.
This is how God showed his love among us: He sent his one and only Son into the world that we might live through him. This is love: not that we loved God, but that he loved us and sent his Son as an atoning sacrifice for our sins.
Dear friends, since God so loved us, we also ought to love one another.
No one has ever seen God; but if we love one another,
God lives in us and his love is made complete in us.
We know that we live in him and he in us, because he has given us of his Spirit.
And we have seen and testify that the Father has sent his Son to be the Savior of the world. If anyone acknowledges that Jesus is the Son of God, God lives in him and he in God. And so we know and rely on the love God has for us.
God is love. Whoever lives in love lives in God, and God in him.
In this way, love is made complete among us so that we will have confidence on the day of judgment, because in this world we are like him. There is no fear in love.
But perfect love drives out fear, because fear has to do with punishment.
The one who fears is not made perfect in love.
We love because he first loved us.

- 1 John 4:7-19 (NIV)

Meditatio:

What is it that you fear? What are you holding onto that God wants you to give to Him so that He can purge that fear from you?

Oratio:

> Use the power of your words in invocation today, blessing God and thanking Him for all He has done for you and through you. Confess to Him anything you have been holding back which has kept you living in fear, letting go and giving it to Him completely.

Contemplatio:

In love, God formed this world, brought forth the plants, the trees, the birds, the animals, and the fish to swim in the rivers and the oceans. When He was done, He declared that what He had made was good and gave it to us as our home. In love, God created man and woman in His own image, designing them to have fellowship with Him and to return the love He poured out on them. In a love that goes beyond human understanding, God sent His own Son to pay the price of sin when mankind chose to be disobedient and bring spiritual death upon itself.

Today, as we are nearing the end of this study by reflecting on God's unending love, take time to simply lie on the Earth, close your eyes, and feel the ground beneath you. Whether the ground is warm with the breath of summer or cold from the winter's touch, let the Earth remind you of God's faithfulness and provision through all the joys and difficulties of life. When you are ready, enter again the innermost chamber of your being with a silent prayer of thankfulness.

Benediction:

- Return slowly and peacefully from *Contemplatio*
- Take time to be thankful again
- Acknowledge that you have completed your time for today and ask God to go with you as you leave this time.

Compline

Reading: *1 Corinthians 13*

Reflection: Why are faith, hope, and love each so important? How do they affect whether you live in fear or with freedom and boldness?

Prayer: Pray aloud again this evening. Pour out your thoughts and cares to God and let His love fill you in return.

REFLECTION

Revisit Your Favorite Passage

Day 7

Reflections on the Week

Reflections on Book Two

Take a few moments to reflect on your spiritual journey over the last fourteen weeks. In what ways have you grown? What are the most important lessons you have learned?

When a soul has advanced so far on the spiritual road as to be lost to all the natural methods of communing with God; when it seeks Him no longer by meditation, images, impressions, nor by any other created ways, or representations of sense, but only by rising above them all, in the joyful communion with Him by faith and love, then it may be said to have found God of a truth, because it has truly lost itself as to all that is not God, and also as to its own self.

- St. John of the Cross
From *The Spiritual Canticle*

Looking Forward

As you come to the close of this book, take a moment to look back at what you have learned and where the Spirit is calling you to go from here. To those who seek Him, God gives the gifts, tools, and passion to become a powerful conduit of His love in this world. Where is the Spirit leading you next in your pilgrimage through this life? What path is He opening up before you?

No matter where your spiritual journey takes you, always remember the importance of spending time each day alone with God, listening to the voice of the Spirit speaking through the scriptures. If you would like to continue the practice of *Lectio Divina*, consider using the third book of the *Vigil* series, the *Lectio Divina Journal*, to continue having your time outdoors each morning.

Don't be surprised if God calls you to help and encourage others on the spiritual journey as well. You may even find yourself feeling called to lead others through a program such as *Vigil*. Just remain open to whatever God has for you, even if it is well outside of your comfort zones.

As you travel the byways of this world in search of knowing God in all His fullness, carry this blessing from *Numbers 6:24-26* with you along the way:

May the LORD bless you and keep you. May He make His face to shine upon you, and be gracious to you. May the LORD lift up His countenance upon you, and give you peace.

Compline

Reading: *Hebrews 11:32-12:2*

Reflection: What has God taught you as you have moved through this book? What is He calling you to do as you move forward?

Prayer: As you pray, open your eyes and look up toward heaven. Talk to God with your whole being, ending with a time of thankfulness.

Week 14

Summary of the Eight Precepts of *Shalom*

The precepts taught in the Bible flow from God's nature and reflect His wisdom for how we are to live together as His children here on Earth. By following these commands, we can experience the fellowship and peace that He intended for us to share as His family, even while we are surrounded by those who are mired in conflict and hatred. When we allow these precepts to flow from us as natural expressions of God's love and mercy, we build here in this world a community of faith that is a picture pointing toward the perfect *shalom* that awaits us when we see our God face to face.

As you study these principles for building peace with those around you, try to focus on the positive actions that God calls you to perform as His child. The *shalom* that God intends for us is not built by just avoiding what is sinful or hurtful; it is built day by day as we love each other, pray for each other, support each other, and act as faithful reflections of Christ each moment.

1. Integrity:

- Be honest and straight-forward. Speak the truth completely and without misleading. Let your love of the truth be a reflection of God's loving-kindness and perfect Truth.
- To the best of your ability, keep your commitments, be on time, and be reliable. Carry out your commitments with a positive attitude, making them an act of service to God.
- Let your *Yes* mean *Yes*, and your *No* mean *No*. Speak and act so that people know they can trust you without question.
- Speak the truth completely and without the intent to mislead by omission, making sure not to be deceitful by leaving out details or emphasizing only the facts that support your own view.
- Treat everyone fairly, regardless of their wealth or social position.
- Make your beliefs, thoughts, words, and actions all consistent so that none can say that your faith is shallow or hypocritical.

2. Peace:

- Speak and act from a place of inner peace.
- Practice the spiritual disciplines in your own life that allow you to carry God's peace with you as you move through your community and that create in you the capacity to listen to the Spirit's voice so you know when you have moved out of that peace.
- When you don't have peace, stop speaking and acting until you address the problem. Go apart to pray and listen to the voice of the Spirit until you can get past any negative thoughts or emotions that you would bring into your community if you were to allow them to influence your words or actions. If you need help in dealing with anger or grief, seek the help of those in your community of faith to find the consolation needed to restore yourself to peace.
- When you cause a problem by acting outside of peace, take responsibility for fixing it. If your words or actions pull someone else out of peace, go to them and make it right. If your actions are causing destruction to God's creation, find a way to stop the damage you are causing and restore what has been lost.
- Your first responsibility is tending your relationship with God and caring for your own mind, body, and spirit. You can't help others when your own altar fire has grown cold. Your second priority is to care for your family and those in your community of faith.
- In choosing how to act and speak, consider the peace of your community both now and to the third and fourth generation. Seek to leave a legacy of peace for your great-grandchildren.

3. Holiness:

- Set your mind upon the things God created for you to do and enjoy. Avoid actions, thoughts, activities, or situations that pull you away from peace and wholeness.
- In deciding your actions, consider the wise course to follow instead of merely asking if something is permissible. When choosing between several options, always try to follow the path that is wise and that will lead your footsteps along the way that God has ordained for you.
- Focus your mind, body, and spirit on what is real, not on a reality filtered by the minds of men. Use computers and phones as tools, not as entertainment. Avoid spending time with TV, video games, and other electronic devices that shut down your senses and that direct your mind through filtered experiences.
- Spend your time in direct contact with people and in unmediated time with God in nature.
- Consider the harm that alcohol, tobacco, and drugs do in our culture and decide how to handle them wisely.
- Avoid immorality, especially sexual immorality that pulls the mind, body, and spirit all into patterns of sin.
- Be a good steward of the Earth that God has given to provide for your needs and for the needs of your children.

4. Consolation:

- When a member of your community of faith is dealing with grief or the negative emotions created by sin, the community should support them in dealing with these issues and help them return to a place of inner peace and right-standing with God.
- Don't try to handle your grief by yourself; you can't grieve fully alone. When you are going through grief, find a member of your community to pray with you and bear witness to your grief. For deeper grief, find those in your community to whom the Spirit has given a gift of consolation and allow them to help you work through the process of grieving.
- Be faithful in supporting others in your community by bearing witness to their grief, praying for them, and helping provide for their physical needs while they grieve.
- The community of faith must act with wisdom and compassion to break cycles of abuse and address the generational grief that is carried by its members.

5. Invocation:

- Let internal quiet become your baseline state, allowing the tongue to move only when it is needed, and guarding it carefully when it does.
- Learn to watch your inner dialog to notice if it turns negative, and correct it when it does.
- Avoid idle chatter. Idle talk dilutes the spiritual power of your words.
- Avoid meaningless arguments. Let your words arise from a place of calm deliberation, considering the impact of your words before you release them.
- In all conversations, strive to be fully present and to make the space between you sacred.
- Guard your everyday language and the way you use humor so that what they invoke is holy.
- Be careful to avoid gossip. Refuse to listen to others gossip as well. The community should hold accountable its members when they bring gossip into the community.
- Use the power of listening to bring peace and healing to those around you.

6. Communion:

- Live in communion with other Believers, sharing the burdens of daily life.
- Practice hospitality and share meals.
- Take care to build strong relationships between the generations, especially connecting the elders with the children and youth.
- Pray and worship together as a community of faith, not letting differences in style or personal preferences become a wedge between you.
- Deal swiftly with those who claim to follow Christ but who refuse to follow His commands. They will bring division and strife to the community.

7. Unity:

- Seek to build unity among all those in the community of faith. Do not put denominations or small points of theology ahead of the covenant we all share as God's children.
- Do not create structures in the community that are designed to allow a few leaders to push through their vision without having to carefully listen to all voices. This is often done in the name of efficiency, but most often results in efficiently ignoring what God is saying.
- Practice discipline and accountability within the community, calling one another to repentance when needed. Also actively practice reconciliation to restore unity between members when conflict or disagreement arises.
- Honor the diversity within the community that God has created. Accept differences in tastes, styles, and expressions, provided they come from the right spirit.
- Look for and develop the spiritual gifts of each member of the community so that the Church can function as one body with Christ as the head, having all the members God intended.

8. Love:

- Love should be visible and active, not distant or theoretical. Anyone who sees your community should come away talking about how the group is defined by the way they show love for each other.
- Treat each other with mercy and forgiveness, offering forgiveness freely, just as you would want to be forgiven.
- Obedience to God's commands should flow first from love for God, not out of fear of punishment. Encourage each other to good works because it is an expression of God's nature, not trying to scare anyone into obedience out of fear.
- Diffuse the power the world has over you and your community by praying for those who abuse you and showing mercy to those who would destroy you.
- Let everything flow from God's love, so that the way in which these precepts are expressed in your community are a reflection of how God loves and cares for each of His children.

THE DAILY PRACTICE OF *LECTIO DIVINA*

Preparation:

- Calm your mind and take a few deep breaths. As you exhale, try to relax and let go of any tension in your body and any thoughts that would distract you.
- Start with a Prayer of Thanksgiving, trying to find something new to be thankful for each day.
- Continue with the prayer, *"Lord Jesus Christ, come to my assistance and protect me in mind, body, and spirit as I seek to know you."*

Lectio:

- Read the entire passage slowly, reading aloud when it helps you to listen more fully.
- Re-read the whole passage, concentrating on any words or phrases that attract you.
- Close your eyes and repeat key passages or phrases, either aloud or silently.
- If you lose the meaning as you read, stop immediately (even mid-sentence). Go back to where you lost track and begin again from there.

Meditatio:

- Ask what specific message God is giving you through the passage.
- Think about how the passage applies to what you will think, say, and do today and throughout the next week. How would you act differently if you fully lived this passage?
- If the passage has a setting or action, try to visualize yourself in the scene.
- Notice any emotions the passage has evoked in you and name them.

Oratio:

- As you finish meditating on the passage, talk to God about the thoughts and emotions the passage has brought out in you.
- Ask God to create in you the heart and mind that the passage shows He desires.
- Talk to God about any thoughts or concerns you have for the day.

Contemplatio:

- Read through the *Contemplatio* section and use the focus it describes to help slow your mind and become more aware of God's presence.
- Once your physical senses and spiritual sense are fully focused, let go of your own thoughts and pay attention to God's presence in and around you.
- As thoughts arise, let go of them gently. Use your sacred word when needed to help you return to the silence.

Benediction:

- Return slowly and peacefully from *Contemplatio.*
- Take time to be thankful again.
- Acknowledge that you have completed your time for today and ask God to go with you as you leave this time.

Compline

- Before you begin, finish all your tasks for the day and be ready for sleep.
- If possible, sit outside for a minute or two to reconnect with what God is doing in creation. Reach out with your senses and take in what is happening, and then return inside to your sacred space.
- Light your candle if you have one in your sacred space. Begin by gently reading through the scripture for the evening in your Bible. Read in a relaxed and gentle way, allowing the words to soak through you.
- Look back over the day, examining your thoughts, words, and actions. Notice anything for which you need to ask forgiveness or be thankful. If you have said or done something during the day that needs to be set right, make a plan to take care of it tomorrow and then let it go for the night.
- Move into a time of prayer, asking forgiveness where needed, being thankful for the day's blessings, and talking to God about any other concerns from the day.
- Finish up with a minute or two of inner silence, allowing yourself to focus fully on God's presence as you prepare for sleep.
- Blow out your candle, turn off your light, and go quietly to bed, carrying the sense of inner stillness with you.

The Welcoming Prayer

- When you realize that you are not in peace, or are acting from a negative emotion, take the time to practice Welcoming Prayer.
- Start by identifying the negative emotion, naming it if possible. Note any sensations in the body (tightness, uneasiness, etc.) that seem to be related to the emotion.
- Acknowledge the feeling and welcome it. Be thankful that the emotion is bringing you a message that helps you understand your own inner desires and motives, even if the desires or motives are negative. Remember, you aren't welcoming bad circumstances or any desires or motives that aren't holy; you are only welcoming the emotion itself. If any negative thoughts or images arise, release them just as you would release a thought during *Contemplatio*.
- Allow yourself to fully experience the feeling until its message is fully received and you are able to create a little space between yourself and the emotion.
- If possible, determine the underlying desire or motive that is causing the negative emotion. Name the desire or motive if you can. If you can't identify an underlying cause of the emotion, don't worry about it. Simply move forward with the next step.
- Give the negative emotion, along with the underlying desire or motive, to God, releasing its attachment to your mind, body, and spirit. Let go of any tightness or tension in your body that is associated with hanging onto the emotion.
- Also give the situation over to the Spirit in prayer. Continue working to resolve negative circumstances, but accept God's will for how the situation will work out.
- Notice the shift in your emotions once you have released everything to the Holy Spirit. You may find yourself subconsciously grasping to take the emotion or desire back into yourself. If this happens, go back through the prayer of releasing and affirm your decision to give it all fully to the Holy Spirit for healing.